MONSTER!

Volume 4 / Issue 23 / November 2015

Cover art: Jolyon Yates
Contents Page: Christian Colbert; **Page 40:** Andy Ross

Contributors: Jolyon Yates, Dennis Capicik,
Mike T. Lyddon, Jeff Goodhartz, Eric Messina,
Michael Elvidge, Troy Howarth, Dawn Dabell, Andy Ross,
Christos Mouroukis, Michael Hauss, Stephen R. Bissette,
John Harrison, Les Moore, Brian Harris, Steve Fenton, and
Tim Paxton

Timothy Paxton, Editor, Publisher & Design Demon
Steve Fenton, Editor & Info-wrangler
Tony Strauss, Edit-fiend · Brian Harris, El Publisher de Grand Poobah

MONSTER! is published monthly. Subscriptions are NOT available.
© 2015 Wildside Publishing / Kronos Productions, unless otherwise noted. All rights reserved.
No part of this publication may be reproduced, distributed, or transmitted in any form or by any
means, including photocopying, recording, or other electronic or mechanical methods, without
the prior written permission of the publisher, except in the case of brief quotations embodied in
critical reviews and certain other noncommercial uses permitted by copyright law.

For permission requests, write to the publisher:
"Attention: Permissions Coordinator," at: Tim
Paxton, Saucerman Site Studios,
26 W. Vine St., Oberlin, OH 44074 ·
kronoscope@oberlin.net.

MONSTER! contains photos, drawings,
and illustrations included for the purpose
of criticism and documentation. All
pictures copyrighted by respective
authors, production companies, and/or
copyright holders.

EDITORIALIZING
GLOBALIZING THE ZOMBIE

In keeping with this issue's somewhat rough idea of a theme, I give you a few of the only "true" Indian zombie films that I know of. The undead pestering mankind is no new theme in their cinema, it's just that the Subcontinent's supernatural lexicon doesn't typically include zombies, *per se*. Sure, ghosts and other similar post mortem beings have been a big part of Hindu culture and folklore going back thousands of years, but the concept of shambling, "dead alive" bodies out to kill and/or eat the living is a much more recent development in Indian cinema.

ILLUMINATI FILMS AND EROS INTERNATIONAL PRESENT

GO GOA GONE

First up is **GO GOA GONE**, a 2013 film which had been on my radar for a couple years, but, since I tend to dislike most zombie films, I had given it a wide berth until recently. To be honest, when I found out that it was a horror comedy—and an *Indian* horror comedy, no less—I considered checking it out, as I've recently been warming-up to that particular genre more. As it turned out, the film wasn't all that bad. In fact, after watching years' worth of ultra-low budget horror films from the likes of Kanti Shah and his contemporaries (featuring the inept "comedic stylings" of Jagdeep *et al*), **GO GOA GONE** was a decidedly different experience.

And it was actually *funny*!

As the film opens we are introduced to two stoner buddies, Luv (Vir Das) and Hardik ([!?] Kunal Khemu), along with their flat-mate Bunny (Anand

Tiwari),[1] who is the breadwinner of the group. They are all watching A. Kodandarami Reddy's **DONGA**, a 1985 Tamil film that features a famous dance number ripped-off from Michael Jackson's John Landis-directed 1982 "Thriller" video.[2] Luv has recently found out that his long-time girlfriend has been cheating on him, and Hardik is fired from

---

1   And, yes, there *are* jokes made about Hardik's name! Luv, on the other hand, is a common Indian name derived from that of one of the deity Ram's twin sons. And as for Bunny, well…it happens.

2   Man oh man, did they ever *LOVE* Michael in India! Indian comedians aped Jackson in film after film, and there's a long list of movies that feature rip-offs of many of the late so-called King of Pop's hit videos. In fact, the Ramsays' horror film **3D SAAMRI** (1986; see *Monster!* #14, p.85) has one of their own poorly-executed "Thriller"-styled musical numbers. It's truly *horrid*! The superior musical number that appeared in **DONGA** was called "Golimar" (*"Shoot the Bullet"*), which is very popular on YouTube and Facebook. Just Google "Indian Thriller", and you'll be on your way!

his job for smoking weed on the premises. Bunny, on the other hand, has been offered to attend a conference in Goa for his job as an MD. Of course, all three drive to Goa, which is sort of the official "party" state in India. There they meet up with some beautiful women and attend a rave on an isolated island off the coast, where a batch of strangely glowing drugs are sold to some of the club's more "beautiful" people. Not only can't Luv, Hardik and Bunny afford the pills, but they also end up striking-out with their dates, too. All three dudes crash-out on the beach then wake up alone and a little hung over...which soon proves to be the *least* of their problems!

The morning after, the island seems deserted, with none of the night before's partygoers in sight. Just then, a bloodied Russian man comes running down the road, wild-eyed and brandishing a sinister blade. Just as he is demanding an explanation (in Russian, of course, which our heroes don't understand), he is attacked and disemboweled by two zombies, whereupon our heroes rightfully take off running. After eventually losing their ghoulish pursuers, the trio try to suss-out just what kind of monsters they're dealing with. Clearly these wrecked versions of humans are some sort of supernatural entities. Our heroes have the following discussion on the matter—

Luv: Hardik, what's going on? What's it all about?
Hardik: Actually, I had seen something similar in a horror film, but I can't remember...
Luv: Hey, I know what they are! They can't handle sunlight. They start burning in the sunlight!
Hardik: [motioning to the clear and cloudless morning sky] This isn't exactly moonlight...
Luv: Guess that's just for vampires. At least we know they're not vampires.
Bunny: Did you see their feet*? Were they turned backwards?*
Luv: Shut up, Bunny! Those are witches.[3] Witches are usually just women.
Hardik: Anyway, none of them were walking backwards.
Bunny: Must be ghosts, then. Ghosts can be seen in the daylight. Mutant ghosts!
Luv: Cross! Maybe they will flee if we show them the cross!
Hardik: I have a cross. But what if they're not Catholic?
Luv: Maybe it was something they ate at the party?
Hardik: I know what they are!
Bunny: What? Evil-deads?
Hardik: They're zombies!
Luv: Zombies? But we only have ghosts and spirits

in India. Where do zombies come from?
Hardik: Globalization! These foreigners have screwed us! First they brought HIV. Now, zombies!

That short discussion is a very important one so far as the history of Indian horror cinema is concerned. Almost all of the supernatural horror movies made in India primarily deal with "ghost and spirits" (*bhoots* and *aatmas*), "witches with backward feet" (*chudails*), occasional vampires (both of the indigenous domestic kind—such as the *Brahmarākṣhasa*—and more Western-type ones), hairy demons, and the occasional ghoul or two. But all-out zombies are something entirely new to Indian moviegoers, at least in productions produced on their own shores as opposed to foreign imports. India's folklore has always had its undead beings, though. Sometimes they come in the form of living corpses that are rotten things which stagger around, usually under the control of some evil *tantric* or other; but never until quite recently were any "true" flesh-eating zombies of the type that invaded our popular culture in 1968 c/o George A. Romero's classic trendsetter **NIGHT OF THE LIVING DEAD** seen in Indian-made movies. The idea of viral or chemical contagion is a very alien concept in their genre films. If there is any sort of spread of zombification from one person to another, it is typically done via some form of spiritual infection (as seen in such films as Ram Gopal Varma's 1996 **DEYYAM** [see *Monster!* #15, p.94]).

Buddies Luv, Hardik, and Bunny meet up with Luna (the stunning Puja Gupta), a woman who was at the rave whose friends took the red pills and turned into walking dead. After a brief skirmish with a group of feisty female zombies, they team up with two muscleheaded, Russian-speaking, gun-toting hardcases, Boris (Saif Ali Khan) and Nikolai. Now armed, they head back to the rave, where the only boat on the island lies on the beach. On the way, Boris lets them in on the secret of the drug, known as D2RF, which was dispensed at the party. They find that the boat has been "commandeered" by a zombie and they are forced to stay the night at a nearby cabin, waiting until morning when they can again make a try for the boat. Of course, now it's time for the zombies to attack again, this time in full force...

GO GOA GONE is one of the wittier Indian comedies—or any horror comedy from anywhere, for that matter—that I've seen in a while. What directors Krishna D.K. and Raj Nidimoru managed here was to manufacture an Indian comedy like no other, and theirs is a wildly original film for their country's industry. About the closest thing I could compare it to would be Simon Pegg's and

---

3 Traditional Indian witches and ghosts have their feet turned backwards. Folklore can be *weird*!

3

INDIA'S FIRST ZOMBIE ORIGIN FILM

The zombie genre is still too alien to make any kind of foothold in Bollywood, as India's movie-going consumer base is still neck-deep in ghosts and witches

Edgar Wright's hit Brit zomcom **SHAUN OF THE DEAD** (2004), from which a few minor episodes were plagiarized for **GGG**. It has a smart script. Good acting. No mugging for the camera. No irrelevant dance numbers. Ergo, it's damn-near-perfect in my book!

We follow that lighthearted and fairly gory little film with the Ford Brothers' **THE DEAD 2: INDIA**, a 2013 film which, like its predecessor **THE DEAD** (2010, D: Howard J. Ford), is an English production. I imagine that the directors must've thought that placing the action in an "exotic" locale would make all the difference in regards to its rather weak script. Like its predecessor **THE DEAD**, which was set in Africa, however, not much of an effort is made to interweave any local folklore or tradition. I am reminded of Lucio Fulci's seminal **ZOMBIE** (*Zombi 2*, 1979 [see *M!* #13, p.60]), which *did* manage to warp Haitian *Vodou* beliefs as a reason for the dead's rising from their graves. And, yes, it was never actually clarified as to why the dead—not just the recently-deceased, but even centuries-old corpses also—returned to (un)life to walk the Earth anew. In that enduring Italo splatter classic, it is less a physical disease which animates the title creatures, and rather a more spiritual one. The Fulci film is as near-perfect a zombie film as I can think of (Dan O'Bannon's **THE RETURN**

OF THE LIVING DEAD [1985] runs it a close third, with Romero's *Dead* trilogy [1968-85] being right at the top). Sure, if you're bitten by one of the rotting corpses, you are doomed. But then again, it is more of a *magical* infection as opposed to some weirdo weaponized biological or chemical carrier, as is the case with O'Bannon's just-cited **TROTLD** and dozens—if not scores—of other movies and TV shows worldwide. **GGG**'s ravers popping designer drugs to get high is just another form of mass-contamination (one which recently showed up as the cause for the undead in the TV show *iZombie*; similar basic elements involving drug-induced zombiedom can also be found in Zach Lipovsky's **DEAD RISING: WATCHTOWER** [2015, USA]).

Still another recent Indian film that attempted to give the undead a go with mixed results is **RISE OF THE ZOMBIE** (2013, Ds: Luke Kenny, Devaki Singh).[4] Sadly, as with **GO GOA GONE**, it fails to utilize any kind of classical regional folklore to help further its zombie plot, which might have been a nice touch. In it, a photographer from Mumbai decides to go on a camping trip alone, only to be bitten by some weird bug that turns him into a form of living dead. The film itself is not very good, and I was hoping for something a little better and a whole lot cooler.

Frankly, I miss the more "traditional" depiction of the undead in films. And to the best of my knowledge, there is no direct cultural connection between the zombie and any entity to be found in traditional Hindu folklore. India indeed does have its vengeful ghosts, but no shuffling corpses to speak of. So, maybe the idea of the Western zombie will never take root in any lasting way, other than as a passing fad prompted by the ongoing Hollywood and international commercial success of films in the zombie horror subgenre. In my opinion, that is not a bad thing, as there are plenty of other indigenous types of monster inhabiting India's rich folklore that can be tapped for more of its horror movies. Now, if only some enterprising director will get off his or her ass and do some cultural mining for some original creature features. I would so *love* that!

~ **Tim Paxton**

4 Another is **ROCK THE SHAADI** (formerly known as "SHAA-DI OF THE DEAD"), a still-forthcoming Bollywood zombie comedy directed by Navdeep Singh, starring Abhay Deol and Genelia in the lead roles. However, this movie has been delayed until further notice, so it remains to be seen when (or if) it gets released.

One should judge a man mainly from his depravities.

Virtues can be faked.

Depravities are real.

COMING IN 2016

MONSTER!

$5⁹⁵ each

Each and every monthly issue of MONSTER! is chock-full of reviews and articles on rare, unusual, and classic creature features from all over this wide and wild world!

WENGSCHOPSTORE.COM
Home of Wildside/Kronos Publications

DOCTOR BLOOD'S COFFIN (CERT X) EASTMAN COLOUR
KIERON MOORE · HAZEL COURT · IAN HUNTER
Directed by Sidney J. Furie · Produced by George Fowler · A Caralan Production
UNITED ARTISTS

DOCTOR BLOOD'S COFFIN
(working title: "FACE OF EVIL")

Reviewed by Jolyon Yates

UK, 1960/61. D: Sidney J. Furie

US poster taglines: *"We Dare You To Look Into* **DOCTOR BLOOD'S COFFIN** *In Gori-est Eastmancolor... Can You Stand The Terror... The Awful Secret It Contains?"*

Although this minor film may set few hearts beating faster—even when said organs are on full display—this is worth a look for horror fans and perhaps something of a zombie milestone. To begin with, this may have been the first zombie movie shot in color. The British Board of Film Classification (BBFC) passed a print dated October 31st, 1960—running 91 minutes and 40 seconds—with the "X" certificate, and it was released to theatres in the United Kingdom in January of 1961, and in the US on April 26th. Whether this beats Barry Mahon's **THE DEAD**

ONE (a.k.a. **BLOOD OF THE ZOMBIE**), also from 1961, remains unknown; at least to me, as I have not yet been able to find that New Orleans zombie drama's exact release date. It is also perhaps the first autonomous, aggressive zombie—as were unleashed *en masse* in Romero's **NIGHT OF THE LIVING DEAD** (1968, USA)—instead of the enslaved victims of unethical obeah men, scientists and aliens of previous zombie films, although if you regard the creatures of Frankenstein as composite zombies then they would set that precedent. However, before zombie fans lurch off to grab a copy of **DOCTOR BLOOD'S COFFIN**, I must inform you that the zombie, although he's a charming fellow, only starts shuffling around in the 85th minute.

Another point of comparison of interest to people like me who should really get out more is a parallel to later, more celebrated British Horror films. Like John Gilling's **THE PLAGUE OF THE ZOMBIES** (1966 [see *Monster!* #10, p.25]), the other "Cornish Zombie Movie", it was shot back-to-back with a snake woman film, the present film's director Sidney J. Furie's **THE SNAKE WOMAN**, which was released domestically in May 1961 and on June 3rd in the US. **PLAGUE** was shot on the same sets as **THE REPTILE**, then double-billed with Terence Fisher's **DRACULA – PRINCE OF DARKNESS** (1965, UK), whilst Gilling's **THE REPTILE** bunked with Don Sharp's **RASPUTIN – THE MAD MONK** (1966, both UK), **DRACULA** and **RASPUTIN** also having been shot back-to-back on the same sets.

Unlike in **PLAGUE**, however, the zombie of Dr. Blood's making is animated by science rather than magic, which again poises it between the progeny of Frankenstein and the ghouls of **NIGHT**, although—as in **PLAGUE**—there is a Transatlantic, shamanistic history to his method, by way of South America instead of Haiti (unlike the 1963 treatment for **PLAGUE**, entitled *The Zombie*; in its final script, Haiti, and Haitian characters, are reduced to background elements). **PLAGUE** would be the last gasp of Voodoo Zombie Movies before **NIGHT** changed the rules; throughout the previous decade zombies had tended to be more the product of brainwashing (Communist or consumerist), Atom Brain implantation or alien dehumanization/replacement/reanimation than the supernatural (1957's **ZOMBIES OF MORA TAU** is an entertaining exception, and features the first zombies to spread their condition to their victims). And while both **PLAGUE** and the present film are set in Cornwall, only **DOCTOR BLOOD** was shot on location, with studio interiors for **DOCTOR BLOOD** and **THE SNAKE WOMAN**

done at Walton-on-Thames (the latter film is set in Northumberland). Locations include the Carn Galver Mine at Penwith and the village of Zennor, on the north coast, known more for its mermaid than the walking dead. The Mermaid of Zennor (named after Saint Senara) was chronicled in recent years by the 2005 Sue Monk Kidd novel *The Mermaid Chair* (filmed in 2006 for the Lifetime channel under the same title, starring Kim Basinger), and can be seen carved into a 15th Century bench-end in Saint Senara's Church in the village. "Moomaid *[sic!]* of Zennor" ice cream is also available. **REPTILE** is set in Clagmoor, **DOCTOR BLOOD** in Porthcarron and **PLAGUE** in Tarleton: all fictional names, although there is a Tarleton in Lancashire in northwest England, and in Porthcarron's case a few beaches in Zennor's area are named Porth-something (Porthmeor, Porthgwidden and Porthminster *[There's also a popular seaside resort in South Wales called Porthcawl; "porth" being a Welsh word whose English translation is "portal" or "gate" – ed]*). Cornwall itself derives the second half of its name from Old English for "Welsh" (Anglo-Saxons referred to the region as "West Wales"), which accounts for the Welsh sound of these place names. I wondered if the "carron" of "Porthcarron" might relate to "carrion", but it's more likely from the Irish for "cairn" (a stack of stones marking a path).

**(WARNING: Spoilers follow!)

The uncredited artist of this Belgian poster for **DR. BLOOD'S COFFIN** seems to have used a still of Karloff as Imhotep in **THE MUMMY** (1932) for reference

8

In Vienna, a researcher in a surgical mask is about to inject a serum into a human subject when he is happened upon by Professor Luckman (Paul Hardtmuth, a German actor who, like several **DR. BLOOD** personnel, worked in **THE CURSE OF FRANKENSTEIN** [1957, UK, D: Terence Fisher; see *M!* #13, p.11]). The Professor throws him out of town. Shortly afterwards in Porthcarron, Dr. Robert Blood pulls up in front of the Tinners Arms (a real pub in Zennor), where locals debate the recent disappearances of two men with the senior policeman in town, Sergeant Cook, played by Kenneth J. Warren, who had appeared in the BBC's *Quatermass and the Pit* television series (1958) and did the rounds of top studios of British Horror with **I, MONSTER** (1971, Amicus, D: Stephen Weeks), **DEMONS OF THE MIND** (1972, Hammer, D: Peter Sykes) and **THE CREEPING FLESH** (1973, Tigon, D: Freddie Francis). Dr. Robert Blood is played by Ian Hunter, who had been in Rowland V. Lee's **TOWER OF LONDON** (1939, USA) and Victor Fleming's 1941 Hollywood version of **DR. JEKYLL AND MR. HYDE**. Running towards the doctor from the crowd is Nurse Linda Parker, played by Hazel Court. The gentle reader is no doubt familiar with Court's work in **DEVIL GIRL FROM MARS** (1954, UK, D: David MacDonald) and aforementioned **THE CURSE OF FRANKENSTEIN**, where she played Elizabeth. At this point she was working in television, most recently in a 1959 episode of *The Invisible Man* (1958-60, UK), and would soon grace the Corman/AIP Poe films **PREMATURE BURIAL** (1962), **THE RAVEN** (1963, both USA) and **THE MASQUE OF THE RED DEATH** (1964, USA/ UK). She would return to Cornwall-filmed horror in a cameo for the hunt scene in **OMEN III: THE FINAL CONFLICT** (1981, UK/USA, D: Graham Baker). I was prepared to accept Court's running nurse introduction as no more than part of the plot, despite the jiggling, but a couple of scenes later the camera is ogling her rear end as the point-of-view of a mysterious stranger who has been stealing glucose and other supplies from her office.

The stranger has the missing men hooked to drip-feeds down in a local mine. As you might have surmised from the pub's name, Cornwall's main produce was tin, and what with all the mines and smugglers' tunnels riddling the ground it's a miracle the county doesn't cave in. Tin mining in Cornwall goes back to the 22nd Century B.C., declining from the mid-19th Century A.D. once mines opened up in Bolivia and the Far East. The spooky remains of old mines can still be seen, and it is easy to imagine they're haunted by the many miners who perished in the lift disasters and floods (mines descended below sea level), or died a protracted death from the arsenic-laced fumes. *[A form of the awful respiratory disease silicosis which is related to that known as "black lung" in coalminers; a variation caused by long-term inhalation of radioactive radon gas is also suffered by uranium miners. Nowadays, special respiration/ filtration devices are worn in workplaces to provide protection against toxic materials in the air which cause such debilitating diseases. – ed.]*

That night the stranger sneaks into the bedroom of George Beale (Andy Alston), chloroforms him and injects him with something, but drops the syringe as he carries George away to the mine lair. The poor man is still alive, but paralyzed. Next morning, a handsome young man (Kieron Moore, the lighthouse keeper in **THE DAY OF THE TRIFFIDS** [1963, UK, Ds: Steve Sekely, Freddie Francis] and hero of **CRACK IN THE WORLD** [1965, USA, D: Andrew Marton], both with Janette Scott) drives his 1959 Ford Zodiac convertible Mk.II up to the doctor's door. Leering at Linda's bum follows. He introduces himself as the doctor's son, Peter Blood: an ominous name for a health care professional, and one shared with another fictional West Country doctor, who practiced in Bridgewater, Somerset *[I was born near there! Pardon the intrusion ☺ -- SF]*, and went on to be known as "Captain Blood" in several books and films (played by Errol Flynn in the terrific 1935 movie). Peter has been away in Vienna for four years studying biochemistry on a research grant. His father is in the back room playing chess with the village funeral director, Gerald F. Morton (played by Gerald C. Lawson, who here reminds me of John Carradine, and appeared in Terence Fisher's **THE MUMMY** [1959], and as "The Seer" in Cliff Owen's **THE VENGEANCE OF SHE** [1968, both UK]). Evidently, reports of anyone named Blood being expelled from Viennese hospitals have yet to reach Porthcarron.

Peter is not entirely saddened to learn that Linda is a widow, her husband Stephen having died a year previously as a result of swerving his car to avoid a child. She seems to like the look of Peter, but he is pulled away to guide a police search of the mines where he played as a young boy, and where George may be hidden. Peter successfully diverts the hunt from the lair, but realizes that George has been able to crawl out. At this point, the mystery of the stranger is over for the viewer, but one might also be noticing the absence of a complete nuclear family in Porthcarron. Peter's mother died when he was small, Linda's husband is gone, there seem to be no children around… The horror here, as in another British zombie film of the time, Terence Fisher's **THE EARTH DIES SCREAMING** (1964), is the disruption of a small community. The family is infiltrated by an evil "Prodigal Son", and its conventional means of producing life is

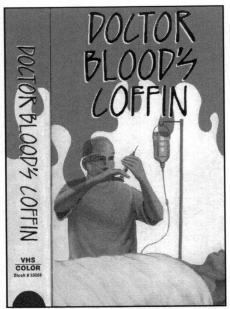

Top: Ye ol' editor Tim *[same goes for ye ol' editor Steve! – SF]* used to have this very VHS edition of **DOCTOR BLOOD'S COFFIN**— recorded in dreaded SLP ("super-long-play") mode—which was released on the ultra-cheap $1 bin-stocker label Alpha Video. **Above:** The film did offer up some gruesome gore during some rather vivid surgical procedures, however

right twice. Anyway, George makes it outside by morning, and Peter gives up. While his father leaves for Plymouth, Devon, to examine the serum found in the dropped syringe, Peter chats-up Linda. She finds his 16th-Century container of curare (*Strychnos toxifera*, used as arrow poison), but Peter explains the bamboo tube is a souvenir of a classmate from his Viennese years, whose great grandfather was a witch doctor from a tribe of the Orinoco River, and that it now contains nothing more than honey. Sgt. Cook rushes in to announce that George has been found, but needs medical help. Peter rushes to the gasping George and slips him some more curare before he can talk, then pronounces him dead. With dad absent, it falls to Peter to perform the autopsy, at Morton's mortuary, where the poor paralyzed man is cut open alive, with no anesthetic, which would have made for a terrifying scene in a better medical horror movie like Georges Franju's EYES WITHOUT A FACE (*Les yeux sans visage*, a.k.a. **THE HORROR CHAMBER OF DR. FAUSTUS**, 1960, France/Italy), but here passes without much impact despite some dutch angles, a bloody chest hole and a pulsing heart. I will say this, though: *scarlet* really pops in "gori-est" Eastmancolor, be it throbbing organs or Hazel Court's lipstick! Director of Photography was Stephen Dale, who stayed with the team for **THE SNAKE WOMAN** and would soon shoot Cy Endfield's **ZULU** (1964) and **THE NIGHT CALLER** (a.k.a. **BLOOD BEAST FROM OUTER SPACE**, 1965, UK, D: John Gilling). Camera operator was none other than Nicolas Roeg, 2nd unit photographer on David Lean's **LAWRENCE OF ARABIA** (1962, UK), DP on Corman's **THE MASQUE OF THE RED DEATH** and director of **DON'T LOOK NOW** (1973, UK/Italy); scarlet playing a fearful role in those latter two movies, as you may shudder to recall. While musing on this lurid scene, I should add that the special effects were handled by Les Bowie— whose Bowie Films Ltd. had handled monster and gore duties for Hammer since Val Guest's **THE QUATERMASS XPERIMENT** (1955, UK)—and Peter Neilson of **FIEND WITHOUT A FACE** (1958, UK, D: Arthur Crabtree).

blasphemously replaced. Other British zombie films were taking a more social, nationwide view, the threat falling from the ruling class on the population below, as seen in Val Guest's **QUATERMASS 2** (a.k.a. **ENEMY FROM SPACE**, 1957, UK [see *M!* #11, p.56]) and aforementioned **THE PLAGUE OF THE ZOMBIES**.

That night, Peter returns to hunt George through the tunnels; which might have been tenser had I not been distracted by the same shot of Peter running being repeated four times, although flipped left-to-

Anyway, Peter's efforts awaken Morton in his bedroom above, where even his dreams must smell of formaldehyde, so he creeps down the spiral stairs and witnesses Peter extracting the heart from a clearly still-living man. Peter tries to argue that conquering death justifies killing worthless boozers like George, there's a struggle and Morton is accidentally killed. George's heart fails in the meantime. Peter stuffs Morton in a coffin (the only one we see in the movie).

On her day off, Linda goes for a drive with Peter, who takes her down his cold, damp mine despite her being clad in a low-cut dress and heels. She really starts to doubt his sanity when he recalls happy childhood days spent lying there imagining himself as an entombed Loki or pharaoh awaiting new life. Luckily for her, a prospector named Tregaye suddenly appears and guides them outside. Tregaye is played by Fred Johnson, a character actor you may well have seen in **THE QUATERMASS XPERIMENT**, as an inspector, or as a grandfather in **THE CURSE OF FRANKENSTEIN**, or the face of **THE ABOMINABLE SNOWMAN** (1957, UK, D: Val Guest). Later, after George's funeral, Peter returns to the mine to clobber Tregaye just in case he's discovered the lair, but the mounting deaths and disappearances have come to seem unusually suspicious in the minds of Blood, Sr., Sgt. Cook and Linda, even for a crime hotspot like Porthcarron village. The Bloods argue, although Cook says, "Don't be too hard on *[Peter]*, Doc. After all, it's all in the family".

Tensions escalate when, for the third time, someone walks in on Peter up to no good, on this occasion Linda, who finds him using curare on Tregaye in the mortuary. Peter reasons that Tregaye is just "a useless tramp", which fails to mollify Linda, who, in the chapel attached to the mortuary, hits him with lines like "You want me to deny God, and instead to kneel down to worship a new god: *Science!*" and "You have the pride of Lucifer!" Moore and Court give the scene all they've got, especially when Peter suddenly claims she is rejecting him because she feels she's betraying her husband as if he were still "alive, not as he is now, pinned down by a gravestone"; which could have been put with more tact. Tregaye interrupts them again, this time through his twitching knocking over the curare tube. Linda escapes and calls on Blood, Sr. and Sgt. Cook. A search is launched, which is an opportune time for Peter to haul Tregaye to his lair and dig up Linda's husband Steve. Tregaye's heart is transplanted, and we finally see the corpse's face, 85 minutes in. By the way, although the gentle reader may question the science of reviving a corpse by sticking a living human's heart in it, back in 1960 human heart transplants were yet to be performed, so perhaps such a thing may have been more credible, or at least just as incredible as any other method. In 1964, a surgeon in Mississippi gave a human patient the heart of a chimpanzee, but the human died less than two hours later. In 1967 the first successful adult human-to-human transplant was performed in Cape Town, South Africa. The patient under Dr. Blood's tender care here, the late Steve Parker, is played by Paul Stockman, who *[wearing one of George "Robot Monster" Barrows' borrowed gorilla suits – ed.]* took the title role of **KONGA** (1961, UK/USA, D: John Lemont), was a guard in Freddie Francis' **THE SKULL** (1965, UK) and somewhere in the crowd

in **JACK THE GIANT SLAYER** (2013, USA, D: Bryan Singer). Makeup artistry is credited to Freddie Williamson, who also worked on above-cited **THE FINAL CONFLICT**.

Top to Bottom: The contents of **DOCTOR BLOOD'S COFFIN**; Kieron Moore as Dr. Blood engages in a literal life-and-death struggle with his lab-created zombie in this detail of a US lobby card; and the film's US pressbook (art unsigned)

11

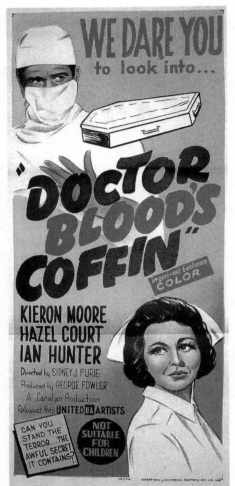

WE DARE YOU to look into...

"DOCTOR BLOOD'S COFFIN"

in gori-est Eastman COLOR

KIERON MOORE
HAZEL COURT
IAN HUNTER

Directed by SIDNEY J. FURIE
Produced by GEORGE FOWLER
A Caralan Production
Released thru UNITED ARTISTS

CAN YOU STAND THE TERROR... THE AWFUL SECRET IT CONTAINS?

NOT SUITABLE FOR CHILDREN

Australian daybill poster (art unsigned)

out to the rocky shore as the search party arrives, and walks off with the remaining Doctor Blood...

The foregoing was directed by Sidney J. Furie (1933-), a Toronto-born Canadian who had worked in television, and after **THE SNAKE WOMAN** helmed **THE IPCRESS FILE** (1965, UK) and **SUPERMAN IV: THE QUEST FOR PEACE** (1987, UK/USA). Although his stylish work in **IPCRESS** shares the mannered compositions of contemporary screen storytelling like *The Avengers* television series (1961-69, UK), and certainly works for that movie's tale of brainwashed zombification, the approach in **DOCTOR BLOOD** is rather understated, as if to mask the ridiculousness of the plot, or perhaps to conceal the gruesome horror within pleasant, sleepy normality, like the dark deeds occurring in the tunnels below sunny Porthcarron.

The story crept from the mind of Nathan Juran ([1907-2002] a familiar name from '50s films like **THE DEADLY MANTIS** [1957, USA]), adapted by James Kelley (**THREE ON A SPREE** [1961, UK], also directed by Furie and featuring **DR. BLOOD**'s Ruth Lee) and Peter Miller, screenplay by Juran under the name Jerry Juran. Kelley went on to write and direct **THE BEAST IN THE CELLAR** (1970, UK). Music director was another Hammer personage, Phillip Martell, who would also work as music supervisor at Tyburn (e.g., **THE GHOUL** [1975, UK, D: Freddie Francis]), and the score is by the Scottish composer whose marvelous name you might have noticed in the credits of **FIRST MAN INTO SPACE** (1959, UK, D: Robert Day) and **FIEND WITHOUT A FACE**: Buxton Orr.

THE INVASION OF THE ZOMBIES

(*Santo contra los zombies* / *"Santo vs. The Zombies"*)

Reviewed by Les "Gringo" Moore

Mexico, 1961. D: Benito Alazraki (a.k.a. Carlo J. Arconti)

While Santo had previously appeared in a pair of woefully sub-par and virtually uneventful Mexican/Cuban co-productions produced some three years prior—ploddingly dull, mundane crime melodramas both—he had not been those films' bona fide "star", even if he had pretty much stolen the show (such as it was). The present film represented the first time that Santo ever received billing on the top line in the

By now it is night, and Peter revives Stephen, who gasps, "Linda...!" so Peter grabs her from her home, and presents her to the shambling, rotten revenant that was her husband. As in James Whale's **FRANKENSTEIN** (1931, USA), our first sight of him is from the back and he shuffles around to face us/Linda. Peter claims "I wanted to make something worthwhile... *This* is what you rejected me for?!" but she fails to be cowed. "You haven't brought Steve Parker back to life, this is something from Hell!" The zombie is not her lover returned, it is the agent of raging evil, as she predicted in the chapel, and it starts throttling her, but it is also the nemesis to Peter's hubris, and quickly turns on him. There's a fight—nicely filmed with a handheld camera in close-up—as the zombie claws at Peter's face and finally throttles him, then collapses. Linda staggers cinema; although he was by this point in his career already well-used to headlining real world wrestling marquees, such was his superstardom. As in the Anglo export version of the Mexican/Spanish co-job **THE SAINT VS. DR. DEATH** (*Santo contra el Dr. Muerte*, 1974, D: Rafael Romero Marchent), for this rare English-dubbed outing courtesy of K. Gordon Murray—sadly, only very few of his adventures were ever post-synched into the vernacular; less than a half-dozen, by our count—El Santo is once again known as "The Saint", the literal English translation of his Spanish handle (no relation to Leslie Charteris' Simon Templar character, needless to say!); as opposed to "Samson" (his other two-time US alias, which made him sound like a peplum strongman hero), "Argos" (as he was billed on Italian releases of his movies), or even "Superman" (in France).

INVASION commences promisingly enough with a lengthy—over 11-minute (!)—ringside sequence, Santo vs. a *rudo* known as "The Black Shadow". Hunksome police hero Armando Silvestre (whose Mexi-monster movie roles are legion) subsequently remarks of a colleague, "He'd rather see The Saint wrestle than have supper with Anita Ekberg!" So you just know the guy's gotta be really into beefy macho men in masks and tights.

The plot proper explains that the scientist father of the glorious Gloria (lovely ex-"Miss Mexico" Lorena Velásquez, reigning Scream Queen of Mexi-monsterdom and leading lady of last ish's magnificently *loco* **SHIP OF MONSTERS** [*La nave de los monstruos*, 1960]) has gone missing while on a Haitian holiday researching material for a book on—what else?!—*zombies*. Now Gloria lives at home with her feeble, blind Uncle Herbert (played by Carlos Agosti, who would shortly be starring as Count Frankenhausen in a wondrous pair of vampire mood-pieces directed by Miguel Morayta). With the scene and players appropriately set, we are then introduced to a trio of men with stiffly expressionless faces and stiff-limbed, synchronized movements as they are dispatched by radio control to raid a jewellery store safe after hours, their automaton-like gaits easily betraying them as the "zombies" of the title. They promptly clean out the vault icebox then stride off into the night, ignoring direct gun-blasts to the forehead and spine while making their getaway. These remote-controlled undead human robots, though far removed from the rotten, maggot-faced E.C. Comics or later Romero/Italo traditions, do owe more than a passing nod to Edward L. Cahn's **INVISIBLE INVADERS** (1959, USA), which was reputedly a direct influence on Romero's **NOTLD**; and also foreshadow next issue's **EL DR. SATÁN** (*"Dr. Satan"*, 1966) and his own dehumanized henchmen. And here, as in that lattermost cited title, the zombies owe their earthly existence to equal parts

Mexican lobby card for **THE INVASION OF THE ZOMBIES**

13

science and magical/alchemical mumbo-jumbo. Co-writer of the original story Fernando Osés—who, as per usual, also appears onscreen in an acting part (that of a *luchador*-turned-zombie)—evidently borrowed more than a few ideas from Eddie Cahn's **CREATURE WITH THE ATOM BRAIN** (1955, USA [see *Monster!* #2, p.21]) for the present tale of walking dead men created using the corpses of executed/murdered criminals.

Down in the voluminous cavern chambers below Gloria's missing father's house, a hooded figure—hmmm, any bets on *WHO* it might possibly be?—oversees the return to the roost of his diamond-pilfering zombies. Elsewhere, representatives of truth, justice and the Mexican way contact Santo/Saint over the hero's video transceiver hotline with an urgent message. However, it's not too urgent that he can't take the time to stop off at the local arena for another quickie ring session to recharge his batteries first. In the audience is Gloria: "Is this the one who's gonna help my father...a...a...*wrestler*?!" she exclaims with some noticeable contempt; a reaction which is ironic considering that Velásquez would soon be plying the noble luchadorean martial art-form herself as another Gloria (therein surnamed Venus) for René Cardona, Sr.'s seminal **DOCTOR OF DOOM** (*Las luchadoras contra el médico asesino* / "The Wrestling Women vs. The Killer Doctor", 1962), as well as in a couple sequels to that film besides.

When the zombies strike again (don't they always!), this time nocturnally invading an orphanage in an attempt to kidnap a bunch of shrieking *chicos* for some indeterminate purpose (*hmmmm...*),The Saint shows up to singlehandedly take 'em on *mano a mano* at last. Sure, bullets may bounce off these dead suckers and mere mortals may tremble in their shoes at the very sight of them, but now they're messin' with The Big Guy! Clenching his fists in open frustration, the anonymous hooded puppet master watches helplessly on the monitor while The Man Masked in Silver thrashes his zombie-men right, left and center. With his similarly-hooded accomplice, the *mucho misterioso* "???" converts one of The Saint/El Santo's upcoming wrestling opponents, Dorrel López (Osés), into a human automaton; a fate

Top to Bottom: In THE INVASION OF THE ZOMBIES, Santo and his frequent onscreen opponent Fernando Osés—here playing a zombified wrestler—come to grips; Santo very nearly gets unmasked by the baddies; the zombies roll up to the jewelry store to commit a robbery; nope, that spot on this robo-zombie's forehead isn't his third eye or a particularly unsightly wart...it's meant to be a bullet-hole!

worse than death (or *is* it?) which Gloria learns also happened to her elderly lost pops (who makes for decidedly the feeblest looking of the zombie posse).

If necessary, the zombies can blip-out and disappear by matter-transmitting themselves back where they came from, and in one scene do just that, confounding the heck out of our hero, who hadn't gotten used to such weirdness yet, it being still so early into his career, at which time he had yet to tackle the va-va-voom Vampire Women, as well as Baron Brákola, Count Drácula, La Hacha Diabolica, La Momia, or any of the other assorted supernatural/paranormal menaces that he would within just a few short years be taking in his stride as all in a day's work, without barely even busting a sweat. In Santo's big bout with Osés herein, the former defeats the latter by (literally) causing a short-circuit in his shorts (wherein his remote-controller is hidden, of all places). His—to quote Kryten the robot from *Red Dwarf*—"groinal socket" region smoldering accordingly, Osés screams out in agony (and you would, too) then drops to the mat like a sack of spuds, stone cold dead.

One wonders why, in the privacy of their own secret lab hideout, that these two hooded villains should be so concerned about remaining covered up…unless of course it's only to generate "suspense" within the audience by keeping their IDs obscured. Gee, who *ARE* these guys? One of them just *couldn't* be you-know-who, could it…? Determined to get to the bottom of the mystery, Santo succeeds in tracing the zombie-controlling short-wave transmitter signal back to its source. At the lab, he almost gets unmasked by some zombies, but a miss is as good as a mile, as they say. A brief glimpse is given here of Santo with his trademark hood pulled half-off (or, if you happen to be an optimist, might that be half-*on*?). I have a sneaking suspicion that a stand-in for Santo was used for this shot, but it might just as easily be the real deal (in real life, he didn't *always* wear a mask, you know). Either way, our hero not unexpectedly manages to retain his own secret identity even as he finally unmasks the hooded ringleader as he who we have long since predicted it would be (*SPOILER ALERT!*): Uncle Herbie.

No stranger to pronounced mood-pieces (see **CURSE OF THE DOLL PEOPLE** [*Muñecas infernales / "Infernal Dolls"*, 1961]), director Benito Alazraki (real name Carlo J. Arconti, of Italian descent) here approximates the *guacamole*-thick monochromatic ambience of Alfonso Corona Blake's or José Díaz Morales' 1960s contributions to the *Santo* series. Director/actor Federico "Pichirilo" Curiel (whose sizeable Mexi-monster filmography includes **EL IMPERIO DE DRÁCULA** [1967; see *M!* #19, p.25]) appears in the present

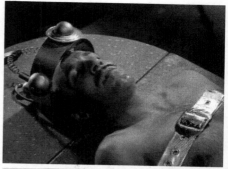

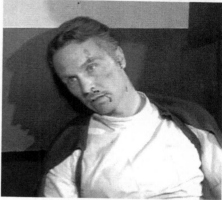

Fernando Osés finds himself strapped to the zombification table, and Carlos Agosti meets his demise in **THE INVASION OF THE ZOMBIES**

film as a night-watchman who catches the zombified safe-crackers in the act and empties his revolver into one of them, to no avail, and then gets karate-chopped out cold (dead?) for his trouble.

As befitting his saintly handle, an uncharacteristically overt "Divine" element is implied for the film's conclusion, as Saint Santo ascends a spiral stairway out of the cavern lab into an exaggerated aura of white light that streams down from the heavens above (perhaps even from very Heaven itself). As our hero takes his leave, in K. Gordon Murray's English-dubbed version, a supporting character remarks, "I guess that's why they call him 'Saint'…" Don't you forget it, evildoers! Be you man or monster, he'll smack some justice into you, make no mistake about it.

If this movie doesn't make a believer out of you, nothing will! It amounts to classic, surreal Mexican horror-*noir* from what is arguably the apex period of the genre, and should not be missed by fans of the shiny-masked S-guy or fun'n'funky flicks in general.

GUESS WHAT HAPPENED TO COUNT DRACULA?

Reviewed by Dennis Capicik

USA, 1969. D: Laurence Merrick

According to the producers of this lowly flick, Count Dracula actually turns out to be Count Adrian (Des Roberts), the *SON* of Dracula and the owner of Dracula's Dungeon, a cheap-looking horror-themed restaurant in Los Angeles. Managed by a host of oddball characters, including an old gypsy fortune-teller and an Igor-type *maître d'*, this culinary chamber of horrors also houses a caged gorilla and even a tiger named Alucard. After being resuscitated by some sort of impromptu "Macumba" ritual, Dracula (oh, sorry, make that Count Adrian!) becomes smitten with the rather dimwitted Angie (Claudia Barron), one of his recent customers, much to the chagrin of her frustrated boyfriend Guy (John Landon).

While this rather clumsy effort actually received stateside theatrical distribution as a GP-rated horror film in 1970 (ad-hype: *"A Giant Terrorama!"*), even as a children's matinee this would hardly elicit any scares. Dressed as a "traditional" bloodsucker with an added van dyke beard, Des Roberts portrays Count Adrian as an escaped refugee from Europe—Transylvania, to be exact—and he doesn't wish to return (quote) "...until the Communists are gone!" Played with a thick European accent *à la* Bela Lugosi ("I try to speak English well, but sometimes I put words in the wrong places!"), Roberts' performance never rises above the dinner theatre style of acting, and rather unfortunately, this takes up most of the film's running time, as he slowly seduces Angie. At one point, he arrives at a surprise party held by Angie's

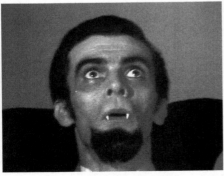

Count Adrian (Des Roberts)

friends dressed in black slacks and a beige smoking jacket, and, unbelievably, hypnotizes Angie into submission then gives her the proverbial "bite". Even though most of the film sticks fairly close to traditional Dracula lore, our Count needs to bite his victims at least three times before they become completely vampirized, which results in Angie suddenly fearing daylight and even chomping on a big, bloody, raw steak. Even Dr. Harris (Robert Branche) doesn't seem too concerned about the "loss of blood" and a "foreign element" in her blood, and simply remarks that the puncture wounds on her neck are the result of a "passionate boyfriend", but then jokingly remarks it could be the work of "Dracula, and all them cats!"

Being a GP-rated horror film, many of the exploitable elements such as nudity and gore never materialize, but despite this rather glaring oversight, it still remains a quite strange viewing experience. Unfortunately, much of the film's eccentricities begin to wear off with long, drawn-out scenes of Dr. Harris and Guy (our kind-of-humble Van Helsing and Jonathan Harker, respectively) *FINALLY* coming to the conclusion that Count Adrian may be a vampire. However, as a humorous aside, Dr. Harris actually turns out to be nothing more than a coward—complete with a girly scream!—instead of the usual hero-type. And yeah, it's no coincidence Angie's boyfriend is named Guy, whose character is quite clearly modeled after John Cassavetes' role in Roman Polanski's influential occult thriller **ROSEMARY'S BABY** (USA, 1968).

In one of present film's oddest touches, Dracula's Dungeon, Count Adrian's restaurant, resembles a travelling circus sideshow—including never-ending circus music playing in the background—and is decorated with all sorts of trinkets and junk, which may have been the filmmaker's intentions; reducing the legendary myth of Dracula to nothing more than a simple sideshow performer. During a "special night of the black calendar", Angie is witness to the "Macumba", a mating ritual with dances that will be, according to Count Adrian, "rather bizarre", but actually turn out to be nothing more than a single snake dancer, with lots of ooga-booga and frenzied camerawork. Bathed in loads of garish colors—Count Adrian's first seduction of Angie has an appropriate red tinge to the entire scene—and swirling lights, the psychedelic-type lighting is definitely indicative of the late '60s/early '70s, and also adds to the carny-like atmosphere. Photographed by Robert Caramico (1932-1997), a very busy DOP throughout the '70s, his colorful shooting style was quite evident in many of his later, and more popular, genre work, such as Richard Blackburn's **LEMORA: A CHILD'S**

TALE OF THE SUPERNATURAL (1973, USA) and Tobe Hooper's candy-colored horror opus EATEN ALIVE (1976, USA). In the latter part of his career, he was predominantly associated with TV, shooting many a teleseries, and movies for the small screen like Gordon Hessler's KISS MEETS THE PHANTOM OF THE PARK (1978, USA).

Director Laurence Merrick's (1926-1977) career was cut short when, according to the IMDb (quote), "he was shot and killed in Hollywood in 1977 by a mentally unbalanced man who was stalking him"; this after he co-directed the acclaimed, Oscar-nominated documentary MANSON (1973, USA) alongside Robert Hendrickson. While never achieving the same success with many of his solo directorial efforts, including BLACK ANGELS (1970, USA), a Blaxploitation biker flick, Merrick's even more obscure DRACULA AND THE BOYS (1969, USA) was apparently, according to one reviewer on the IMDb, a gay porn film, which eventually morphed into the GP-rated GUESS WHAT HAPPENED TO COUNT DRACULA?, an unsubstantiated—but possibly true—account of this film's ultimately bland and bloodless nature.

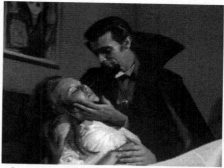

Count Adrian (Des Roberts) and the love of his life, Angie (Claudia Barron)

"There, across the desert, was where I had my first experience. As I looked out into the beautiful hills beyond, beyond the beautiful hills, I saw a panorama of beautiful hills. However, as beautiful as they may seem, death lurked behind the beautiful hills, behind the beautiful hills."

In a cave in one of those "beautiful hills, beyond the beautiful hills", a lone coffin houses our titular Dracula (Vince Kelley), or Alucard (which the credits so redundantly remind us is "Dracula spelled backwards"), who doesn't so much resemble a

DRACULA, THE DIRTY OLD MAN

Reviewed by Dennis Capicik

USA, 1969. D: William Edwards

Back in 1966, long before *Mystery Science Theater 3000* began riffing on bad movies, Woody Allen acquired an old Japanese spy film and redubbed the entire soundtrack with his improvisational and unique sense of humor. This concoction, which now focused on the discovery of some sort of chicken salad recipe (!), became his first film, the now rather infamous WHAT'S UP TIGER LILY? (1966, USA), which director William Edwards, rather inadvertently, tried to emulate with his nudie-monster flick, DRACULA, THE DIRTY OLD MAN (1969, USA), an astonishingly inept effort that makes some of Edward D. Wood, Jr.'s efforts seem like the work of his idol, Orson Welles.

Following some rather kitschy opening titles, it becomes apparent very quickly that this take on the Dracula legend will be—for lack of a better word—a very "distinctive" effort. The clumsy and maddeningly awful (to put it mildly) narration starts things off, and really needs to be quoted to get the full effect:

Kelley as Count Alucard *[top]*—or is it Pepé Le Pew?!—about to bite one of his victims in her (quote) "good place" *[above]*

17

SHOCK NUDIE SHOW the CENTURY!

From Out Of A TIME ROTTED TOMB crawls...

DRACULA THE DIRTY OLD MAN

SWV's VHS box art (taken from an original US pressbook ad)

Apparently conceived as a straight-up nudie-monster movie, in a last ditch effort to salvage the film, this troubled production had to resort to overdubbing the entire soundtrack. The improvisational and poorly post-synched dialogue sounds as if three or maybe four people performed it in a single afternoon without any edits or polishing, and, although funny at first, it wears out its welcome rather quickly. Taking liberties from Lew Landers' **THE RETURN OF THE VAMPIRE** (1943, USA, see *M!* #22, p.58), which also had Dracula (well, actually Armand Tesla, played by Lugosi) utilize a werewolf as a servant, **DTDOM's** primary motivation is the nudity, of which there is plenty. Beginning rather innocently, the film becomes progressively sleazier as Dracula strips and then straps his victims to wooden crosses and bites them on their nipples or "...right here in your *good place*". Venturing into "roughie" territory, even Mike as the "Jackal-Man" gets in on the sleazy action when he rapes an unfortunate housewife in a rather uncharacteristic and prolonged scene featuring some quite risqué female nudity for the time. Naturally enough, Mike is instructed to get Ann ("...she's the best one yet"), which results in the obligatory, climactic monster battle between old Drac and the Jackal-Man and then one last, approving, congratulatory romp between Mike and Ann on a dirty old blanket.

William Edwards seemed like a one-shot director who got the filmmaking bug in 1969, but then seemed to disappear forever after. **DTDOM** was indeed his only directorial effort, but he was also the writer and producer of yet another monster-mash, Oliver Drake's **THE MUMMY AND THE CURSE OF THE JACKALS** (1969, USA), which had a more upscale cast, including Anthony Eisley and John Carradine, and then, that very same year, he also wrote and produced **RIDE THE WILD STUD** (1969, USA), a "roughie" western, which was once again directed by Drake. In an interesting bit of trivia, the "Jackal-Man's" rat-like werewolf mask was also used in **THE MUMMY AND THE CURSE OF THE JACKALS**, which at one point, was available on VHS through Academy Entertainment (under the slightly altered title of **MUMMY & THE CURSE OF THE JACKAL**) but, unfortunately, has yet to find a home on DVD.

Unbelievably awful, **DRACULA, THE DIRTY OLD MAN** still manages to retain some mild interest for fans of early sexploitation flicks or monster movies, and even though most of the jokes and deadpan humor fall woefully flat, the sheer madness of this concoction is still intriguing enough, and perfectly encapsulates the spirit of the late Mike Vraney's Something Weird Video.

"dirty old man", but rather a cross between Pepé Le Pew and Bela Lugosi, who, through a cartoonish Yiddish accent remarks, "It was one of those days, you know". We are then introduced to Mike (Bill Whitton), a reporter who is out on a date with his new girlfriend Ann (Ann Hollis), but, later that night, when Mike drops Ann off at home, Dracula spies on her as she strips down to her underwear ("Take it off! Take it *all* off!"), after which he turns into a plastic toy bat. In true Bram Stoker fashion, Mike is summoned by Dracula to Nelson's Landing (it actually turns out to be Bronson Caves, a popular location of many a low-budget flick) to report on the opening of a new mine, where Dracula continues to hang out with one of those "outdoor fireplaces indoors". More would-be comedic narration occurs as Mike ponders his current assignment: "As I sped towards the mine shaft, little knowing what awaited me there, I knew I was going to get shafted!" Sure enough, Mike's deductions were correct, and he is turned into a "Jackal-Man"—a poor man's werewolf—and ordered to "get a different girl every night". The rest of this mercifully short film has our Jackal-Man abducting women and bringing them back to Dracula's cut-rate lair, where Dracula, the old perv, proceeds to put the bite on 'em.

AMITYVILLE 2: THE POSSESSION

Reviewed by Eric Messina

USA, 1982. D: Damiano Damiani

This sleazy haunted house filled with demonic pigs, Christ-hating invisible ghoulies, incest and Burt Young, who looks a lot like my own scary father, has always made a ghastly impression on me as someone who grew up in Long Island and has heard creepy stories about the title house since kindergarten. The first one you can keep; it has some creepy moments, but it sucks, as far as I'm concerned. Just like **THE WAR OF THE GARGANTUAS** (フランケンシュタインの怪獣 サンダ対ガイラ / *Furankenshutain no kaijū – Sanda tai Gaira*, 1966, Japan [see *Monster!* #12, p.24]) and **THE EMPIRE STRIKES BACK** (1980, USA) this sequel—or rather prequel—surpasses the original.

The spooky Lalo Schifrin score of ghostly little singing kids instantly makes you nauseous and unsettled, which sets the uneasy tone of this stressed-out, fanatically-religious true crime account of the Ron "Butchie" Defao, Jr.

murders. Man, did they ever take liberties with the facts behind this case! This film is actually based on a fictional account of the real crime by parapsychologist and ghostbuster Hanz Holzer... Confused? I was too! This kind of factual butchery shouldn't be allowed, but the producers didn't want to give George and Kathy Lutz any more publicity, so they distanced themselves from their case and went with this prequel instead. Butch is called Sonny Montelli here, and Burt Young as the abusive father couldn't have been a better casting decision.

So—*YAY!*—everyone's excited about the new move. But why is it so *cheap*, anyway? And—"Oh God, no!"—why are paint brushes floating around drawing punk scrawls of a psychedelic pig with a skin-crawling intermezzo accompanying the disobedient "dishonor thy father" statement written in the corner of the art project? That part is one of the most twisted and unnerving moments in horror cinema; it kind of looks like a finger-painting by the Manson Family. But wait, it gets worse, because Sonny's sister Patty (Diane Franklin) does some freaky-deaky shit with her brother. As I mentioned before in my review of **TERRORVISION** (1985, USA [see *M!* # 14, p.49]), this was the moment I developed a crush on Mrs. Franklin, which I realize is very disturbing, but that's the way it happened— I'll consult my therapist on this matter!

The Jackal-Man and his master, Count Alucard

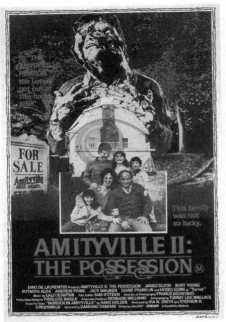

Australian poster

This sensationalized account inspired by real sister Dawn Defao's persuasive relationship with unstable sibling Butchie is totally mental! Defao, who was a major junkie loser, might have conspired with Dawn when he gunned down his family, but who knows if they really had an incestuous relationship—it's pure speculation by Holzer. No one is sure if they actually planned out the slaying together, because she was also killed in the shootings and Butch pinned the blame on voices in his head, which commanded him to murder his own family.

If only this family wasn't so Catholic, maybe the demons would stop loudly knocking at three in the morning. They even cause an earthquake when the family prays at dinnertime. The Satanic forces imbedded in the house feel very threatened by all the iconography. The Montellis seriously need counseling, because right from the minute they first move in, they are already at each other's throats, and it doesn't take much to inspire the son to defend his victimized siblings from their tyrannical father by pointing a rifle at his neck. What this family really needs is professional help or a nice divorce settlement instead of a priest to bless the house, but of course that's what happens, which is like putting a Band-Aid over an open wound! This film is really psychologically traumatizing for me, because the extremely angry dad looks like mine. His name is Anthony like my father, and it's set in Long Island,

where I grew up. Thankfully there were never any guns in my house, but unfortunately there's an entire rack in the basement here!

Down in the muddy, dank, fly-and-shit-covered basement, Sonny sees a severed arm pop out of a brick wall, which is never explained. The only part where they sort of go into the backstory happens at a library where the chipper worker tells the priest that the house was built over an Indian burial ground (which is another Holzer fabrication [this plot point was evidently inspired by a similar one in Steven Spielberg's and Tobe Hooper's *POLTERGEIST*, which was released earlier in '82, just a few months prior to *AMITYVILLE II* – ed]). This might be the only time where fiction embellishes and enhances the storyline of a true case. In every Amityville story I've ever heard, as someone who doesn't believe in ghosts, I mostly chalk it up to drug abuse or insanity. Just watch the recent documentary **MY AMITYVILLE HORROR** (2012, USA) about Daniel Lutz, the abused man who really lived in the house as a child a few years after the murders, and tell me that he wasn't on LSD (or worse)! Lutz believed as a kid that he saw flying pigs, (*Oink! Oink!*), a ghostly brass band, and red eyes staring from out of his window. My theory after witnessing the erratic behavior of this man is that the whole thing was the result of George Lutz, a tyrant who controlled his children with drugs and invented the whole thing for publicity.

Back to the movie's storyline: so anyway, after simultaneously getting defiled and possessed by an invisible force that caves in his stomach muscles, this immediately causes Sonny to commit incest with his pretty nubile sister Patty (Diane Franklin). The green and reddish lighting here is a nice touch, and the way the camera whirls around the room makes you feel claustrophobic. The part where they get down'n'dirty inbred-style is so sleazy and revolting that it makes you want to take 40 showers!

Rutanya Alda as the mom is constantly hyperventilating as blood rather than holy water shoots out of the priest's aspergillum. The poor woman is a nervous wreck, and—BLECCCHHH!—she also witnesses her son grabbing his sister's butt! For a long time this film really skeeved me out, and I attribute some of it to Alda's anxiety-ridden performance, which just gives me the heebie-jeebies. In fact when I saw her in the trailer for William Lustig's **VIGILANTE** (1983, USA), I wasn't sure if I wanted to see the film, her shrieking had that much of a damaging effect on my psyche. **AMITYVILLE 2** is just an unpleasant, sick experience that can be only enjoyed by a handful of weirdoes (myself included). Thankfully, I gave that

Lustig classic another chance, and it now remains one of my absolute favorites.

In the first **AMITYVILLE** film, you begin to realize that it's supposed to be the former tenant possessing James Brolin. In this prequel, however, it gets wonky, because we're dealing with reality, and the actual killer was a junkie. Although we never actually do see Sonny shoot up, his arm and face contort in a hideous, mangled way. It's just a theory of mine, but the demonic force herein seems to be a metaphor for drug use. There's also a Cronenberg-like element of body dysmorphia that makes it all so fascinating and bizarre. Tommy Lee Wallace, the scriptwriter, penned this and **HALLOWEEN III: SEASON OF THE WITCH** (1982, USA [see *M!* #10, p.21]), which he also directed; they are both sequels that originally divided horror fans but that have recently been reevaluated as misunderstood classics. Sonny is commanded by the evil voice—which always growls—from his Sony Walkman to shoot "the pigs", a.k.a. his own family. Eventually, the evil spirit decides it can't wait anymore and time is of the essence, and deforms his face so that it looks as if he's had extreme plastic surgery and Botox (recent photos of Scott "Carrot Top" Thompson spring to mind)! Jack Magner, the actor who played Sonny, vanished from the acting scene after he appeared in this. He does an amazing job in this massively disturbing role. Why he gave up acting is not known. Moses Gunn from **THE NEVERENDING STORY** (1984, USA, D: Wolfgang Petersen) shows up, but sadly doesn't contribute much to the film.

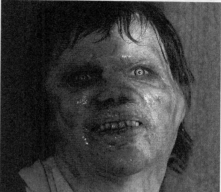

The last 30 minutes degenerate into a full-blown **EXORCIST** rip-off as Father Adamsky (James Olsen), without the consent of the Catholic Church, assumes the role based on Max Von Sydow's character. There are so many odd religious fantasy elements throughout this flick: for example, when the priest goes back to his car, his Bible has been mysteriously torn to ribbons. (Silly demons, don't you know you can go to any hotel and pick up another one?!) Sonny is finally arrested after the incident, but what really burns my bacon is the notion that if this serial killer is *really* insane, then he should be locked-up forever in an asylum, not put under the care of an irresponsible rogue priest

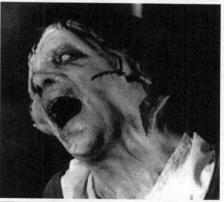

Right, Top to Bottom: Unlike the previous film with its swarm of flies and haunted pig, this first *AH* sequel went totally off the rails, and there was some decent full-blown monster action to be had. In these 4 images, Jack Magner transforms from human to inhuman, in the bottom shot being replaced by John Caglione, Jr.'s special makeup FX

like Olsen's character, who loses his marbles and begins to see the ghost of Patty (Franklin) bathed in blue light greeting him at the entrance to the jack-o'-lantern-eyed title mansion.

After that swift descent into madness, the film gets even more bonkers as Sonny's lawyer, played by bristly-mustachioed actor Ted Ross—a.k.a. "The Cowardly Lion" from **THE WIZ** (1978, USA, D: Sidney Lumet)!—actually takes the advice of the crazy padre, who persuades him not to plead insanity, but rather tell the court that his client Sonny is "possessed by demons"! Of course, they are all laughed out of court!

THE POSSESSION should end with both priest and victim in the same nuthouse! As Olsen goes through the fire-and-brimstone holy motions, I love how Sonny's face begins to mutilate and crack like a giant flesh-and-blood-covered egg until the demon underneath is revealed, which looks like the distant relative of a **C.H.U.D.** (see p.33). The creature gleefully smiles beneath the human mask with its jagged teeth. SFX makeup artist John Caglione would later rework this demon (which sprang from the basement pool in the weak-ass **AMITYVILLE 3-D** [1983, USA, D: Richard Fleischer]) into those aforementioned infamous '80s acronym beasties.

Logic in this movie just flies off the cliff as Sonny transforms into a slutty-looking Diane Franklin and sexually tempts the priest, who should just go into another line of work! It all ends on a nihilistic note as the house ignites into flames and Father Adamsky—who really should let bygones be bygones—is totally *fucked*! This film is very Roman Catholic, and even if you're not religious it's just unpleasant and totally ludicrous. That's why it's one of my favorite sequels—it can be only be enjoyed by the truly demented.

NIGHT CLAWS

Reviewed by Michael Elvidge

USA, 2013. D: David A. Prior

Ad-line: *"Survival Is Not An Option."*

A young couple is making out in a vintage automobile, only to have the woman abruptly interrupt their make-out session, thinking there is someone lurking outside the car. The young man is then grabbed by a hairy humanoid/hominid monster and pulled out through the window, and in a schlocky scene his horrified girlfriend is left holding the young man's severed ankles. Finally, the monster offs her as well, then the opening credits roll. Police investigate the murder of the young couple and find some strange animal hair at the location amongst the mutilated body parts. Sheriff Joe Kelly arrives, talks with his deputy/lover, Roberta, concluding that they should shut down the parks in the area. When Joe discovers

Caglione's fully-transformed **AH2** demon is a most impressive animatronic creation

that what were apparently claws have ripped-up the hood of the young couple's car, he rightly assumes that some sort of wild animal is to blame for the savage killings. Lurking nearby in the forest are three armed men, who secretly observe the police investigation.

At a neighboring park, two couples are set to take part in a Survival Retreat. They are the Chadworths, Edward and Linda, and the Parkers, Charles and Cindy. Their guide for the excursion is Sharon Farmer, who will take them up into the mountains, where they will live off the land for three days with a GPS device at hand in case they encounter any trouble. Elsewhere, Professor Sara Evans of the National Museum of Anthropology gets a phone call about the attack, whereafter she and her assistant Thomas (A. Wade Miller) head to the park to investigate. Sheriff Joe is told by the town's mayor to keep the whole incident hush-hush. Shades of Murray Hamilton's mayor in Spielberg's **JAWS** (1975), he's worried that it might interfere with the township's "Pumpkin Fest", which attracts 100,000 visitors annually, and he doesn't want media there either. Prof. Evans arrives in town, representing a special government unit called Search For New Species (SFNS). Joe allows Sara to review any evidence they have gathered, then decides to examine the bodies at the coroner's. The coroner is of the opinion that some species of powerful animal could be responsible; the prof believes the perpetrator might well be a Sasquatch or Bigfoot. Investigators also found a big footprint at the scene, and after examining it they estimate that the beast stands around 10 feet tall. Prof. Evans is subsequently informed that a local drunk named Cooter has info about sighting a Bigfoot, but he stipulates that he will only talk with her if she buys him beer! He claims there isn't just *one* Bigfoot but several living in the area. A short time later, a woman is grabbed and dragged away by a Bigfoot, and things go from bad to worse before they get any better. If you want to learn any further details of **NC**'s plot, you'll have to seek it out yourself, as I don't want to spoil things for you by redundantly relating the entire synopsis here.

NIGHT CLAWS is a compelling B-film that, over the course of its 83-minute runtime, keeps you guessing what the final outcome will eventually be, and it contains some cringe-worthy gore. Shots of the creature during most of the action are presented blurrily and fast-paced, with close-ups of drooling fangs and large, sharp claws. They never really reveal the Bigfoot's full appearance till near the end of the film. **NC** released on DVD in Japan on May 2, 2013, and it is also known as **APEX PREDATOR**.

As for the actors in **NIGHT CLAWS**, the rundown is something like this: Sheriff Joe Kelly is portrayed by Reb Brown. This actor has had a lengthy career in TV and feature films, including playing the title hero of the made-for-TV movie **CAPTAIN AMERICA** and its sequel **CAPTAIN AMERICA 2: DEATH TOO SOON** (both 1979, USA). Another role was in **HOWLING II: ...YOUR SISTER IS A WEREWOLF** (1985, USA), and he appeared in many action-oriented films, including "Anthony M. Dawson"/Antonio Margheriti's trashy **STAR WARS/QUEST FOR FIRE** rip-off **YOR, THE HUNTER FROM THE FUTURE** (*Il mondo di Yor*, 1983, Italy/Turkey) and "Vincent Dawn"/ Bruno Mattei's notorious poverty row **ROBOCOP/ PREDATOR** rip-off, **ROBOWAR** (*Robowar – Robot da guerra*, 1988, Italy). Leilani Sarelle co-stars in **NC** as Prof. Sara Evans, and she works both on television and in film. Her credits in the latter medium include **NEON MANIACS** (1986) and **BASIC INSTINCT** (1992, both USA), and she has more recently appeared on the TV series *Glee* (2012, USA). Ted Prior plays Charlie Parker in **NC**, which was directed by his late brother David A. Prior. Ted starred in such movies as **SLEDGEHAMMER** (1983), **SURF NAZIS MUST DIE** (1987) and **MUTANT SPECIES** (1994, all USA). Sherrie Rose appears herein as Deputy Roberta Glickman, and she has acted in many TV shows (e.g., *Miami Vice* [in 1989] and *Married With Children* [in 1990]) as well as other films (e.g., **TALES FROM THE CRYPT: DEMON KNIGHT** [1995, all USA]). David Campbell appears as Hunter

Crawford the ex-military Bigfoot hunter. Campbell has done much work in B-grade films, including **KILLZONE** (1985), **DEADLY PREY** (1987) and its sequel **DEADLIEST PREY** (2013, all USA). Frank Stallone has a small role as a character named Testi in **NC**. He is best known for being the brother of actor Sylvester Stallone, and has made a name for himself in the field of acting, appearing in **ROCKY** (1976), **BARFLY** (1987, both USA), **THE PINK CHIQUITAS** (1987, Canada) and **HUDSON HAWK** (1991, USA). More recently he performed the voice for the character Thunderhoof in the cartoon TV series *Transformers: Robots In Disguise* (2015, USA). Tara Kleinpeter appears as Sharon Farmer, **NC**'s Survival Retreat Tour Guide. Tara has only been in the film industry for the past 15 years or so, and also works on the production side. She worked on **RELENTLESS JUSTICE** (2014) and **DEADLIEST PREY** (2013, both USA), and was also a producer on **NIGHT CLAWS**. Alissa Koenig stars in the film as Cindy Parker, and she can also be seen in **ZOMBIE WARS** (2007) and **EYES OF THE WOODS** (2009, both USA). Edward is played by Edward Saint Pe', who has worked as both a TV weatherman and a University professor. His film acting work includes roles in **THE BIG EASY** (1986), **THE ONE WARRIOR** (2011) and **ZOMBEX** (2013, all USA). **NC**'s score was composed by Chuck Cirino, who has worked on the soundtracks of films like **CHOPPING MALL** (1986, USA), whose music has recently

been released as limited edition colored vinyl LP record on Waxwork Records.

To end this piece on a sad note: the day following my viewing of **NIGHT CLAWS** and writing the bulk of this review, I learned online that the film's director—David A. Prior (1956-2015), who also wrote/produced films and co-founded Action International Pictures—had died. During the 1980s and '90s, Prior directed a lot of action, horror and other B-movies; over 30 of them in total. His filmography includes the likes of **KILLER WORKOUT** (1987), **MUTANT SPECIES** (1994) and **ZOMBIE WARS** (2007, all USA). Since his passing, we can only be grateful for the legacy of films he has left for us to enjoy.

BLOOD THIRST

(a.k.a. BLOOD SEEKERS; THE HORROR FROM BEYOND)

Reviewed by Michael Hauss

USA/Philippines, 1971. D: Newt Arnold

The thing I love about the DVD releasing company Vinegar Syndrome is they release some pretty obscure shit on their label. This obscure film is in black and white, and as far as I can ascertain was

Terror In The Trees: Those **NIGHT CLAWS** can kill you just as well in broad daylight

filmed around 1965, but not released until 1971. It was filmed entirely in the Philippines, and has Pinoy exploitation great Vic Diaz in the cast. Diaz here plays inspector Manuel Ramos, and is best-known for his turns in many films as a fat, oily, sadistic villain. Jack Hill's **THE BIG BIRD CAGE** (1972) and Eddie Romero's **BLACK MAMA, WHITE MAMA** (1973, both USA/Philippines) are just two of his 130 acting credits. Besides the present one, he also appeared in other Pinoy-shot monster movies too, including opposite John Ashley in Romero's pseudo-werewolf tale **BEAST OF THE YELLOW NIGHT** (1971), playing no less than Satan himself.

In **BLOOD THIRST**, murders are being committed where the victims—attractive young women all—are being killed exactly the same way each time, and left drained of blood. Inspector Ramos calls for his personal friend Adam Rourke, who is known by every detective in the world because of a book he wrote entitled *Sex Crimes, Motivation and Investigation*. The fact that Rourke is a sex crime expert helping a friend to investigate crimes that evidence no sexual abuses seems a bit odd, as the murders were more ritualistic and occult-connected rather than sexually motivated. The little-known actor Robert Winston—who looks a bit like Dana Andrews—plays Adam Rourke and, while not turning in a great performance, does a passable job in the role. The Rourke character is definitely a product of the times, kissing and slapping his woman Sylvia (Katherine Henryk) into loving him after a bit of friction when they first met. His lighthearted banter had angered the woman, who is the Caucasian sister of Filipino Inspector Ramos (she was adopted by the family in her youth). She sparred with alpha male Rourke verbally, but—as the world was in those days, at least in the movies—a good slap was a sure sign of some good lovin' coming her way.

A club called the Barrio seems to have a connection with the murders, as some of the murdered girls worked there. Rourke offers to go undercover at the club, posing as an American journalist, who wants to do a story on the latest murder victim, Maria. While at the club, Rourke tries to get the proprietor, Mr. Calderon (Vic Silayan), to buy his fake journalism story and submit to some questioning. While he is there, a beautiful thin blonde named Serena (Yvonne Nielson) is introduced doing a tantalizing dance for the ecstatic club patrons. The truth revealed is that Serena, despite all outward appearances, is actually hundreds of years old, and uses the blood of her victims to prolong her life; lifeblood taken from one woman to sustain the youth and beauty of another. Blood combined with electricity derived

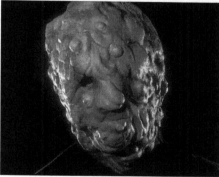

Top: US double-header one-sheet, on which **BLOOD THIRST** was co-billed with the equally-less-than-wonderful Brit "vampire" film **BLOODSUCKERS. Above:** BT's lumpy-headed Filipino horror, a distant cousin to the more famous denizens of Blood Island

from solar energy—the killings were committed as sacrifices to the Sun God, you see—keeps golden goddess Serena alive. Right at the beginning we are introduced to a monster with a prune face that commits the murders and draws blood from the victims in order to supply its master, Serena. The blood is placed in a vat and the goddess adds some kind of magic powder, this and the blood being key to her continued rejuvenation. The ending is so out-there and stupid that it won't be revealed here; buy the disc and find out for yourself!

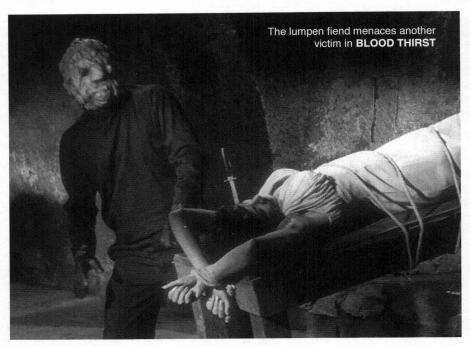

The lumpen fiend menaces another victim in **BLOOD THIRST**

BLOOD THIRST was dull and no suspense was built, for the simple reason that the killers' identities were obvious as soon as they appeared onscreen. This is not really a straightforward horror film, as it throws in spy gadgets, such as a decoy dummy named "Harvey" which Rourke carries around with him, that he uses as his stand-in in dangerous situations. The film also has some light comedy that falls flat, as well as some *film noir* traces, with Rourke's cynical quips, his fast fists and trusty gun. The monster of the film's face looks rather reminiscent of the transformed nerd in **THE TOXIC AVENGER** (1984, USA, Ds: Michael Herz, Lloyd Kaufman). **BT** has some nice camera work and is well-done on the technical side. The video transfer is nice, albeit with a few scenes where the blacks get too deep and grainy, while the audio track—which boasts a nice breezy jazz score (composer uncredited)—does have a few spots of overt audio hiss. Struck from original 35mm film elements and presented widescreen (1.66:1), the film is part of the "Drive-In" collection from Vinegar Syndrome, and is included on a dual disc with another made-in-the-Philippines horror which contains some analogous themes, **THE THIRSTY DEAD** (1974, D: Terry Becker), starring John Considine.

Although **BT** has been made previously available on domestic DVD in scrappy, fullscreen pan-and-scan transfers by several budget labels (Alpha Video and Retromedia included), the fact that this obscure monster movie has now been released in much more optimal form by VS is recommendation enough to pick it up.

CEMETERY OF TERROR

(*Cementerio del terror*; a.k.a. **ZOMBIE APOCALYPSE**)

Reviewed by Les "Gringo" Moore

Mexico, 1985. D: Rubén Galindo, Jr.

The opening to this film, which I initially saw in its original Spanish on a VHS rental tape back in about 1990, exhibits a decidedly American/Italian influence: perhaps that's why a former *compañero* of mine once called it "a cross between **FRIDAY THE 13TH** and a zombie gore film". If nothing else, I was interested in seeing this rare late entry in the Mexican horror stakes on basis of its more recent vintage than the usual more Golden Age Mexi-monster fare which is covered here in *Monster!*'s pages. At the height of the home video boom back in the '90s, most of the readily available genre films from Mexico seemingly sprang from the '50s, '60s and early '70s, and anything produced before or after those decades was generally much more difficult to see (although nowadays quite a number of pre- and post- examples are readily available for viewing on

YouTube, albeit typically of less-than-ideal picture quality; but we can be thankful they are at least viewable in some form. That said, there used to be a fairly decent copy of **COT** uploaded at said site under its original Spanish title given above [*sans* any English dubbing or subs], but it since seems to have been taken down, so those interested in seeing the film will have to look elsewhere, I'm afraid).

As **COT** begins, late at night in a darkened living room illumined only by a flickering TV set, one Dr. Camilo Cardán (Hugo Stiglitz) dozes restlessly in an easy chair: he dreams of a lumbering, slow-moving figure—whose face as-yet isn't revealed—pursuing a young woman through an apartment building and brutally clawing her to death in an elevator. Police bullets don't faze the killer, who somewhat resembles your common-and-garden variety zombie in its mode of locomotion (hint-hint). This is the obvious Italian influence showing through (by no means coincidentally or accidentally, the film's above-listed Anglo alternate title likewise has a distinctly Italo ring). Star Stiglitz (hereon billed as "Stieglitz") was by this point no stranger to dealing with zombies, having already starred in Umberto Lenzi's popular splatter shocker **CITY OF THE WALKING DEAD** (*Incubo sulla città contaminata*, a.k.a. **NIGHTMARE CITY**, 1980), which was an Italian/Mexican/Spanish co-production. In fact, also in '80, Stiglitz co-starred in René Cardona, Jr.'s crime actioner **UNDER SIEGE** (*Traficantes de pánico*), another joint-job produced by those same three nations. And speaking of Cardona, his son René Cardona III (the late René Cardona, Sr.'s grandson) appears in a supporting part in the present film as Oscar, who gets his belly slashed open by the razor-clawed head zombie, causing his intestines to partially splork out through his ruptured abdominal wall (not as visually gruesome as it sounds, although it looks pretty painful nonetheless). Also, Andrés García, Jr., boyish son of the popular Mexican muscly macho man action star, appears as the horny Pedro, who's too preoccupied chastely making out with his GF to notice the carnage going on all around them.

As for the US slant? This manifests itself in **FRI 13** form when the urban locale of the opener abruptly shifts to backwoods Mexican lake regions, where overaged La*teen*o substitutes do the Spring Break bit (or whatever passes for it south of the border, anyways). A carefree carful of "teenagers" (all at least 25, if they're a day) stay over at an isolated, spooky-looking manse which stands nearby to the title cemetery, while on the soundtrack imitative two-key piano plonking with accompanying humming

You Axed For It! Andrés García, Jr. is about to get the chop in this Mexican lobby card for **CEME-TERY OF TERROR**, a mediocre mash-up of the slasher and zombie genres (art by F. Cerezo C.)

27

Top to Bottom: Scenes from **CEMETERY OF TERROR**'s best sequence. A clutch of Italo-style zombies go for a late-night stroll; one of the film's cooler zombie makeups (note eye-worm!)—too bad it's barely seen onscreen!—and a ghoul-gal, back from the grave and ready to party!

synth-swells further emphasize the already patently obvious "stalk'n'slash" / "slice'n'dice" timbre of the proceedings. When not slavishly imitating other people's music (e.g., Tangerine Dream and Goblin, etc.), composer Chucho Sarsoza's original compositions are sometimes quite inventive, if betraying rather crude production. As if to stress the American connection all the more, the overgrown kids' antics are periodically punctuated by blasts of cheezy '80s-style electrobop and chintzy sub-Chuck Berryesque instrumental riff'n'roll from their cranked-up boombox (which, back in the days when I had one, I used to call a "ghetto-blaster"; but I'm pretty sure the PC Thought Police zombies would tell me that's no longer a politically correct term, which is entirely the reason why I used it. In fact, last I heard, even "politically correct" is now politically *in*correct. There's just no satisfying these authoritarian SJW buzzkills! But I digress…).

Soon after their arrival, one of the party animals wanders off alone to explore the darkened house—man oh man, didn't these witless whippersnappers see **HELL NIGHT**, fer chrissakes?! He shortly happens across a musty old volume (*El libro negro* / "The Black Book"), so, right as a nocturnal thunderstorm whips up, just for shits and giggles the not-too-smart party hearties perform a "resurrection" ceremony in the nearby cemetery by reading aloud from this tome of terror's pages in the devil's name ("*…el señor del tinieblas… ¡Satanas!*" ["The Lord of Darkness… Satan!"]). Before you can scream "*THE EVIL DEAD!!!*" their ill-advised graveyard disturbance invokes a walking corpse (which the clueless partiers had previously stolen from the local morgue, just for kicks). The revived stiff—possessed of a gait not unlike a certain J. Voorhees—turns out to be (natch!) that of a recently killed maniac Satanist, and not only that but is the very same killer from Stiglitz's nightmare, in which the black book also figured (cue opening strains of the *Twilight Zone* theme in your mind's ear here). Having been supernaturally reanimated, him known as "Devlon" (the tall, bushy-bearded and very sinister-looking José Gómez Parcero) obliges us by diminishing the ranks of obnoxious non-teens with extreme prejudice, evidently highly ungrateful about having been so rudely awoken from The Big Sleep, even though he seems in no big hurry to return to the grave.

More ominous double-note piano (*ding-dink* / *ding-dink…*) is heard as the resuscitated devil-worshipping psycho killer goes for "a little walk", as Bramwell Fletcher from Karloff's **THE MUMMY** '32 might put it. Later, still more dumb, disrespectful kids—these ones actual juveniles—come to chillax in the cemetery of terror, which raises the obvious question: Hey, don't you brats have a *MALL* to hang out in?! (Or better yet, go play in traffic.)

Elsewhere back at the haunted *hacienda*, the "teens" settle in for a night of hot partying/make-out action, seemingly forgetting all about the trouble they took lugging that corpse over and totally ignoring the slim possibility that their invocation might have been successful. Stupid damn kids! Don't they know that children shouldn't play with dead things? (Evidently, no one saw *that* movie, either…except for **COT**'s screenwriter, that is, because some of the plot similarities are just too close to be mere coincidence). One-by-one, as per the usual rigid template, gory mangled teen-impersonators are found, all victims of the super-strong undead slayer. Naturally, the fill-in-the-blanks / paint-by-numbers script ensures that plenty of foolhardy victims stroll off all by their lonesomes to trip over the righteously shredded booties of those that went before. Before long, most of the youngsters have been permanently silenced by the slashing-taloned, devilish Devlon (who also evidently has the handy ability to render himself invisible when called for; either that or he can simply move objects via telekinetic means, I couldn't tell for sure). Things really strained my personal "suspension of disbelief" credo when one guy (i.e., García, Jr., who bears a quite strong familial resemblance to his actor pops) gets his cranium cleft in two by a medieval battle axe hefted by the invisible man(iac), or possibly animated by the power of his mind. In what amounts to about the goriest scene, all up-close-and-personal like, Devlon manually rips the guts out of a shrieking starlet.

To top off all the other obvious plagiarisms herein, the story is based during the night of the Mexican equivalent of Halloween: *"La noche de las brujas / Witches' Night"*. At one point, a quintet of younger, trick-or-treating children swing by the boneyard, get spooked and also end up seeking refuge in the adjacent old dark house, only to encounter Jason— *oops, sorry!*—Devlon, instead. This leads into a succession of cheap, manipulative kid-in-jeopardy shocks: gosh, will that poor li'l tyke climb out the window in time? Omigod, I sure hope so. The punch-line to this one-joke movie—amounting to by far its most entertaining sequence—has a whole slew of relatively well-rendered if rather (*er*) lifeless zombies clawing their way up through the six-foot dirt to reenact a passable **RETURN OF THE LIVING DEAD PART II** imitation (*ding-dink / ding-dink…*); quite the feat, considering that movie hadn't even been made yet. Unlike the older twentysomething "kids" that preceded them, who all got slain, these five cutesy tween and preteen trick-or-treaters all make it out alive for the conclusion, although there's a whole lot of bawling and terrified, teary-eyed moppets leading up to it. Having been injured in the leg, Stiglitz limps along using a cruciform wooden grave marker as a crutch while deploying a shiny silver crucifix to keep the walking dead "horde" (read: dozen-or-so) at bay while the kiddies make good their getaway.

Now, might this be (1) a haunted house flick, (2) a slasher flick, or (3) a zombie flick, people? Don't you believe them if they try to tell you it's an "innovative, novel amalgam of many classic horror subgenres" or some such twaddle. Not for a minute. It makes for a watchable enough time-waster, but give me the more singular oeuvres of a Méndez, Baledón or Curiel over this any day. **COT** is just too unoriginal and heavily reliant on tried-

Above Left: *Splitting Headache!* In **CEMETERY OF TERROR**, Andrés García, Jr. suffers sudden acute brain-pain (serves him right for thinking with his little head instead of his big one). **Right:** *Spoiler Alert!* For the film's expected final "twist", we get this freeze-frame of star Hugo Stiglitz, now no longer his former nice self

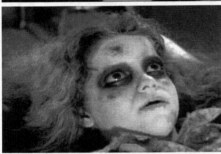

Top to Bottom: One minute they're perfectly normal, the next—*MUTANT*! *Quick!* Look behind you, Jody! (Too late!); and one of the film's mutants, a little girl, shows all the symptoms…and it ain't the measles or mumps she's got; hero Wings Hauser

and-trusted *gringo* influences for its own good. Although most classic Mexi-horrors derived plenty of their inspiration from Hollywood models, they also managed to infuse and invest their proceedings with something distinctively *méxicano* that at their best tended to bring its own "exotic" flavor…a quality which this film sadly sorely lacks. Shit, the ending even leaves itself open for a potential sequel, as if in hopes of turning things into a franchise; which is perhaps this movie's ultimate display of Americanization.

At the very least, this flick is competently constructed with a professional sheen, which makes it all the more bothersome that it's so derivative, unimaginative and therefore thoroughly predictable in the extreme. In summation, **CEMETERY OF TERROR** doesn't have enough gonzo gore to meet the expectations/requirements of either the modern zombie *or* slasher meat markets (hell, there isn't even a lick of nudity, either), and it must remain just another buried, mediocre obscurity for completist video grave-robbers like myself to exhume and vivisect in zines like this one.

MUTANT
(a.k.a. **NIGHT SHADOWS**)

Reviewed by Michael Hauss

USA, 1984. Ds: John "Bud" Cardos, Mark Rosman

US trailer narration: *"From the depths of the Earth, through the shrouded mist, it is coming—the final phase of an accident of nature. It is unexplainable, unbelievable, and uncontrollable. You can't see it in the darkness, or hear it in the silence, but you can feel its presence and sense the danger… MUTANT: Its time has come! MUTANT: Any one of us could be one of them! There is no place left to run, nowhere left to hide, there is no escape… Mankind's deadliest threat will not come from the skies."*

This film stars the freakin' awesome Wings Hauser, fresh off his psychotic role as Ramrod in the crime actioner **VICE SQUAD** (1982, UK/USA, D: Gary Sherman). Unfortunately for Hauser, any performance of his that I would catch after viewing **VICE SQUAD** would unfairly be measured against that unhinged role. So, in this film I expect me some Ramrod beating the shit out of somebody, *anybody*, please…but what I got was a kinder, gentler Hauser. He still has that goofy psychotic grin, those shifty eyes and that high energy level, but here he plays a good guy and does not turn the psycho ass-kicking thing on until late in the film, when zombies attack.

MUTANT for me never fulfilled its potential. It has plenty of avenues to expand upon, but it always just left good plot devices unfulfilled or cut too short. Two youthful brothers, Josh (Wings Hauser) and Mike (Lee Montgomery), are travelling through some southern backwater town when their car is forced off the road, down an embankment and into a creek by a truck full of trucker-hatted, bib overall-wearing rednecks, and they are forced to walk to the nearest town—ironically called Goodland—for help. The redneck angle is never fully explored or developed, and the further confrontations between the boys and rednecks are always shortchanged, never given enough development to build the potential tension properly. I didn't want to have them boys squealing like pigs, mind you, but resolution of a conflict is always a rewarding outcome. While we're on the uncomfortable **DELIVERANCE** (1972, USA, D: John Boorman) pig-squealing subject, as the boys walk to town they are picked up by a local man named Mel (Stuart Culpepper), who tells them he hunts for little green men and perverts. While letting Mike and Josh off outside of town, Mel turns Mike's thank you handshake into a long, awkwardly uncomfortable hand-fondling display.

The community of Goodland is a virtual ghost town, with many of its townsfolk currently down with the flu; which in reality are the side effects of a company called New Era dumping toxic waste into the ground and making people sick. Those stricken first develop flu-like symptoms, then eventually it turns them into...*zombies!*

Mike disappears after telling Josh he loves him in another awkward moment, this time a scene of "brotherly love", and Mike is subsequently snatched by an unseen creature from his room in the inn they are staying at, which is run by a creepy old woman whose daughter may or may not be dead. Mike is pulled headfirst under the bed by *something* in a very well-executed scene. When Josh awakens the next morning and finds that his brother is not in his room, he goes into town looking for him, only to find the place deserted. The only place open in town is the tavern, where he meets Holly Pierce (Jody Medford), who is covering the bar for her sick uncle Jack. She is also a school teacher at the local elementary school, but it seems the whole school is out with the flu. Josh and Holly become romantically involved and must join together with drunken sheriff Will Stewart to defeat the zombie horde. Sheriff Stewart was once a big city cop who shot a young man—perhaps drunkenly—and is now resigned to his fate serving as lawman in some godforsaken redneck backwoods town. Bo Hopkins, who plays the sheriff, is a true good ol' boy, with a slow southern drawl and a twangy voice. He appeared in many films, and is best-known for his performances in Sam Peckinpah's **THE WILD BUNCH** (1969) and Joseph Sargent's **WHITE LIGHTNING** (1973, both USA).

The film's zombies are blue-skinned with fast movements, even able to run. They attack for blood, but blood is never shown and none of their attacks on persons ever show the outcome, most times cutting away quickly. A bloodless film about blood-

Quick-draw Goodland sheriff Bo Hopkins thinks the only good mutant zombie is a DEAD mutant zombie!

Better leave that car window rolled up...this guy ain't here to wash your windshield

craving zombies speaks volumes about **MUTANT**'s deficiencies. While the cast are all decent in their roles, Hauser as the lead is what fuels this film and kept me entertained throughout. His mannerisms and facial expressions are golden as he twitches and grins and cracks smiles at the most inappropriate times. The zombies develop an orifice in their palms, through which they ingest victims' blood. Young northerner Josh and southern belle Holly must fight together to save themselves and humanity from the zombie infiltration, the north and south bonding with one another to save the world. To this end, Josh and Holly investigate the New Era dumping site, which is patrolled by shotgun-wielding thugs, only to have Mel show up again, this time as the man in charge of a crew dumping yellow toxic waste into a pit in the ground. Josh is caught snooping around and, just as ol' Mel and his good ol' boys are attempting to toss him into the toxic sludge, Holly crashes her car through the warehouse door and rescues him, and Mel and his men get covered by the spraying yellow waste. The scene cuts away before we see the effects of this waste on Mel and his crew...*another* lost opportunity!

The ending resembles Romero's **NIGHT OF THE LIVING DEAD** (1968, USA), with the young lovers being attacked by zombies at the local gas station where they have holed-up. Just as their demise seems inevitable, they are saved by the sheriff and an assembled group of cops, who shine lights on the station and then open fire. Interestingly (or perhaps just inconsistently?), the zombies in this flick can sometimes be killed by gunfire and at other times not; some fall after a shot or two while others are shot multiple times and survive.

Director John "Bud" Cardos was also a stuntman and an actor, appearing in that latter capacity in many of Al Adamson's movies, including **BLOOD OF DRACULA'S CASTLE, FIVE BLOODY GRAVES** and **SATAN'S SADISTS** (all 1969, USA). Cardos also directed the fine nature-gone-wild film **KINGDOM OF THE SPIDERS** (1977, USA), which stars the great William Shatner.

The present movie, also known as **NIGHT SHADOWS**, was filmed in Norcross, Georgia for a reported $2,500,000 (which was a pretty generous budget for an indie movie of the time). Like I said earlier in this review, it is a film of unfulfilled possibilities. For instance, the redneck antagonist angle needed further exploration and development; through what precise process the townsfolk had become infected was left undisclosed; the zombies with the orifices on their palms needed to be properly explained, and also should have at least been shown feeding via said orifices; plus the so-called New Era company setting needed major beefing-up, as it appeared to be little more than a barn full of rednecks, not some powerful global corporation.

But the one thing **MUTANT** has going for it—its definite saving grace—is Wings Hauser, and he does not disappoint as the twitching, grinning hero. Hauser is still actively performing today, and to date has some 100+ television and film appearances to his credit, including **DEADLY FORCE** (1983, USA, D: Paul Aaron), **NIGHTMARE AT NOON** (1988, UK/USA, D: Nico Mastorakis) and **THE CARPENTER** (1988, Canada, D: David Wellington), among others.

The thing that kept running through my mind as I watched this underachieving film was, "What would Ramrod do?" One thing's for sure—he'd have beaten some life into this dead film!

C.H.U.D.

Reviewed by Eric Messina

USA, 1984. D: Douglas Cheek

This poster blurb clarifies the film's acronymic title: *"(Cannibalistic. Humanoid. Underground. Dwellers.)"*

Does there exist a better urban mutant hobosploitation film? I offer a resounding *"NO FUCKING WAY!"* I first saw this one at the same place where I saw every movie that traumatized me as a youngster growing up in Long Island, NY: over at my friend John's house. This is the same dude whose mother rented Fulci's **ZOMBIE** (*Zombi 2*, 1979, Italy) and porn for him. *[Read Eric's personal reminiscences about said Fulci flick—and his childhood buddy John—in* Monster! *#13 [pp.59-62] – ed.]* I've since re-watched this grimy urban monster flick numerous times, and any time my shower gets clogged or I see a sewer cover, I'm instantly reminded of this classic.

Before the credits roll, a woman and her dog are viciously dragged beneath the ground; we later learn that the victim is Captain Bosch's wife. Incidentally, a funny thing happened to me one day while shopping at Berkeley Bowl when I wore my C.H.U.D. shirt (which is available from *http://www.redbubble.com/people/hydraalpha*). Someone stopped me and said, "Hey, I'm friends with Chris Curry, the actor who played 'what's-his-name' in that movie". In reply, I said, *"Bosch!"* I mean, they say his name *so* many times in the movie that if you played a drinking game you'd end up barfing in under an hour! John Heard from **CAT PEOPLE** (1982, USA, D: Paul Schrader) plays George Cooper, a cranky fashion photographer who's tight with the underground homeless people, and they need weapons right quick.

Daniel Stern (who played Cyril, my favorite character in Peter Yates' melodramatic sleeper **BREAKING AWAY** [1979, USA]) is A.J. Shepard, a conscientious soup kitchen "Reverend" who's also aware that the derelict moles all need protection from the titular subhuman creatures taking massive chunks out of kneecaps and causing the already miserable and downtrodden still more oppression and death. The synth score by Martin Cooper and David Hughes is atmospheric and bleak. It's one of my favorites, and Waxworks Records finally released it on vinyl after years of it lying in obscurity collecting dust. The sewer locations and greasy-looking homeless people look very authentic. The makeup by Ed French, Doug Drexell and John Caglione, Jr. is mind-melting. Caglione handled the main design of the monsters, and French, who did some of his best work here, created the hideous victims. One scene with a severed head and an assortment of burped-up appendages and sinews is particularity gruesome. French has a very entertaining podcast on YouTube, where he goes into intricate detail about how he created the film's gore effects, mentioning that he never uses real animal brains or innards and makes everything from scratch. I find that admirable.

The **C.H.U.D.** design is magnificent! I love the pointy ears, bulbous neon-fluorescent eyeballs and the frightening way the monsters spin around at

US one-sheet poster

lightning speed and take bites out of the surface dwellers. I also like how when a creature attacks someone it just floods the screen with bloody meat and teeth and blurts out an unearthly gurgle! The monsters' forefathers are the Morlocks from H.G. Wells' *The Time Machine* (1895), as they are subterranean cannibals who once were human but now feed off each other and those living aboveground. Providing a direct link between **AMITYVILLE 2** (1982, see p.19) and **C.H.U.D.** are the makeup effects by John Caglione, a protégé of the father of almost all cinematic "Grande Illusions", Dick Smith. Virtually every effects artist owes their craft to Smith, who taught most creature creators the tricks of their trade. Even though the C.H.U.D. look slightly like the demons from **AMITYVILLE 2** and **3** on steroids, it's fine for Caglione to get some more mileage out of his own creations, because here they get to wreak consistent havoc and aren't designated to just one measly scene.

In the DVD commentary track, it's slightly depressing how the cast goofs on the film and they kind of trash it; I don't share their lack of enthusiasm! Although I understand where they are coming from, because originally the script by Parnell Hall was just a haphazardly thrown-together outline, and, according to an interview with Daniel Stern conducted by *TheOnionAvclub. com*, they improvised a lot of situations on the spot and it was a real collaborative effort. The original creature designs by Tim Boxell were very strange, and in them the creatures looked kind of like zipper-faced phalluses. Andrew Bonime, who was the producer, argues on his site *chudfacts.com* (which has since been [temporarily?] taken down), that his vision of the film was compromised by Douglas Cheek and Daniel Stern. Bonime mentions in an interview how he felt that the C.H.U.D. designs (quote) "sucked", and he had envisioned something

more like **ALIEN**, which to me would've been too derivative and not very impressive. It appears as if the cast, makeup man and crew were divided on this film and felt animosity toward Bonime. He seems very bitter to me, and mentions in an interview with *Bloodygoodhorror.com* that now neither the cast nor John Caglione wants anything to do with him.[1]

The determined Captain Bosch—who won't rest until he solves the mystery of his wife's (and dog's) disappearance—joins up with The Rev, and they become quick friends. Down in the tunnel, they discover a nuclear waste-seeking Geiger counter and almost get devoured by the neon-flashbulb-eye-socketed ghouls. Heard and Kim Greist as a combative couple are equally hostile toward each other, and they give off a certain unappealing level of chemistry.

And in this film it's not even safe for cops to order a cheeseburger at a greasy diner! John Goodman makes an early cameo in this scene, which was tacked on as a surprise-attack ending whenever I saw it on cable, or even on VHS. The sequence has since been reinserted toward the midway point, where it belongs.

The NRC (Nuclear Regulatory Commission) bureaucrats get wind of the situation and eventually show up. They scoff at Bosch and all seem pissed-off or deprived of sleep; it's obvious that these dicks are the cause of the underground homeless folk's mutations as a result of irresponsible toxic pollution. Mr. Wilson the stern-faced jerk, reveals what "C.H.U.D." stands for, but it later turns out to be a false acronym. The Gov. garbage men all look guilty as fuck because they are covering up the whole mess. George Martin the actor played

1 *http://www.bloodygoodhorror.com/bgh/inter-views/03/05/2008/andrew-bonime*

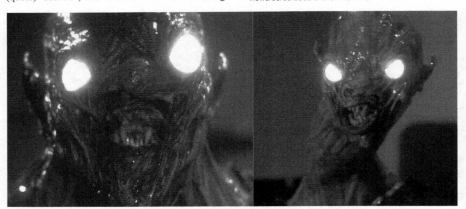

Bright Fright: John Caglione, Jr.'s memorable chuds turn their high-beams on

Nope! It's **Not** Bud The Chud: The film's "Cannibalistic Humanoid Underground Dwellers" didn't start out as bug-eyed monsters, but rather as more humanoid/penile (*ahem*) in appearance; then when the budget for the film increased, the creature creators were called in. These preliminary conceptual sketches were rendered by Tim Boxell (comic book artist and future director of the mutant lizard-monster movie **ABERRATION** [1997, New Zealand])

Wilson the main villain—not The Beatles producer or the *Game of Thrones* writer, needless to say. *[Or the pseudonymous Spanish-born paella/spaghetti western star of the same name, real name Francisco Martínez, either! – ed.]*

This film is kind of a Reaganomics fantasy about the local Gov. infecting the homeless, the mentally ill and transforming them into cannibalistic monsters to erase the problem—*no leftovers!* I mean, if we can round them all up, lock the manhole covers and have the mutants devour the underground population, we get rid of the problem and help fund big business and the military industrial complex, am I right? Of course, maybe I'm giving this film too much credit and reading too much into it...or *am I*? Maybe this is Presidential candidate Trump's current plan to decimate liberals, women and immigrants—But wait! Now I just sound like some whack-job conspiracy theorist!

Down in the catacombs, sluicing around in bum entrails and sinew is Victor, played by Bill Raymond, the guy whose knee was practically chewed-up beyond repair, who runs into Cooper (Heard) and the Rev. (Stern) in mid-transformation.

There's an expository scene where they reveal the genesis of the C.H.U.D. plague, and I completely forgot that this ever happened until I re-watched the film a few years ago. The concept of a victim (d)evolving into an irradiated creature would again rear its ugly head in the sequel **C.H.U.D. 2: BUD THE CHUD** (1989, USA, D: David Irving)... whose existence I *refuse* to acknowledge!

The humanoid menace is a plague that's spread through biting. What's interesting is that the monsters are easy to kill, yet ballistic and super-strong, so they don't usually leave enough of their victims to join up with the toxic horde. Greist, left all by herself in the apartment while her boyfriend is out snapping photos and barely making it out of the sewer in one piece, takes a shower with a clogged drain that ends in a gore-soaked mess. Also, a creature on the prowl shows up at her flat and makes it clear that these ghouls have a ridiculously easy weakness: it extends its neck toward the ceiling like a hideous-pustuled extraterrestrial and cleanly gets its head hacked off by a sword. If only Cooper and The Rev had samurai swords, they could've easily sliced-and-diced their way through the scuzzy tunnels of NYC.

The ending is pretty nihilistic, because basically nothing is resolved. It's also set up like a video game, where (*SPOILER ALERT!*) Bosch shoots the right target and Wilson's van sinks into a manhole and explodes—*GAME OVER!* Actually come to think of it, I wonder why Atari didn't jump on this opportunity. Maybe because it wasn't a kiddie-friendly affair?

Despite its shortcomings, this film is one of the best of the '80s, and it holds up as a true trashterpiece.

Editor's Note: The following movie was previously covered by Les "Gringo" Moore just a few issues back in Monster! #20 (p.28), but because our newest contributor Jeff Goodhartz had some extra details to offer about it, we figured it was well worth getting a second opinion on this lesser-known Mexi-monster movie. Take it away, Jeff!—

THE INVASION OF THE DEAD

(*La invasión de los muertos* or *Blue Demon y Zóvek en La invasión de los muertos*, a.k.a. **INVASION OF DEATH**)

Reviewed by Jeff Goodhartz

Mexico, 1973, D: René Cardona, Sr.

It seems no matter what I do, I just can't steer clear of the wild and wonderful world of cut-and-paste cinema. Despite a change of genre, country— or in this case even zine—I just keep coming back for more. However, unlike the Frankenfilm monstrosities of IFD and Filmark studios in Hong Kong which I cover in *Weng's Chop*,[2] the genesis

2 In Jeff's ongoing column entitled "Pimping Godfrey Ho" - ed.

Mexican pressbook ad for
THE INVASION OF THE DEAD

of this part-time Lucha Libre pic from Mexico falls under somewhat less exploitative and decidedly more somber circumstances.

THE INVASION OF THE DEAD was originally conceived as a project for one of Mexico's local living legends (of sorts), Zóvek. First a little backstory on our subject: Zóvek (real name Francisco Xavier Chapa del Bosque [1940-1972]) became a household name back in 1969 as a Houdini-like escape artist, and appeared several times on local TV showing off amazing physical feats which included doing an impossible 1,780 sit-ups nonstop over an eight-hour period (while holding his secretary over his head for the last 200!), swimming non-stop for another eight hours in order to raise money for the red cross, and skipping rope for nine hours straight for the same cause. Other feats which may or may not have been televised: Zóvek stopped eight motorcycles dead in their collective tracks using chains, his teeth and a biting device to hit bullseyes. This, by the way, was accomplished while being blindfolded. He also drove a motorcycle in the same manner with obstacles placed in his way, such as poles with protruding knives set ablaze. On top of this, he was also a martial arts practitioner and apparently created his own system, which he used to train the Mexican military.

Zóvek's fame understandably skyrocketed, and his fans wanted more. Movie studios were obviously listening, and promptly signed the prodigy to a nine-picture contract. Sadly Zóvek's career lasted less than two films as, tragically, he suffered a 200-foot drop out of a helicopter midway through the making of **TIOTD**. What makes it even more of a shame is that, judging by the footage that he shot for his one-and-a-half-film career, it revealed a lot of promise at least and the next big local star at most. His debut film, **EL INCREÍBLE PROFESOR ZÓVEK** (1972, Mexico), likewise directed by Cardona, was a hugely enjoyable showcase for his skills, as the filmmakers added ESP and escape artist traits to his considerable physical skills. The film pits our hero against an *Island of Dr. Moreau*-like villain, complete with fanged manimals of both the normal and midget (of course!) variety. This particular combination of action and horror was so sharp and so much fun (one of the best examples in the genre) that it was a no-brainer to repeat the formula in the follow-up feature...

For **TIOTD**, director René Cardona takes to inspiration from George Romero's groundbreaking shockfest, **NIGHT OF THE LIVING DEAD** ([1968, USA] you may have heard of it!). Over the credits, a narrator babbles on about life in the

Mexican lobby card

universe before quoting Genesis 22 in *The Bible*. The film opens with Zóvek on a motorcycle investigating the mysterious deaths of two cops who had just witnessed a fireball crash-land. The scene is exciting, but meaningless, as said fireball has nothing to do with the remainder of the story. But no matter (in best "*Monty Python*" voice, but that's not what our story is really about), as we are later introduced to one Professor Bruno Volpi (Raúl Ramírez), who, while exploring territories with his daughter Erica (gorgeous German actress Christa Linder, who can also be seen in René Cardona, Jr.'s **THE NIGHT OF A THOUSAND CATS** [*La noche de los mil gatos*, 1972, Mexico]) spots some strange markings on a cliff. Unable to translate their meaning, Volpi enlists the aid of Zóvek. Using his considerable mental powers, Zóvek interprets the carvings as a warning of a cosmic tragedy that will soon be upon us (something to do with one of the five elements not being represented; it was a bit confusing even with the benefit of English subs). It doesn't take long for the prophecy to come to fruition as a radioactive satellite (possibly alien; it's never made entirely clear) crashes in Mexico, causing the recent dead to rise—shot during a rainstorm and making for a particularly effective sequence—and immediately go on a killing spree against the living.

It should be mentioned here that, unlike contemporary zombie films of the time, there are no instances of flesh-feasting; sorry, gorehounds! What separates these local ghouls from others in the genre is that they are capable of driving cars and flying helicopters! Although the idea isn't brought to the forefront as it might have been, the mere fact that this crazy concept is even introduced places the film in the need-to-see category. For his part, Zóvek finds himself getting into several memorable tussles with the undead, none more so than in an atmospheric cavern which ends with our hero jumping into an underground river to escape as the sheer number of zombies prove to be too much to handle. Speaking of which, it is impressive to see just how many extras were utilized for these scenes. At one point, Zóvek and company are being chased across a field by what looks to be at least a hundred of the shambling nasties. (*SPOILER ALERT!*) Late in the film, the good professor is killed by the legion of undead, only to come back as one of them and attack his daughter. It's predictable, but well-done. Ultimately, Zóvek realizes where the source of the problem lies and drives a pickup truck into an electric line pylon, causing the high tension wires to come crashing onto the offending globular object, which thusly explodes. The undead all fall simultaneously as the cosmic tragedy is averted...temporarily anyway, as Zóvek fears that

these events are likely to repeat in other parts of the world.

Upon re-watching **TIOTD**, it seemed the Zóvek footage was enough to create a whole picture from. His intro scenes were filmed, as well as the climax and several fight and dialogue sequences. If left alone, it likely could have been edited into a tight, roughly 45-minute film without anything of note missing. Unfortunately, it was simply too short to release as a feature. Thus the filmmakers were left with a decision to make as to how to pad the length of what would be Zóvek's second and final feature. One way could have been to use a double, *à la* Bruce Lee in **GAME OF DEATH** (死亡游戏 / *Sei mong jau hei*, 1978, HK, Ds: Robert Clouse, Bruce Lee) or Bela Lugosi in **PLAN 9 FROM OUTER SPACE** (1959, USA, D: Ed Wood)—I should just drop the proverbial mic and leave right now, as I've just mentioned Bruce and Bela in the same breath! Ultimately, it was decided to shoot 30-odd more minutes of new footage with a new costar and make it appear as if he's interacting with the main hero. For this, wrestling legend Blue Demon was recruited. Sadly, his early scenes which take place in a lab of sorts cause the first half of the movie to drag. Someone reports a UFO, someone else reports the discovery of a headless body, only for it to vanish, and Blue merely pontificates until the original footage kicks back in. All the while, Blue must deal with his ultra-annoying sidekick, played by Polo Ortín. Polo is your typical hastily-drawn, over-the-top Mexicomedian, who is told repeatedly by Blue—who speaks for most of us, I would imagine—to shut-up. Things do pick up for our masked hero once he's out in the field combating the reanimated dead along with Zóvek (but never side-by-side, for obvious reasons). It's obvious here that Cardona put a genuine effort into matching the footage, which brings us to the biggest headscratcher in the film: Among the zombies in the new footage is the appearance of a couple of hairy, fanged monsters that are in no way connected to our living dead antagonists. Blue's fight with these beasties is fun, but—*what*

Children Shouldn't Play With Dead Mexican Things! **Top Left:** The bearded guy is Francisco Lara, a.k.a. "Cacama", a Mexi-monster movie regular. **Pic 2:** Beefy monster-player Gerardo Zepeda shows up in **THE INVASION OF THE DEAD**'s insert scenes as an inexplicable werewolf. *Go figure!* **Pic 3:** The severely-undermanned Mexican Army is attacked by fanged beasties that may have wandered into the wrong movie. **Left:** What would a Mexican monster movie be without dudes in masks!

the hell?! It made zero sense whatsoever...eh, why ask why? Another effective moment in the new footage features a small group of soldiers being murdered by the zombies, only to return as...you get the idea. It's an effective visual, seeing zombies in military gear, and lofty thoughts would suggest it's an allusion to the Vietnam War, which was raging at the time... Nah, probably not! And after my previous (and well-deserved) Polo Ortín bashing, there is a semi-amusing sequence late in the film where Polo, surrounded by the undead ones, fools them by acting like them and marching along with them. It made me grin, so gotta give props where it's due...I guess.

THE INVASION OF THE DEAD may not quite be all it could have been but, given the circumstances, it's still an above-average entry in the Lucha genre and a fitting final tribute to Zóvek and his all-too-brief film career. It's also a pretty decent zombie film.

The mighty Zóvek comforts heroine Christa Linder in **THE INVASION OF THE DEAD**. A detail of a Mexican lobby card

LA HORDE

Reviewed by Andy Ross

France, 2009. Ds: Benjamin Rocher, Yannick Dahan

Zombie cinema as we know it today began not— as many would argue—with George Romero's **NIGHT OF THE LIVING DEAD** (1968, USA), but rather through its far superior follow-up, **DAWN OF THE DEAD** (*Zombi*, 1978, Italy/USA). A genre benchmark, **DAWN OF THE DEAD** sought to explore the plight of those not affected by the contagion and how, through a concerted effort, they could cast aside their differences and confront a common foe. A film that really cemented the enduring popularity of the zombie, **DAWN OF THE DEAD**'s post-apocalyptic scenario was one that would become increasingly associated with the cinematic genre. An archetype that literally shambled through its early incarnations, had Romero not possessed the resolve to envisage his cadavers as flesh-eaters, zombies would have remained quite firmly in the realms of folklore. An enduring favorite with cinema audiences, the zombie has never been more popular nor culturally significant as it is in the 21st Century. Gracing console games, comic-books, television shows and board games, the emergence of the "zombie walk" came to substantiate its role in contemporary pop-culture. Though not strictly a zombie movie, Danny Boyle's **28 DAYS LATER** (2002, UK) was to overhaul the construct by abandoning its lumbering

ambulations and, where sheer numbers had once been their main asset, the addition of speed was to make them far more fearsome. A curious hybrid of Romero's *Living Dead* series and the New French Extreme, of the countless zombie films that have emerged in the new millennia, **LA HORDE** remains one of its most savagely relentless. With a straightforward premise laying down the foundations for an unexpected turn of events, whilst **LA HORDE** borrows heavily from its American and Italian cousins, its intrinsic Gallic flair proffers a rough diamond of contemporary zombie cinema.

Seeking to avenge the murder of a colleague, a

Japanese poster for **LA HORDE**

LA HORDE

group of plain-clothes police infiltrate the high-rise hideaway of a notorious Paris drug dealer. Entering the premises with a minimum of fuss and making their way towards the top floor, a well-meaning interruption from the building's superintendent alerts the gang to their presence. Finding themselves at the mercy of the felons, the situation takes a turn for the worse when the building is besieged by a zombie horde. Forced into an alliance despite their underlying differences, the group soon find themselves on the back foot. With the wider city succumbing to chaos and martial law declared, the isolated combatants steel themselves for the battle ahead.

A crime/siege/horror drama, whilst **LA HORDE** brings nothing thematically original to the table, its artful blend of genre and intense physical performances make for some seriously compelling viewing. With its zombies akin to the swift-moving creations of Danny Boyle, the pace of the action and the desperation of the situation rarely lets up. A film that plays best in its natural tongue with English subtitles, **LA HORDE** is a masterful French horror-shocker. Like **HIGH TENSION** (*Haute tension*, 2003, France/Italy/Romania, D: Alexandre Aja) and **MARTYRS** (2008, France/Canada, D: Pascal Laugier) before it, that the movie doesn't shy away from its more intense episodes was to gift the production with a gritty and streetwise realism. In true **DAWN OF THE DEAD** fashion, whilst firearms remain the first line of defence against the antagonists, a rather unique aspect of **LA HORDE** was to come via its frenetic displays of unarmed combat. If Joe Prestia (from Gaspar Noé's **IRREVERSIBLE** [*Irréversible*, 2002, France]) as José therein taking down two zombies singlehandedly isn't impressive enough, witnessing Aurore (Claude Perron) unleashing merry hell on a zombie housewife is, frankly, breath-taking. Hitting her opponent with everything from a cupboard door to an ashtray and even a refrigerator, whilst her fighting style may be unorthodox, its effectiveness is undeniable. Suffice to say, the best of these scenes is reserved for the towering Nigerian, Adewale (Eriq Ebouaney of Jason Statham's **TRANSPORTER 3** [2008, France/UK/USA, D: Olivier Megaton]). Enraged to discover the zombie José feeding off his brother's innards, Adewale slams the creature's head repeatedly against a concrete pillar. Filmed in a similar vein to the fire-extinguisher attack in **IRREVERSIBLE**, as witnesses to the spectacle, we are left aghast.

Hard As Nails: As Aurore, the badass antiheroine of **LA HORDE**, Claude Perron makes Furiosa look like Little Orphan Annie by comparison. Likening her to Sigourney Weaver on steroids doesn't quite cover it!

A raw display of human resilience, **LA HORDE** saves its most poignant moment for the third and final act. Descending into the basement of the apartment complex, when the survivors' road to freedom is blocked by a mass of walking dead, Ouessem (Jean-Pierre Martins of **IN GOLD WE TRUST** [*600 kilos d'or pur*, 2010, France, D: Éric Besnard]) runs headlong into the impregnable mass. Climbing atop the roof of a car and delivering a performance worthy of Bruce Campbell's Ash in Sam Raimi's **THE EVIL DEAD** (1981, USA), when his pistol ammo runs out he resorts—in vain—to the well-honed blade of a machete.

Presenting two opposing factions forced to unite in the face of a greater threat, the "enemy of my enemy is my friend" soliloquy is perhaps no better exemplified than it is in **LA HORDE**. A turbulent and often incendiary relationship, the emergence of René (Yves Pignot, from Jean-Paul Belmondo's **THE PROFESSIONAL** [*Le professionnel*, 1981, France, D: Georges Lautner]), a veteran of the Franco-Vietnam conflict, provides a unifying influence on the combatants. As mad as a barrel of monkeys, René has been busily booby-trapping the corridors in a one-man war against the zombie incursion. Referring to the zombies as "chinks" (a slurring comment on the Chinese supporters of the NVA), the former soldier has determined that the sickness is spread through the bite of the creatures. Sharing a bottle of mature brandy with his visitors, it is at this juncture that we realize the sheer extent of the contagion. With an erratic television signal reporting the declaration of martial law and the streets awash with panic, the view from the veteran's window is hopelessly apocalyptic.

Whilst it's true to say the male police officers (with their jaw-clenching intensity and impressive facial hair) wouldn't have looked out of place in the massed ranks of Napoleon's Imperial Guard, the sole female protagonist displays an equal amount of "balls-to-the-wall" resilience. Striking a blow for sexual equality, Perron as Aurore doesn't let the little fact of her being pregnant stand in the way of her kicking ass. And given the amount of testosterone on display, it's rather fitting that she makes it through to the film's (tragically) unresolved climax. Intense, action-packed and bloody as hell, **LA HORDE** packs enough punch to keep even the most seasoned of horrorphiles happy. In an age where TV's *The Walking Dead* (2010-, USA) continues to enjoy global acclaim, fans of the zombie genre will quite literally eat this one up.

Zombies headbutt their way through windows to get in at their live human prey!

It ain't called **LA HORDE** for nothing!

GRYPHON

(a.k.a. **ATTACK OF THE GRYPHON**)

Reviewed by Christos Mouroukis

USA, 2007. D: Andrew Prowse

Ad-line: *"The fate of two kingdoms rests in their hands."*

One question I often return to when I am about to write a review is: Does film criticism really *matter* anymore? In order to avoid becoming an alcoholic, the answer I return to again and again is that:

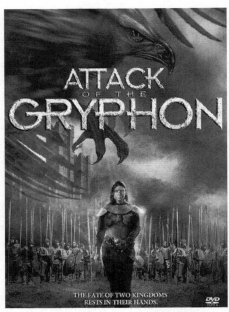

Alternately-titled poster for **GRYPHON**

It really depends. It depends on what you review, where you publish it, and maybe—just maybe— how you review it. For the first part, I tend to avoid reviewing (or even watching) mainstream fare such as **MAN OF STEEL** (2013, USA/Canada/UK, D: Zack Snyder), not only because I'm a snob (this is irrelevant here), but also because my review would not change anything. It wouldn't, because with the millions of dollars spent on advertising it is before-hand roughly calculated how many asses the studio will put in seats (and how many discs they will sell etc.); it also wouldn't, because, usually the consumer demographic such films are targeted at generally consists of people who don't read film journalism too much; and it also wouldn't because most of the outlets that host such material focus on trailers and "news" material about who went out for dinner with who and whatnot. Speaking of that, we come to the second part, which is where you publish it. I publish here and in *Weng's Chop*, where I know that the people who buy those magazines read them cover to cover because they care about genre films. And (last and least) the third part, about how you review it, is easy to explain: you have to have an angle, because—guess what—many already went to internet forums and expressed their opinions, so you have to have something to say, otherwise no one will bother. So, bottom line is, review things that most people either could not or would not, express your opinions honestly, and publish them in a relevant outlet.

This film is set in olden times (I don't believe that it is anywhere clear when or where, but it doesn't really matter), and two sisters fight against each other over the inheritance of their father's kingdom. It isn't long until evil magician Armand (Larry Drake, who in this film resembles King Tut from the *Batman* [1966-68, USA] TV series) uses his powers to bring the titular beast to life. Said monster was well-guarded in the form of a statue, but it has now become reanimated, and carnage will ensue. In case you are curious, the creature is just a gigantic eagle; but with murderous intentions. The only way poor humans can make it alive out of this situation lies at the hands of the heroic Prince Seth of Delphi (Jonathan LaPaglia from **DECONSTRUCTING HARRY** [1997, USA, D: Woody Allen]).

This was shot on 35mm by cinematographer Viorel Sergovici (**ELVIRA'S HAUNTED HILLS** [2001, USA, D: Sam Irvin]), and it shows, as this is one of the very few aspects in this production that actually works. The CGI FX are so cheesy that I can't help but feel sorry for the poor guy who had to put a trailer together; you can simply not pick up a single good shot out of this mess! At some point one character says to another that he will see things he never even dreamt of; all I could think of was that what the audience gets to see is not dreamlike at all…more like a bad nightmare. To be fair, there are several attractive ladies in the cast (including some that show a lot of skin, albeit never any actual nudity), but I suspect that this is not enough of a reason for a monster fan to sit through this. Sometimes I think that, even if you're the Sci Fi Channel (this premiered on that network in January 2007), how on Earth do you find the guts—or have the nerve—to broadcast something as *BAD* as this?!

Director Prowse also made **DEMONSTONE** (1990, Philippines / USA / Australia). **GRYPHON**, which was shot in Bucharest, Romania, was written by Kenneth M. Badish (who also produced), Tim Cox (**MAMMOTH** [2006, USA/Romania, D: "Tim"/Abram Cox]), Sean Keller (**GIALLO**

[2009, USA/UK/Spain/Italy, D: Dario Argento]), and Boaz Davidson (who also executive-produced with Danny Dimbort, Avi Lerner, Trevor Short, and John Thompson).

ICE SPIDERS

Reviewed by Christos Mouroukis

USA/Germany, 2007. D: Tibor Takács

Ad-line: *"Hell Has Just Frozen Over."*

Sometimes I see people describing this or that Hollywood director as "experienced" when he's done five or six major-studio films by the time he's 50. I find this to be irrelevant, and I will elaborate. Although it is fascinating that someone managed to put together one film, let alone five or six, it is still a number which says that said director spent more time scrounging for money and butt-kissing studio executives rather than actually being on a set and filming things. On the other hand, people like Fred Olen Ray? Yeah, *that's* what I call experience. This kind of filmmaker has made dozens of films, so they have actually spent more days on sets shooting actors and actresses.[3] One such case is the present film's director, Tibor Takács (I reviewed his **THE BLACK HOLE** [2009, USA/Germany] in *Monster!* #16 [p.33]), who has been making notable features since the 1980s, including the fan fa-

---

3 Come to think of it, people who make industrial videos or work at local TV stations are even more experienced in my book, but I digress…

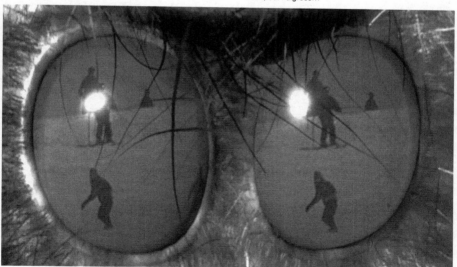

Icy Stare: Unsuspecting skiers are reflected in the watching eyes of…*what?*

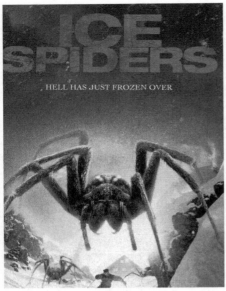

US Poster

there is quite a bloodbath, as we're talkin' R-rated material here.

When a director is shooting a conventional piece (it being a feature, a short, an industrial video, etc.), he has to have coverage. Coverage is pretty much standard business for conventional affairs, but directors need to take into account the subject matter on hand in order to adapt. The method of coverage is often dictated by the era in which the subject is shot. One example that comes to mind is the zoom lens, which every filmmaker jerked-off to back in the '60s (instead of shooting a wide shot and then a close-up, they were simply shooting a wide shot and then zoomed into the actor's face). Zoom was new, so everyone wanted to use it (from people who mastered it, such as Jess Franco, to virtually every other idiot on the face of the Earth). But around the same time, the spaghetti westerns were popular too. But it wouldn't make any sense if you'd put those two together, because the zoom lens gives an artificial sense, while the westerns are traditionally period pieces. Yet because they coincided in time, zoom was used so much in spaghetti westerns that it became the norm (if not—dare I say—a style). Similarly, you would think in this era of straight-to-TV monster movies that CGI would be a stupid choice, because you simply cannot do them properly on such puny budgets. Yet this happens on dozens of occasions and still money comes in (from advertisements, DVD sales and whatnot), so it is now the norm.

This film was produced by Sylvia Hess (**WOLVES OF WALL STREET** [2002, USA, D: David DeCoteau]) and Jeffrey Schenck (**FINDERS KEEPERS** [2014, USA, D: Alexander Yellen]), and was first broadcast on Sci Fi Channel in June 2007, hitting DVD a few months later.

vorites **I, MADMAN** (1989, USA), **THE GATE** (1987, Canada/USA) and its sequel **THE GATE II: TRESPASSERS** (1990, Canada/USA).

In **ICE SPIDERS**, a bunch of teenage ski champions (led by Noah Bastian from **THE ADVENTURES OF FOOD BOY** [2008, USA, D: Dane Cannon]) go to a Utah mountain in order to get trained for the upcoming Olympics. Near this resort, a top-secret facility has been set by evil Professor Marks (David Millbern from **THE SLUMBER PARTY MASSACRE** [1982, USA, D: Amy Jones]), who is experimenting with...yep, *spiders*. Dr. April Sommers (Vanessa Williams from **CANDYMAN** [1992, USA, D: Bernard Rose]) also works at the lab, but her motives are more honest, and she believes the project will be beneficial to humankind. Needless to say, six gigantic "ice spiders" will break out and start slaughtering the good folk at the ski resort. Luckily for everybody onboard, Dan "Dash" Dashiell (Patrick Muldoon from **STIGMATA** [1999, USA, D: Rupert Wainwright]) also works there, and he is a badass who will kick some major arachnid butt.

This was shot on 35mm by cinematographer Barry Gravelle (**BLEEDERS** [1997, Canada/USA, D: Peter Svatek]), but you can't tell because everything is a bit flat (and those CGI spiders don't help, either). The story by Eric Miller (**NIGHT SKIES** [2007, USA, D: Roy Knyrim]) is as predictable as they get, and strictly by-the-numbers. What makes the whole watching experience a bit endurable is the fact that

THE IMMORTAL VOYAGE OF CAPTAIN DRAKE

Reviewed by Christos Mouroukis

USA/Bulgaria, 2009. D: David Flores

Ad-line: *"Once thought banished forever, winged, fire-spitting creatures are resurrected and immediately begin wreaking havoc on a port city."*

Once upon a time I used to fight really hard the desperate fight of finding financing for one of my feature-length screenplays. One of them actually got optioned by a US company, but nothing came out of it. Nowadays I still fight the good fight, but not as much, because I have a steady job which I have to keep if I want to pay the rent. The point I'm trying to make is that it is really *hard* out there. I've done the meetings in Cannes and Berlin, and to get something produced is near impossible. If you are lucky enough to have something produced, you should put your heart and soul into it, and try to make the best film possible. Yet some people choose to go the formulaic route. I really don't understand that, why one will not try to make the next cinematic masterpiece (succeeding or failing is another discussion altogether, and is irrelevant here). Many would say "Oh, I only had a budget of $100,000 and a week to shoot in the Balkans," but this is, sincerely, horseshit. Roger Corman had two days (and the night in-between) to shoot **THE LIT-TLE SHOP OF HORRORS** (1960, USA) and he even discovered Jack Nicholson[4] while doing so, so there are no excuses. People will pay approximately the same amount of money—and, more important-ly, *time*—to buy a disc of **ANT-MAN** (USA, 2015, D: Peyton Reed) or one of your film, so, although the competition isn't fair, you should at least try and make a good one…which is something that the filmmakers here clearly never thought of!

This film is set in 1592, but takes place in several places around the world (mainly around Europe, but elsewhere too), although it focuses on the ongoing battles between Captain Don Sandovate (Temuera Morrison from **FROM DUSK TILL DAWN 3: THE HANGMAN'S DAUGHTER** [1999, USA, D: P.J. Pesce]) and Sir Francis Drake (Adrian Paul, who played Prospero in **MASQUE OF THE RED DEATH** [USA, 1989, D: Larry Brand]). These two characters and their men will go on a journey of multiple adventures, in which they will face several monsters: a dinosaur-like alligator that resembles a dog with glowing eyes (found in the path of Osiris), a gigantic aquatic arthropod, a dragon that comes out of the ground (think of **TREMORS** [USA, 1990]), a snake that comes out of a tree once an apple gets eaten (read your bible), and some briefly seen monstrous sea turtles.

The cast also includes performers such as Wes Ramsey (**DRACULA'S GUEST** [2008, USA, D: Michael Feifer]), Daniel Kash (*Thirtyish* [2013, USA, Ds: Deena Adar, Kai Collins]), Sofia Pernas (who was only 20 at the time this was made, but she really made an impression on me with her stunning looks; she recently appeared in Roger Corman's **OPERATION ROGUE** [2014, USA, D: Brian Clyde]), Nick Harvey (**MEGA SNAKE** [2007,

USA, D: Tibor Takács]), and Vlado Mihailov (**WRONG TURN 3: LEFT FOR DEAD** [2009, USA/Germany, D: Declan O'Brien]).

Most of this thing is played as a comedy, and you should always remind yourself that you are watching a film that is primarily aimed at kids. It is not a *good* family film by any means, but it is trying to be appropriate and relevant to such an audience setting, because a lot of trivial historical references are made (supposedly to educate?); some accurate, some…er, *not so*.

A big problem here, as usual, is the cruddy CGI, which resembles that seen in bad commercials or—even worse—third-rate video games. I can be very forgiving with such things, but this was distributed by Universal Studios, so there is no reason to be. To be fair, sometimes it has the "feel-good" attitude of films such as **RAIDERS OF THE LOST ARK** (1981, USA, D: Steven Spielberg) or **PIRATES OF THE CARIBBEAN: THE CURSE OF THE BLACK PEARL** (2003, USA, D: Gore Verbinski).

Shot on location in Sofia, Bulgaria, **CAPTAIN DRAKE** was written by Rafael Jordan (**YETI: CURSE OF THE SNOW DEMON** [2008, USA/Canada, D: Paul Ziller]) and it was directed by David Flores (**LAKE PLACID 2** [2007, USA]). It was produced by genre veterans Phillip J. Roth and Jeffery Beach.

Japanese DVD cover for **THE IMMORTAL VOYAGE OF CAPTAIN DRAKE**

---

4 Actually he discovered him a couple of pictures before, but this is beside the point here.

SANTO CONTRA LA MAGIA NEGRA

(*"Santo vs. Black Magic"*)

Reviewed by Steve Fenton

Mexico, 1973. D: Alfredo B. Crevenna

English translation of the tagline to the French-Canadian theatrical release (as **MAGIE NOIRE À HAITI**): *"Interpol grapples with the evil power of Zombies..."*

As well as helming **AVENTURA AL CENTRO DE LA TIERRA** (1964 [see *Monster!* #16, p.6]), one of the grooviest Mexi-monster movies ever, amongst others, seasoned Mexploitation director Alfredo Crevenna also made one of the Mexi-wrestling movie genre's finest and most actionful crime potboilers: **SANTO CONTRA LOS VILLANOS DEL RING** (1967), which well makes up for its complete lack of monsters with some majorly kickarse *mano a mano* wrestlers-versus-gangsters slugfests.

Although it doesn't rank right up there with either its director or star's best work, **SANTO CONTRA LA MAGIA NEGRA** nonetheless amounts to one

Spanish—as in Spain—pressbook
(art by Montalbán)

of the better monster-themed Santo adventures of the '70s, a time when ever-increasing budgetary restrictions and governmental pushback (the latter due to the perceived detrimental effects of such movies' violent content on their primarily youthful audience) forced the once-thriving genre to an all-time low, production-wise. The present film was directed on authentic Haitian locations by Crevenna some two years following the death of the nation's hated long-time dictator, François "Papa Doc" Duvalier. At the time the film was shot, his son Jean-Claude "Baby Doc" Duvalier, who succeeded his father as President, was in power (he was overthrown in 1986). One can only wonder how much—if at all—the Duvaliers' notoriously repressive régime (although, Baby Doc was supposedly more lenient than his papa) might have affected movies shot in Haiti by incoming foreign filmmakers, and what types of official restrictions—if any—may have been imposed on "tourist" productions such as the one presently under discussion. Presumably there would have been special shooting permits to be applied for and fees to be paid, on top of all the other costs (both over-the-counter and under-the-table) incurred by the producers.

During an interview conducted with the star by journalist José Xavier Navar for issue #26 of Mexico's *Cine* magazine *circa* the 1970s (as translated from the Spanish for me way back when by my ex-wife's friend, Héctor Osorio), "Santo"/Rodolfo Guzman Huerta had this to say of the troubled shoot:

"Well, look, SANTO CONTRA LA MAGIA NEGRA, a film that they told me was going to be the best that we would ever do, they told us that they were going to start filming in Haiti... well, we arrived in Haiti, and then nothing that I was promised was going to be done was done. The 'fabulous production' that they told us about didn't exist, and then we began to improvise. Because of that, many times you feel that you just want to finish a movie and get out of there. One would love to make a great movie, but nevertheless they have no media, they have no money, there is nothing. So, whatever that movie turned out to be, the truth is that I didn't like it at all. It was done with very little funds."

The opener to this superior Santonian horror effort—which, if far from outstanding, is still noteworthy, despite its star's dislike of it—consists of a lengthy pre-credits montage of travelogue shots firmly establishing the location as Haiti (its capital Port-au-Prince in particular, as an opening zoom-in on a map emphatically informs us; evidently the bulk of the budget was spent on transporting the cast and crew to said exotic clime for the occasion, leaving little in the way of leftovers for "extras", hence the decidedly no-frills results). The authenticity of the Caribbean setting thus established and the boring opening titles out of the way with, action starts immediately thereafter with a red-robed, raven-haired Latina "voodoo priestess" (luscious 1970s Mexi-sexy movie star Sasha Montenegro, a hot tamale who could hotten-up even a zombie's cold blood) exalting Damballah as if she thinks she's Allison Hayes as the horrid-but-torrid Tonda in **THE DISEMBODIED** (1957, USA, D: Walter Grauman). IMDb identifies Montenegro's character herein as Bellamira, although to me it sounded more like "Dejamira" *[sic?]* the one time I heard it spoken on the film's audio track; but their guess is as good as mine, so we'll give said site the benefit of the doubt and refer to her as Bellamira from here on in. Her pitch-ebony tresses and vivid scarlet robe (low-cut, natch!) really set off the alabaster paleness of her complexion; in fact, she's so pale she almost resembles a zombie herself...albeit the best-looking one you ever saw! (At the risk of appearing gauche, let's just say she'd—*ahem*—smooth out the wrinkles in any red-blooded male's *ouanga* bag.) As well as her more formal ceremonial attire while plying her profession, Bellamira also chillaxes at the beach in a bikini which would have been the height of chicness in the early '70s, but in this the let-it-all-hang-out era of the C-string (and even less) seems positively demure.

The soundtrack frequently throbs with frenetic native bongo percussion, sprinkled with that familiarly cheezy Farfisa organ sound so common to the Santo flix of this period. Total stunner Montenegro as Bellamira—who is far from the priestess with the leastest—gazes into a bubbling sacred jungle pool, and is offered a glimpse of happenings elsewhere on the planet: here, Santo is planning a working vacation in Haiti—on the trail of a number of nuclear physicists who have (oxymoron alert!) turned up missing—and the inimitable landing airliner shot (that oft-used plot contrivance intended to eat up running times and spare directors the bothersome chore of having to shoot more interesting footage) announces his arrival. Lurking outside the airport is a shady black guy—if you look none too closely, you can spot the cameraman's silhouetted reflection in the lenses of this dude's sunglasses!—who spies on Santo's advent, thus establishing the required sinister mood.

Again working as an Interpol agent, as he did in many of his 50-odd movies, I believe the S-man's in town trying (amongst other things) to discover the formula for creating zombies, as had a minor

Top to Bottom: Believe it or not, this is supposed to be an idol of Damballah, and not merely a plastic dimestore skull (!); Elsa Cárdenas doesn't wear much else to bed but her cross; the film's Mexican poster (art unsigned)

47

character mentioned during Benito Alazraki's **THE INVASION OF THE ZOMBIES** (*Santo contra los zombies*, 1961, Mexico [see p.12]); and as did adventurer Wade Davis (played by Bill Pullman) in Wes Craven's later **THE SERPENT AND THE RAINBOW** (1988, USA).[5]

Shortly following Santo's arrival, Montenegro's smoky *juju* priestess—known as a *Mambo* in the vernacular—conjures up a momentary flurry of bad weather which forces his rental car to veer out of control off the road and blow a tire. As The Silver-Masked One attempts to fix the unexpected flat, several men of color emerge from the bush, their shambling, lugubrious gait and expressionless cornstarch complexions clearly identifying them as "zombies" (or *zuvembi*). When Santo hefts a tire-iron to belt one of them upside the brainbox, his undead assailants shield their eyes and shrink from the cruciform tool, repelled by the symbol of goodness it represents to them. This unorthodox deployment of a makeshift religious icon echoes imaginative (if amusing) scenes found in José Díaz Morales' mood-thick **ATACAN LAS BRUJAS** (*"Attack of the Witches"*, 1964, Mexico). Therein Santo had scared off malevolent supernatural beings simply by standing with his body and limbs held in the shape of a cross—legs together, arms outstretched at either side—essentially forming a human crucifix! **MAGIA NEGRA**'s storywriter and supporting actor (and real life pro wrestler) Fernando Osés, who is also on view in aforementioned **THE INVASION OF THE ZOMBIES** (see p.14, top pic), which he also helped co-write, likewise had his prolific pen in **ATACAN**'s story, so possibly such inventive improvisation was one of his recurrent pet concepts. As an associate of Santo's frequent onscreen sidekick and real-life off-screen manager Carlos Suárez (here appearing as a villainous accomplice of Mambo Bellamira), Osés appears in the present film as a sinister special agent in the employ of a foreign power, but doesn't really get to do much this time out; Suárez on the other hand at one point appears made-up as a phony zombie in charge of the "real" ones which initially beset Santo.

In response to our hero's impromptu improvisational defensive measure at roadside following his blow-out, the zombies retreat this time, but frequently the face of their crimson-clad Mambo mastress is briefly inserted into the action in order to impress upon us the

Top to Bottom: Only Santo Baby could pull off a stylin' ensemble like this, so don't even try it, panty-waist! In a dressing table mirror, **SANTO CONTRA LA MAGIA NEGRA**'s succulent sorceress Sasha Montenegro conjures up a flaming upside-down cross; Elsa Cárdenas' zombified onscreen daddy (Guillermo Gálvez) comes to give her a bedtime hug

5 A world authority on the subject, the real Wade Davis filled an advisor's capacity in Jacques Holender's acclaimed Canadian documentary **VOODOO** (1992), about the oft-misunderstood/misrepresented religion (more correctly known in Haiti as *Vodou*, it is referred to as Voodoo in Louisiana). Said doc provides the real dope about the subject, with no sensationalistic/pulpy Hollywood crap-trappings tacked on.

full extent of her omnipotent supernatural influence over them. **MAGIA NEGRA** was produced in the months following release of 007's **LIVE AND LET DIE** (1973, UK, D: Guy Hamilton), and it was clearly intended to at least partially capitalize on the lurid voodoo themes popularized by that hit Bond film, as several cheap knockoff scenes here attest (coinkydink doesn't quite cover it). Much like always happens to James Bond, certain parties in the present film seem to have a vested interest in seeing Santo dead—so what else is new!—and an attempt is made by a Haitian *vodou* worshipper to do just that by introducing a venomous snake (black mamba?) into the jet-setting *luchador*'s hotel room (shades of a similar if more elaborate sequence involving Roger Moore in the above-cited 007 movie). After Santo contemptuously pitches the irksome serpent off his balcony—Moore much more spectacularly puts paid to his hisser intruder using an aerosol can and cigarette lighter as a makeshift mini-flamethrower!—next comes the familiar intrusive nightclub sequence highlighting the "infectious" Caribbean sounds of a Haitian show band (the movie's main title theme seems to be the only tune they know, which they play over and over, *ad nauseam!*).

Elsewhere, the native voodoo gurus enact a pagan occult ceremony, presided over by their stygian-tressed white priestess Bellamira, who may indeed be *bella*, but whose beauty definitely only runs skin deep. This scene basically records an apparently anthropologically authentic magic ritual (albeit, despite the ensuing scene of animal butchery, one of a "white" nature rather than "black", as per the title). The film loses points for insisting on dwelling in loving close-up on the ritualistic sacrificial butchering of a black goat; although such sacrifices are a routine part of *vodou*/voodoo worship, so conceivably the killing here wasn't merely specially staged for the film, and would have been done anyway, whether the camera was present or not; so, although the creature's death throes are sad and unpleasant to witness, being overly judgmental about its inclusion so long after the fact seems rather beside the point. The goat's throat is slit and bled into a bowl, and its tail is hacked off, all while the poor animal is still half-alive and twitching spasmodically as its life ebbs away... Ultra-Realist mondo—or should I say *mundo?*— imagery that is quite uncalled for in the simplistic, surreal comic book universe of a Santo movie. Other than for this dubious inclusion, which is shot full-on and unflinchingly with documentary-like matter-of-factness, seasoned director Crevenna is to be congratulated for bothering to gain access to these genuine religious rites, despite mandatory sensationalized Hollywooden inserts

of Montenegro's casually malevolent priestess stabbing a voodoo doll, as per the usual stereotype. Regardless, this is generally a hell of a lot more convincing than such fetishistic, racist scenes found within '70s Continental "voodoo" thrillers lensed on Haitian locations—for instance, Osvaldo Civirani's sleazy if zombieless **IL PAVONE NERO** (*"The Black Peacock"*, 1975, Italy), starring Karin Schubert—wherein everything was invariably faked and milked for maximum T&A potential; in fact, a version of that just-cited example was released which included very non-fake XXX interracial sex inserts (pun intended). That pulp porno made doo-doo of voodoo and was less concerned with depicting the living dead than with actresses giving head (hey, I'm a poet and didn't know it!). But on that sordid note, let's get back to **MAGIA NEGRA**, shall we...

Here, in keeping with long-established tropes, Professor Jordan (Guillermo Gálvez), the father of wholesome heroine Lorna (played by voluptuous Elsa Cárdenas, resplendent under a mountainous wig of tumbling dark-auburn curls) gets rubbed-out when his tiny waxen effigy is punctured in the chest region and a bloody hole appears at the corresponding spot on the man's body. In a scene brimming with incestuous overtones (or maybe it's just me), he subsequently returns from the grave to menace his scantily-clad daughter in her bedroom after dark. Just when it appears as though her own father (albeit in slow-moving zombie mode) is about to tear off her skimpy nightie—don't get excited, he's actually just reaching for her throat, despite all initial implications—he espies the twinkly gold cross nestled betwixt her buoyant bosoms, causing him to beat a not-so-hasty retreat. Even though they've already previously witnessed some zombies first-hand themselves, for some reason Santo and secondary hero César del Campo appear skeptical when Lorna tells them her recently deceased pops had paid a nocturnal visit to her boudoir. But Santo later becomes a believer when Montenegro as Bellamira tries to do him in by stabbing his wax doll effigy with an icepick. No such luck, witch-bitch!

It seems the main motive for Montenegro's sect to manufacture zombies is in order to command a cheap (i.e., unpaid), non-union workforce to toil for them as laborers (a traditionally servile role for zombies that goes back in historical documentation and folklore even earlier than Lugosi's **WHITE ZOMBIE** [1932, USA, D: Victor Halperin]), which is generally regarded as the first "true" zombie movie. Given incentive by a whip-wielding overseer of their own race, at a local rock quarry which is little more than a glorified gravel pit,

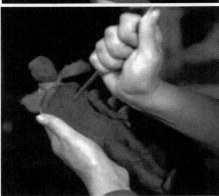

Voodoo Doll: In Alfredo B. Crevenna's **SANTO CONTRA LA MAGIA NEGRA**, black magic woman Sasha Montenegro—whom many a guy might gladly get prodded with an icepick by—conducts a fatal ceremony which causes heroine Elsa Cárdenas' onscreen pops Professor Jordan (Guillermo Gálvez) to croak. He thereafter rises from his coffin at nightfall, having been reanimated as a...well, *y'know*

zombies dig for *uranio* with shovels (trust me, back in my younger days I mined Canadian uranium close to 3000 feet underground for two years, and it *ain't* that easy! It requires big pneumatic drills, blasting powder and shit like that to get it out of the ground; although "muckers" sometimes shoveled raw ore that had been broken up small enough [known as "muck"] by shovel, if a scoop-tram and Jarko truck weren't able to haul it away. Okay, sickeningly nostalgic digression over!).

Later in **SANTO CONTRA LA MAGIA NEGRA**, seemingly from out of nowhere, an ominous inverted burning cross appears on the vanity mirror of Cárdenas as heroine Lorna, whereupon her fingers instinctively stray to the protective crucifix around her neck (clearly just an excuse for an emphatic close-up of said religious bauble nestled in the deep, dark cleavage of her low-cut baby-doll nightie! Let's just say that's it's no wonder "Bloody" Sam Peckinpah once had the major hots for this actress while they were an "item" for a time. Too bad she later got so much plastic surgery done that her face now looks like a total train-wreck ☹). The previously mentioned blasphemously Satanic image promptly vanishes as Lorna prays. Then, her recently-interred dearly departed dad pops out of his coffin and pays the aforesaid nocturnal visit to his daughter's room and attempts to throttle her.

On a different note, seeing Santo on the crowded Port-au-Prince streets during real-life Carnival time, one wonders if the natives' seeming nonchalance at his "larger-than-life" enmasked appearance might stem simply from the assumption that he's merely another one of the teeming garishly-costumed celebrants, which is why they scarcely seem to notice him, mask and all. This as opposed to footage seen in Fernando Orozco's **SANTO CONTRA LOS ASESINOS DE LA MAFIA** (*"Santo vs. The Mafia Killers"*, 1973), which was lensed in South America, where he would have been an easily recognizable celebrity—*because* of his trademark mask, not in spite of it—to untold numbers of people on the street. During "real-life" street scenes in that film, passing pedestrians are shown to stop and gawp or do double-takes in disbelief at sight of The Silver Maskman strolling confidently along the main drag. However, it's hard to believe that Santo could have had much of a hardcore Haitian fan base (?), though stranger things have happened (according to reports, the wrestler/actor had a strong Lebanese fanbase, and there were movies made in Turkey featuring a Santo "lookalike" rather than the genuine article, so he was definitely known further afield than Mexico, if not exactly so far and wide as to span the entire globe). In the present film, despite the man-in-the-street's seeming indifference to his

50

presence in crowd shots, we are treated nonetheless to an edited-in ring interval taking place at a humongous, very packed and allegedly Haitian arena (*not!*). Although wrestling is nowadays highly popular in the Caribbean as elsewhere, I find it hard to swallow that even El Santo could have jam-packed such a massive foreign venue. Judging by the noticeable dearth of Negroid faces in the crowd (although, in the interests of veracity, some quick shots of cast members seated amidst native extras are self-consciously and clumsily inserted into the fight footage), **MAGIA NEGRA**'s *lucha libre* inserts were doubtlessly canned back home in Mexico then spliced in here so as to hopefully help endow Santo with that "international" superstar image befitting his pseudo-007 persona. That said, the wrestling sequence is dispensed with relatively quickly, but not before Santo uses his signature hold—the formidable "*el re del caballo*"!—on his agile opponent (this entails the star straddling the small of the other wrestler's back while pinning him flat on his stomach with his arms incapacitated; in essence, "riding" him like a horse, the animal from which the unbreakable and inescapable clinch derived its name. Not only did Santo frequently use the *caballo* pin-down technique in real-life bouts, but in many of his movie ones too).

While it does provide some local color, the Carnival sequence seen elsewhere goes on for *waaaaaayyy* too long (Crevenna no doubt wanted to can every peso's worth of location footage he could squeeze into the running time, considering the low budget and that the producers had splurged for the cast and crew's "vacation" on location). As a whole though, I must confess to finding **MAGIA NEGRA** quite an engaging and enjoyable effort, which, as well as containing its share of quite stylish moments and some occasionally inventive imagery, benefits greatly from the genuine locales and the relatively rare inclusion of bona fide zombified walking dead in the storyline. Musical atrocities abound, however. For example, an extended non-choreographed cabaret "tribal dance" features coffee-colored Nancy Saliba and her highly-trained gyrating pelvis (obviously included simply because the hyperactive Nancy was/is either the wife, daughter or sister of the film's presumably Haitian co-producer, one Mr. Joseph Saliba).

So far as the female principal cast is concerned, as if two sexy *señoritas* in the curvaceous forms of Montenegro and Cárdenas weren't enough, we also get a third in the form of Gerty Jones (a sultry milky-mochatone African-Hispanic [Haitian?] actress making what is apparently her sole screen appearance) as Michelle, a local "white" voodoo (*magia blanca*) shamaness who lends an invaluable

assist by giving El Santo some pointers about how to combat *la muy maldita magia negra*. More incidental views follow of Ms. Cárdenas as Lorna our heroine "busting out" of still another short'n'sheer lingerie ensemble, which leads into her being captured by Sasha's zombies just as this one-gal voodoo doll squad is about to impale a wax simulacrum of El Santo, as described above… Accompanied by throbbing conga riddims, Lorna winds up bound to a post as a prospective—judging by her pure-white gossamer gown, presumably virginal—sacrifice to the great *Loa* Damballah; much as happened to the similarly white-draped Jane Seymour in **LIVE AND LET DIE**. That film didn't go so far as to include any actual walking-dead (more's the pity!), but it did give us a pseudo-zombie in the skull-faced form of a bogus "Baron Samedi" (played by Trinidadian actor Geoffrey Holder).

Our shiny-headed hero shoots to the rescue like a speeding silver bullet. Sloppy fist violence follows (under-cranked, for that sped-up, "dynamic" look),

Cross Of Iron: Much to Santo's surprise in **SANTO CONTRA LA MAGIA NEGRA**, a cruciform auto tool proves to ward off the film's walking dead men, causing pasty-faced Haitian zombie extras to recoil at sight of it

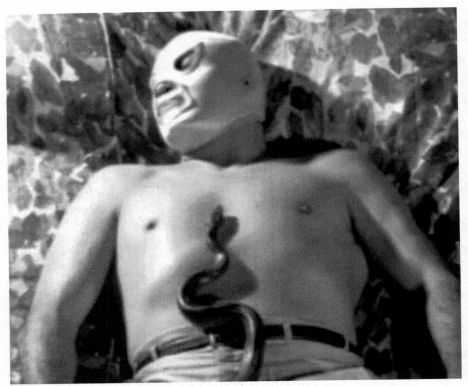

Trouser Snake? Santo has sweet dreams of Sasha Montenegro, until...

as Santo—ably opposed by karate-chopping usual *compañero* Carlos Suárez—delivers his patented brand of 500-lb. justice down on the squishy-soft heads of the no-account villains. Things get more frantic back at the voodoo ceremony, with native women rolling about on the dirt floor and showing their pantyhose and knickers with unabashed heathen fervor. Evidently being above sharing in these festivities herself, Montenegro observes it all from the sidelines with dignified Caucasian restraint (sarcasm alert!), until it's time to pull out the ceremonial dagger to perform the ever-popular virgin-slice. Will Santo arrive in time? Will our heroine ever get the opportunity to wear more racy lacy lingerie? Why, *of course* he will, and *of course* she will!

For the finale, Montenegro's Mambo mama and big daddy Santo engage in a "snake duel" (for wont of a better term): each allows themselves to be bitten by a highly poisonous specimen of serpent, and it becomes a battle of nerves and willpower—and of course whose immune system has the greatest built-in resistance to the toxicity of the venom—to decide who can overcome the ordeal and endure.

Who do *you* think endures…?

Considering the lows previously plumbed by such Mexican/S. American Santonian joint-jobs as **MISIÓN SECRETA EN EL CARIBÉ** (*"Secret Mission in the Caribbean"*, 1969) or **LA MAFIA DEL VICIO** (*"The Vice Mafia"*, 1970) from the same general period, **SANTO CONTRA LA MAGIA NEGRA** prevails as an entertaining early 'Seventies Santo bout. And it's sure as shootin' more involving than Crevenna's own horror-tinged mystery melodrama **SANTO Y LA TIGRESA** (*"Santo and the Tigress"*, 1972), made the year previous; which takes the unsuspecting viewer to new nadirs of video voodoo zombiedom, and will have you somnambulant if not outright snoring faster than an overdose of Sleep-Eze insomnia pills washed down with a half-bottle of tequila.

52

RE-KILL

Reviewed by Brian Harris

USA, 2011/2015. D: Valeri Milev

A few years back it was announced that After Dark Films would be producing a slate of horror films to be premiered on the SyFy Channel. Dubbed "After Dark Originals" (a play on "SyFy Originals", I would assume), these films offered up a healthy selection of horror beasties, including scarecrows, banshees, leprechauns, psychic twins, aliens, cults, vampires and zombies. At least, we were *supposed* to get zombies. However, Valeri Milev's **RE-KILL** was never released, causing quite a stir amongst way-too-entitled horror fans. Was Milev's film so epically awful that After Dark buried it? Perhaps it was just so amazing they pulled it from the Originals lineup and were planning to give it a major push? Or was it so violent, so brutal, so positively insane that no distribution company wanted to touch it for fear of being run out of dodge by the establishment? Some even posited that After Dark were simply biding their time to capitalize on the minor controversy surrounding Milev's **WRONG TURN 6: LAST RESORT** (2014, USA)—all initial releases of that film on disc were pulled after the unauthorized photo of a real missing girl was used. Nobody is saying, so one guess is as good as the next, I suppose.

In **RE-KILL**, the world has become a war zone; a major outbreak of a deadly virus turns people into raging Re-Ans ("Re-Animates"), and humanity barely avoids mass extinction. Bombs are dropped, cities destroyed, and billions die. *Re-Kill*, a reality TV show, introduces this new world to R-Division, the brave men and women tasked with both ridding the world of the Re-An menace and entertaining the hell out of cable viewers with their roughneck antics.

While executing an order to stop a semi truck which is suspected to be filled with Re-Ans, R-D Team 8 discover that the drivers were headed for a destination within "The Zone" (previously Manhattan Island), a government quarantined no-man's-land filled with zombies. R-Division's Operation & Command Central learns the Re-Ans were to be used for a mysterious experiment known only as "Judas Project". Now it's up to R-D Team 8 to enter "The Zone", locate the destination and uncover this nefarious project, all while fighting against unfathomable odds to stay alive. Can they stop the Judas Project, or is the world facing Outbreak 2...?

All conjecture and fan theories aside, **RE-KILL** was completed around 2011, despite being listed on IMDb as a 2015 production. Older trailers don't show some of the elements currently in the film, such as the lost child opening, reality TV show or the faux commercials. I'm thinking the film may have been held back and recut with new material. Whatever the case may be, **RE-KILL** has been released with the newest batch of *8 Films To Die For*—now being distributed by Fox instead of Lionsgate—and it's an entertaining little entry in a worn-out subgenre; but I'll take this film over the last three Romero films any day of the week.

What worked for me? Well, for starters, while I normally find that low-budget pseudo-documentaries miss their mark, this was highly

Top: Brit actor Scott Adkins as **RE-KILL**'s lead grunt Parker, complete with in-joke flak vest.
Above: We don't *actually* have to tell you what this is, do we...?

...ditto for this one, too (hint: something beginning with Z...)

reminiscent of Fox's *Cops*, featuring slick, modern graphics and jerky handheld documentary-style filming. It was well produced, and the post work was a grand slam. Swap the zombies out for drug cartel cronies or a terrorist camp, and this would fit seamlessly into the programing of stations like Spike, A&E, or Nat Geo. It was made to look like a TV show, and it does.

I'm also a fan of the faux commercials shown between segments. Once again well-produced, they look fantastic, and they're spot-on for the concept. In a world recovering from a zombie apocalypse, one would expect to see a news station devoted to outbreak news (Outbreak News Channel), specials featuring everyday heroes with stories of bravery and commercials that encourage sex (for repopulation), guns (for home protection), cigarettes (for the nihilists), wonder drugs (for the suckers), trauma clinics (for troubled survivors), and recruitment (for the patriots). Some may find the commercials a bit annoying, and I suspect that's somewhat the point, as real commercials on real TV are as equally annoying.

Unlike the tried-and-true shamblers of the past, these are the fast-and-furious breed of zombie, and they do come off pretty intimidating. There's something about a roaring, sprinting mass of zombies that just screams, "*Kiss your ass goodbye!*" Most zombie films normally feature a small handful of a dozen or so extras as zombies, due to their budget, and fail to convince viewers of an apocalypse milieu. If you really want people to notice your zombie swarm, it helps to have a few hundred on hand. I can't be certain how many extras really were used here, but they did an impressive job of beefing-up their hordes. One particular shot shows *thousands*

of them, and it's pretty damn convincing despite there obviously being visual effects at work.

Now, for the downside: After Dark dropped the ball by not pushing the hell out of this as a Scott Adkins film. Right now, he's a relatively hot commodity. He's no Iko Uwais (**THE RAID: REDEMPTION** [2011, Indonesia/France/USA) or Yayan Ruhian (**THE RAID 2** [*The Raid 2: Berandal*, 2014, Indonesia/USA, both D: Gareth Evans]), but he's certainly what I'd consider amongst the top martial arts action stars, alongside Marko Zaror (**REDEEMER** [2014, Chile/USA, D: Ernesto Díaz Espinoza]), Yanin "Jeeja" Vismitananda (**CHOCOLATE** [, 2008, Thailand, D: Prachya Pinkaew]), Rina Takeda (**HIGH-KICK GIRL!** [ハイキック・ガール! / *Hai kikku gâru!*, 2009, Japan, D: Fuyuhiko Nishi]) and Tony Jaa (**ONG-BAK: THE THAI WARRIOR** [องค์บาก, 2003, Thailand, D: Prachya Pinkaew). I mean, to basically just throw this out there without really tapping his fanbase seems a bit lazy but, to be honest, his acting was spotty. There were times when his accent—like Bruce Payne's—was totally unconvincing, and his character was flat-out unlikable. I suppose being likable doesn't have to be a big requirement, but consistent accents and sound acting are required to execute those unlikable characters. Those were missing. As a matter of fact, sub-par acting and bad voiceovers are what really knock this film down a peg or two. The last thing I found myself being a bit bothered by involved a specific zombie character ("Elvis") integral to the Judas Project being introduced and then pretty much disappearing. A victim of the ol' "snip-snip", perhaps? Possibly. Instead of becoming the face of Outbreak 2, the bane of mankind, Elvis just up and...*vanishes*. Shame. (Just like his namesake.)

RE-KILL doesn't reinvent the undead wheel, but it doesn't need to. Writer Michael Hurst, no stranger to B-horror (e.g., **PUMPKINHEAD: BLOOD FEUD** [2007, USA], which he also directed), keeps all the familiar basics in place. It just has to provide action and gore, which it does. Everything else is just icing on the cake...a very small, not-so-tasty cake. Its low-budget entertainment that may be quickly forgotten but is still surprisingly satisfying, like a Taco Bell meal when you're drunk. Yeah, it's *that* kind of film. Honestly, this is one of the best zombie films I've seen this year, which isn't really saying much but...hmmm...yeah—damn!— it's been a slow year for zombies. If a TV show essentially featuring the soldiers from **STARSHIP TROOPERS** (1997, USA, D: Paul Verhoeven) or the Colonial Marines from **ALIENS** (1986, USA/ UK, D: James Cameron) doing their thing sounds like fun, give it a shot.

MAGGIE

Reviewed by Brian Harris

USA, 2015. D: Henry Hobson

Most folks weren't all that surprised when Arnold exited politics and made the decision to return to cinema. Seemed almost inevitable. Plus, with today's culture being so ravenous for all things "retro", action stars like Arnold, Sly, Van Damme and Dolph were once again cool, so the man would have to be stupid not to recognize that there was money to be made exploiting his own past celebrity. And why the hell not?! If somebody was going to make money on "The Mighty Oak", it may as well *be* "The Mighty Oak", right?

Now, don't take that to mean people were eager to see him act again, because honestly nobody really watched him for his acting. At least I didn't. I didn't care about his thespian skills, I watched him for his muscles, one-liners, and ass-kicking badassery. Like most kids back in the day, I just wanted to *be* Arnold Schwarzenegger and do the shit he did onscreen. Course, I grew up, and while I still loved watching some of his blockbusters, I also realized

he was a dreadful actor. Always has been, always will be. Or *will* he…?

Small town farmer Wade Vogel (Schwarzenegger) journeys to the big city, now overrun by ravenous zombies, in search of his runaway daughter Maggie (Abigail Breslin, from **ZOMBIELAND** [2009, USA, D: Ruben Fleischer]). He locates her at a hospital, but she's far from safe and sound. Having been bitten by a zombie, she now faces deterioration and an unstoppable transformation into a flesh-eating monster. Wade is faced with handing her over to the government quarantine—where she'll be unceremoniously put down—or keeping her at home until her final moments and ending it himself. Like any good father desperate to hold on to the last few days with his dying daughter, he chooses to defy the law, but must now watch as his daughter slowly begins losing her humanity.

MAGGIE tries to offer something unique to an uninspired subgenre, instead of treading the same old tired ground. It's not heavy on action or gore; there's almost none at all. Instead it focuses on the human element, an angle that seems to have really gained wider acceptance from fans, thanks to shows like *The Walking Dead*. At one time, barely showing a zombie and mainly focusing on the emotional toll a zombie apocalypse would take

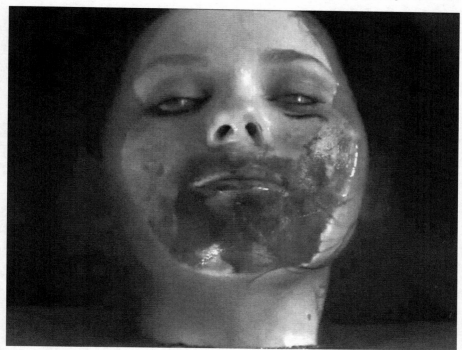

Abigail Breslin is **MAGGIE**

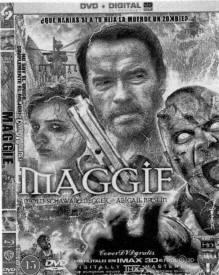

Top: In a rare turn of events, Arnie sheds a solitary tear for **MAGGIE**, his zombified daughter. **Above:** Hispanic DVD jacket

scene to scene, the blurry, colorless sequences create a real sense of melancholy and loss. You mourn with Wade, you feel Maggie's regret, and you can also sense (and see) the growing fear her stepmother Caroline (Joely Richardson) is experiencing as well. As the film progresses, and Maggie slips back and forth between loving daughter and hungry monster, you feel just as helpless as poor Wade does. Like him, you know that in the end there won't be any miracles awaiting this family. Schwarzenegger and Breslin certainly did a wonderful job, and director Hobson should be commended for really bringing out the chemistry between the two actors.

It was a heavy film, no doubt about it. It was also a bit of a bore, and a *huge* bummer. That's not necessarily a negative thing for a film, to take its time and build up to something substantial, but I must admit to being just a wee bit bored—and a whole lot bummed—as it plods along with only a few stops for subplot along the way. You'd have to be blind not to see everything ending on a tragic note.

MAGGIE is a good film, a very good film, and certainly one of the better films in Arnold's filmog to showcase his acting. But I did have a few small problems with it, outside of my boring/bummer comment. I can't say I was blown away by David Wingo's score, which for me is a letdown, as I'm a score junky, but it I do recall it being adequate enough to move things along. Some may find an understated, subtle score to be a good thing, but I'm always looking for the kind of scores that stand out and leave an impression. This one didn't. Another issue I had was the so-so acting from some of the cast. Schwarzenegger, Breslin and Richardson were solid, but there was the occasional actor that had me going, "*Huh*". It was all certainly far better than the usual indie amateur hour-type stuff, but it was, at times, noticeable. I'm getting overly picky in my old age, I suppose.

If you want something outside the norm—and a damn sight more thought-provoking than anything Romero has come up with in the last 15 years—you may find **MAGGIE** a winner. I don't think I'll be seeing it again any time soon; I got my fill. It definitely has me looking forward to more from everybody involved, but this just wasn't my kind of downbeat. Be sure to give it a spin at least once, though.

on survivors would have been unthinkable and met with, "What the fuck, dude?!!" **MAGGIE** is about a father wracked with guilt and mourning the eventual loss of his daughter, and a daughter just wanting to live the remainder of her life as a normal teen. I admit, when I found out a zombie film starring Arnold Schwarzenegger was coming out, I was a bit hesitant. To me it sounded like a train wreck, with Arnold riding in the cab. Think **END OF DAYS** (1999, USA, D: Peter Hyams) with zombies. Thankfully, I was *wrong*. Cast against type, Schwarzenegger spreads his wings and proves that he is capable of a certain amount of depth in his roles. Old dogs can indeed learn new tricks!

Watching **MAGGIE** was a bit like watching someone's nightmare unfold. As you float from

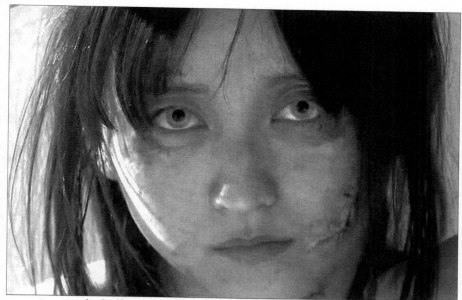

Ayaka Komatsu is **MISS ZOMBIE**...but she'd rather she wasn't

MISS ZOMBIE

Reviewed by Brian Harris

Japan, 2013. D: Sabu

There aren't a ton of Asian zombie films out there, are there? I mean, I know there are quite a few, but far less than we have coming from the States. From memory, I can probably name five of them, if that. I could use Google, but that would be cheating, and I'm far too lazy. That could be an interesting article: "Dead Men Don't Eat Rice". *WOW!* Was that *racist*? Man, it is *late*...

So, I caught wind of a Sabu (Hiroyuki Tanaka) zombie film a while back and, seeing as how I liked his film **UNLUCKY MONKEY** (アンラッキー・モンキ / *Anrakkî monkî*, 1998, Japan), I figured I'd give it a shot. It was B&W—which always makes films more fun—and a few comments I'd come across stated it was a zombie version of **I SPIT ON YOUR GRAVE**. How could I resist? It was indeed in B&W, that part was true, but the latter was absolutely *not*. If you've seen mentions of this sharing similarities to **ISOYG** as well, disregard them. Anyhow, like any cheapskate Asian cinema addict, I waited for the Korean release and snatched up a copy. Forget paying those Japanese import prices! The premise is interesting enough, though Sabu (a.k.a. SABU, all in block caps) doesn't offer

a ton of insight into the zombie apocalypse that preceded his film's setting. Still, it works without it just fine.

After Dr. Teramoto (Toru Tezuka, from Miike Takashi's **ICHI THE KILLER** [殺し屋1 / *Koroshiya 1*, 2001, Japan], which also features the present film's director Sabu in an acting role) agrees to do a favor for a colleague, he and his family receive a crate containing a female zombie (Ayaka Komatsu)—a zombie apocalypse seems to have kicked-off and then burned-out—and he's asked to keep it/her for a few days. He immediately puts the shambler to work doing chores around the house and on the grounds. It doesn't take long before the hired help notice the zombie's "assets", and begin taking liberties with her. When the doctor catches on, instead of chastising them, he decides to get a little yuck-yuck on the side for himself. Even the locals have taken to having their fun, which includes daily stonings and nightly stabbings.

Life around the house takes a turn for the worse when Teramoto's young son drowns in a pond, and his wife Shizuko (Makoto Togashi, from **GUILTY OF ROMANCE** [恋の罪 / *Koi no Tsumi*, 2011, D: Sion Sono]) has the zombie bring the boy back to life. He returns, but not...unchanged. To add insult to injury, Shizuko inadvertently witnesses his amorous tryst with the zombie. The only thing left for all of them is madness, loss and death.

초인종이 울리고 우리 집에 좀비가 배달됐다!

미스좀비

Japanese poster

MISS ZOMBIE looks great, and I really enjoyed Sabu's use of whites and light to signify life and health and the blacks and shadows to signify decay and death, symbolically separating Teramoto's living family from their undead housemaid (at least, I *think* that's what he was doing). During the day, Teramoto's home and family are always seen in their white home, in bright white rooms, wearing white clothing, embodying healthiness, happiness and vivacity. Once the day has ended and the zombie finishes her work, she heads back to her storage unit room to retire to the darkness, usually to sew-up gaping wounds that will never heal. When she reminisces, she's shrouded in inky black shadows. She's mired in memories of lost love and

doomed to rot away alone and in silence. I liked the contrast, if that's what he was going for.

Obviously with a title like **MISS ZOMBIE**, the film should have a riveting lead zombie worth watching for 85 minutes, and it does. Ayaka Komatsu held my attention throughout, her dedication to this slow, expressionless shambler was impressive. The film does get a bit repetitive as our zombie shows up to her job, works, and shuffles off home again a few times before the drama kicks in, but once it does you can't help but feel for this poor creature and her plight. Go figure: another film that makes you feel for the zombie! This is becoming a trend (see also Arnie's **MAGGIE**, p.55)! Komatsu never utters a word or breaks character, even when the light of optimism enters her life and a whole new world of possibilities opens up to her. You genuinely *want* her to be happy, despite her predicament, but you know it's not to be. The film is not really a tear-jerker, but it certainly had me thinking and feeling, which in my book is a good thing.

MISS ZOMBIE is a low-budget film, but the production looked nice, shots were clean and creative, and the zombie's makeup was well-done. The acting was passable, and thankfully not overly melodramatic either—as Japanese acting in genre cinema can often be. Nor was it overly talky; dialogue is kept to a minimum. I really can't come up with anything that I didn't like about this film. I mentioned it does get a bit repetitive, but the payoff is worth it. Otherwise, an interesting offering from Sabu, and a zombie film worth checking out at least once. I wouldn't say I have buyer's remorse or anything, but if I had seen it before purchasing, I might not own it. It's certainly a reprieve from the same old same old, but not nearly good enough for me to tell you all to run out and purchase it for yourselves. If possible, wait until it hits the States, and maybe Netflix it.

NEXT ISSUE:
Crazy Dino action, Monstrous Toys of Yesteryear, Bollywood's Off-Kilter Vampire Epics, insanely rare films reviewed, and load more monster movies!

TÍO JESS & THE LIVING DEAD

by Troy Howarth

A VIRGIN AMONG THE LIVING DEAD (*Une vierge chez les morts vivants*, 1971/73, Belgium/France/Italy/Liechtenstein) is one of the more recognizable titles by the late, great Jesús "Jess" Franco (1930-2013). This is down to the obvious mash-up of exploitable elements promised by its title, as well as the more-prominent-than-usual availability of the film in the US. In truth, however, the film that many of you have seen reflects very little of what Franco originally had in mind; and for that matter, the version that survives which best reflects his original intent is not entirely in line with his original vision, either.

It was part of a clutch of titles Franco made in the wake of the death of his beloved fetish actress

Soledad Miranda (1943-1970). Miranda's shocking demise in a car crash in August of 1970 sent the director reeling. She had been at the forefront of some of his most imaginative films, and she was poised to take center-stage in many more—and then, just as suddenly as she had emerged, she was gone, a promising life and career robbed of its full potential by a cruel trick of fate. To say that Franco took her loss badly would be an understatement. There is nothing to suggest that Franco and Miranda were anything but close friends and colleagues, but they had a remarkable working relationship and brought out the best in each other. Very few of Miranda's films for other directors are memorable today for the simple reason that other directors didn't seem to recognize her awesome potential. Franco saw

59

Une VIERGE *chez* LES MORTS VIVANTS

A VIRGIN AMONG THE LIVING-DEAD

Top: French pressbook for **A VIRGIN AMONG THE LIVING DEAD** (art by Spataro?). **Center:** Therein named, funnily enough, "Uncle Howard", Howard Vernon was Franco's go-to actor for practically any role that needed to be filled, be it a mad doctor, a suave villain and/or a slimeball. **Above:** Christina von Blanc, the sweetly innocent object of a twisted family's deadly desire

the poetry in her black eyes and constructed films around her unusual presence. With Miranda cruelly deprived from him, Franco threw himself into work and started producing films at a faster clip than ever before. These films ran the gamut from jaunty spy adventures (**X-312 – FLIGHT TO HELL** [*X-312 – Flug zur Hölle*, 1970]) to moody thrillers (**THE DEATH AVENGER OF SOHO** [*Der Todesrächer von Soho*, 1971, both West Germany/Spain]) to sardonic sex films (**VIRGIN REPORT** [*Jungfrauen-Report*, 1971, W. Germany]), but none of them were worthy of the peculiar brilliance exhibited in the best of the Franco/Miranda films—with *one* noteworthy exception...

VIRGIN started life in 1971, with Franco wearing several hats as director, writer, producer and supporting actor. Precisely where the financing came from is something of a mystery, though it has been suggested that the film was made with funds "borrowed" from German producer Artur Brauner during the making of the aforementioned (and decidedly undernourished) **VIRGIN REPORT**.[1] The actual production company, as such, was one of Franco's own fly-by-night ventures, Prodif Ets., supposedly based out of Liechtenstein, though this was apparently done for tax purposes. In any event, the director was able to interest his friends at Eurociné in acquiring the film, though whether this turned out to be a fortuitous move is open to speculation. The film was shot fast and loose on location in Portugal, utilizing some locales which the director would revisit for films like **THE EROTIC RITES OF FRANKENSTEIN** (*La maldición de Frankenstein*, 1972, Spain/France). According to the director, it originated under the title "THE NIGHT OF THE SHOOTING STARS" ("*La nuit des étoiles filantes*"), a poetic moniker which nevertheless didn't seem destined to suit the film's eventual audience. In essence, it tells the story of a girl named Christina (Christina von Blanc) who is summoned to the estate of her father (Paul Müller), who has recently passed away. While there, she becomes acquainted with an assortment of weird relatives and servants and comes to realize that everything may not be as it seems. That's the bare bones of it, anyway: if you've seen it, you don't need a recap; if you haven't, put this magazine down and rectify that—*right away!*

Like all of Franco's best movies, **VIRGIN** is less about plot than it is about atmosphere and mood. For a director known for his obsession with sex in its various forms, Franco is nevertheless a fairly melancholy man at heart. Many of his best films

1 Thrower, Stephen and Julian Grainger, *Murderous Passions – The Delirious Cinema of Jesús Franco, Volume 1: 1959-1974* (London: Strange Attractor Press, 2015), p.277.

focus on characters who seem a bit lost. **VIRGIN** is no exception. The character of Christina is very much a lamb to the slaughter, working her way through the labyrinthine convolutions of the plot as she attempts to find some closure with regards to the death of her absent father. The tone of the film is very somber indeed, but there is some dark humor on display, notably with regards to the characters played by the gorgeous Britt Nichols (as a kinky cousin who seems to have a thing for Christina) and by Franco himself (as the dimwitted family retainer). The clash between the absurd and poetic makes the film very peculiar, if not downright bizarre. It's like an art film that almost functions as a spoof of the form. However, it's not fair to suggest that the film is flippant in its attitude, either. In fact, the film is pretty much obsessed with the theme of death and decay. In this way, it functions as something of a forerunner to Mario Bava's masterpiece **LISA AND THE DEVIL** (*Lisa e il diavolo*, 1973, Italy/W. Germany/Spain); and really, if it weren't for the fact that Bava likely never even heard of the film (especially in its original form!), I wouldn't be adverse to suggesting that the Italian *Maestro* may have been influenced by Franco's film. What is more likely, however, is that both Franco and Bava were inspired by Antonio Margheriti's unsung Gothic gem **CONTRONATURA** (1969, Italy/W. Germany), which deals with a faintly similar sort of scenario. Or, alternatively, perhaps the long arm of coincidence is simply working overtime and I as a film buff am merely straining to create links between some of my favorite genre films; yeah, I rather think that's the ticket, honestly.

The ensemble assembled for the film is small but gifted. Christina von Blanc has the role of her short-lived career as Christina. She is the ideal wide-eyed naïf, and she is tremendously likable, as well as being very photogenic. There's something ethereal about her which probably made her tricky casting in general, but she couldn't have been better cast than she is here. The great Howard Vernon (1908[2]-1996) is on hand to play one of his best roles for Franco as the acerbic and creepy Uncle Howard. Vernon's stoic demeanor is wonderfully contrasted with the bizarre nature of his character's actions, and he clearly relished the opportunity to play a role with some substance following some rather minor character bits for the director in the likes of **THE DEVIL CAME FROM AKASAVA** (*Der Teufel kam aus Akasava*, 1970, W. Germany/Spain)

My dear child.

Top: Paul Müller as Ernesto Pablo Reiner, Christina's disturbed, deceased father.
Above: French poster (art unsigned)

and **VIRGIN REPORT**. Paul Müller (born 1923) makes a strong impression as Christina's father. The veteran actor—familiar from the likes of Riccardo Freda's and Mario Bava's **I VAMPIRI** (a.k.a. **THE DEVIL'S COMMANDMENT**, 1957) and Mel Welles' **LADY FRANKENSTEIN** (*La figlia di Frankenstein*, 1971, both Italy [see *Monster!* #17, p.5])—as well as numerous Franco outings—doesn't have a lot of screen time, but he makes the best of what he is given. The images of his ghostly body floating through the forest, his head stuck in a noose which serves as a reminder of his sin of suicide, is one of the most potent and poetic in all of Franco. Britt Nichols (born 1951) and Anne Libert (born 1946), two of the most underappreciated fetish actresses in the Franco canon, are both very well-served here. Nichols is fantastic as the slutty and

---

2 Or was Howard Vernon really born in 1914? Or might it have been 1918? Differing sources give differing answers. In an interview conducted with Franco in the mid-1980s, the puckish filmmaker claimed that Vernon was, at the time of the interview, 104 years old. No doubt he was just having a laugh at the interviewer's expense, but even so, there doesn't seem to be any definitive answer on record as to when, in fact, the man was really born.

And then there is Franco himself, again self-cast, as was often the case, in a comedic supporting role; herein as Basilio, the perpetually-dazed maniac manservant of Monteserate mansion. (It's easy to imagine much the same expression on the director's face while he watched the version of his cinematic vision which Eurociné under Marius Lesœur scissored-and-Scotch-taped beyond recognition!)

sardonic cousin with sex on her mind, while Libert makes a powerful impression as the sultry figure of death. And then there is Franco himself, again cast in a comedic supporting role; Franco is legitimately amusing, but he also has a few moments which are truly alarming, and he delivers quite well on that front, as well.

The film was shot on a very low budget—not as low as something like **NIGHTMARES COME**

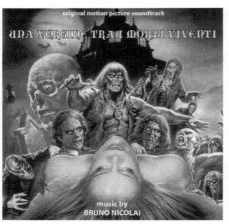

AT NIGHT (*Les cauchemars naissent la nuit*, 1970, Liechtenstein) or **EUGÉNIE** (*Eugenie de Sade*, 1970, Liechtenstein/France), for example, but still very low. Franco enlisted the assistance of cinematographer José Climent to shoot the picture; Climent had already worked with the director on **NIGHTMARES COME AT NIGHT** and **VIRGIN REPORT**, and he would come back to shoot a few more films as well, including **DRACULA, PRISONER OF FRANKENSTEIN** (*Drácula contra Frankenstein*, 1971) and **DEVIL'S ISLAND LOVERS** (*Quartier de femmes*, 1972, both Spain/France). Franco didn't utilize him as much as, say, Manuel Merino ([1918-2001] **COUNT DRACULA** [*El conde Drácula*, 1970, Spain/W.Germany/Italy/Liechtenstein]) but they created some fabulous images together. **VIRGIN** is not an especially lush-looking movie, but the imagery is imaginative and frequently striking: the images of Müller's ghost in the forest come to mind, but there's also the fantastic sequence of a wake being carried out while Nichols

Left: CD cover of Bruno Nicholai's freakishly wonderful experimental jazz-rock score for A **VIRGIN AMONG THE LIVING DEAD** (art by Spataro—with bits and pieces lifted from other sources, like the monster from the cover of *Tales of the Zombie* #7 [1974], art by Earl Norem)

dominates the foreground, painting her toenails while pretending to sing along with the rest of the group. The final act also abounds in memorable images, including the bizarre black mass and the image of the "living dead" congregating in the marsh. It's the sort of film that sums up the rough-and-ready approach typical of Franco's cinema, but it's perhaps not quite as zoom-happy as some of the films photographed by Merino, for example. There are no sets, really, just interesting, judiciously-chosen locations: Franco always had an eye for this sort of thing, and **VIRGIN** definitely shows him using this talent to its full potential. Special effects work is minimal, and viewers expecting rotting-faced cadavers of the Romero or Fulci school will surely be disappointed: these living dead folks are more recognizably human, even if they are ghoulish in their own right. Arguably the film's single most outstanding attribute, however, is its soundtrack by Bruno Nicolai (1926-1991). Nicolai rose to prominence as the favorite orchestrator for *Maestro* Ennio Morricone (born 1928), but he was also a terrific composer in his own right. He had already provided magnificent scores for a number of Franco's films—notably **EUGENIE – THE STORY OF HER JOURNEY INTO PERVERSION** (*De Sade 70*, 1969, Spain/W. Germany) and **COUNT DRACULA**—but **VIRGIN** is arguably his best work for the director. The score alternates between the insistently creepy—the opening titles—to the seductively loungey (during Christina's skinny-dipping scene; come on, it's *Franco*: it can't *all* be doom and gloom!) without ever hitting any false notes. Franco would recycle some of Nicolai's music for later films like **DRACULA, PRISONER OF FRANKENSTEIN** and **DEVIL'S ISLAND LOVERS**, but this would be the last time that he and Nicolai actually worked together on a project. As such, it's a fitting end to their collaboration.

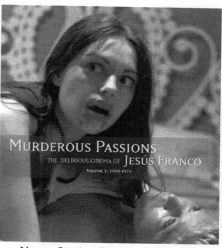

Above: Stephen Thrower's and Julian Grainger's tome of exceptional research work

Bearing in mind that trying to pin down chronology and production dates with Franco can be an exercise in futility, I nevertheless bow to the exceptional research work done by Stephen Thrower and Julian Grainger in their remarkable book, *Murderous Passions – The Delirious Cinema of Jesús Franco, Volume 1: 1959-1974*. As best as can be ascertained, it would seem that the film was shot in 1971, with Franco submitting his original edit that same year. Given the somewhat unusual nature of the subject matter, it's not exactly surprising that the producers didn't quite know what to do with it. It seems to have sat and gathered dust for the better part of two years, during which time co-producer Marius Lescœur (1911-2003) brought in one Pierre Quérut to "spice

Anne Libert as the sullenly sultry, sinisterly sensual "Queen of the Night" prowls the wee small hours, looking for lost souls to steal

Inspired by zombie films like **DAWN OF THE DEAD**, Franco's original film was slightly reconfigured to match its new 1983 title, **A VIRGIN AMONG THE LIVING DEAD**, whereupon scenes of ghoulishly grimacing, greasepaint-faced zombies *[top & center]* were shot by fellow fantasy filmmaker Jean Rollin and edited in. Makeup-wise, these leering "living dead" sort of resembled the Nazi zombies from Rollin's own **ZOMBIE LAKE** *[above]*

up" the film by shooting some new sex scenes. Body doubles were hired to stand in for von Blanc, Vernon, Nichols and others, and a completely nonsensical would-be-arty orgy scene was filmed with Alice Arno (born 1946) presiding over the action. Arno, of course, would go on to appear in a number of Franco films—notably **COUNTESS PERVERSE** (*La comtesse perverse*, 1973, France), where she infamously stripped nude and hunted humans with a bow and arrow—but she did not work directly with Franco on these inserts, as he was already at work on other projects. The added nude scenes did little but disrupt the flow of the narrative, and the film did middling business upon its release in France in 1973, under the title **CHRISTINA, PRINCESSE DE L'ÉROTISME** (or "*Christina, Princess of Eroticism*"). Around that same time, another edit, which hewed closer to Franco's original cut, was released under the title of **UNE VIERGE CHEZ LES MORTS VIVANTS**. Whether this edit got much in the way of theatrical play is unknown, but the fact that it was preserved was essential in later allowing Franco's fans to see a version which at least resembled what he had originally had in mind; more on that in a bit. It then disappeared into obscurity for a number of years, until Lesœur, inspired by the run of living dead films inspired by the success of George A. Romero's **DAWN OF THE DEAD** (*Zombi*, 1979, Italy/USA), decided to reconfigure the project once again, this time as a zombie film. Around this same time, Franco had bailed on a project titled **ZOMBIE LAKE** (*Le lac des morts vivants*, 1981, France/Spain), and the reins were quickly handed over to Jean Rollin (1938-2010), Franco's so-called "rival" in the field of erotic horror films. Rollin also found himself in the position of having to add in some scenes featuring shuffling zombies menacing a not-very-convincing von Blanc stand-in for what became **A VIRGIN AMONG THE LIVING DEAD**. Actually, to say that the stand-in is not very convincing is being charitable: unless you're color-blind, the odds of your not realizing that the new actress' hair is a shade darker than von Blanc's is very slim indeed. Mismatched continuity is the least of the worries in this new footage, however. Rollin was a gifted director in his own right, but he also knew when he was handed something unworkable and could do no more than complete the assignment in a workmanlike fashion and cash his paycheck.

The best one can say for his additional material here is that he managed to get it in the can. The zombies are a sorry-looking bunch, and they're never as legitimately alarming as the more human-looking ghouls in Franco's original edit. The scenes featuring them lumber terribly, and they simply *do not* fit into the scheme of things *at all*. Unfortunately, this is the version most fans first became aware of. It was at this time that Lesœur finally decided to spring for an English dub, which meant that this was the first time the film would be accessible to fans outside of Europe. This was the version that was acquired by Gorgon Home Video of the US in the 1980s, and it attained a reputation as one of those films that may have been pretty interesting in its original form, but which had been pretty much ruined through excessive tinkering. Curiously, the Gorgon version had all of the nudity optically fogged or zoomed-in throughout, so it is not clear whether this was how that edit was always intended to play, or if their transfer was sourced from a TV print; believe it or not, the film did indeed play on TV upon rare occasions in the early 1980s, thus necessitating that a "softer" version be prepared. As part of the softening of the material, some scenes were also altered by means of artificially slowing down certain shots as a way of extending the action prior to cutting away from any potentially offensive material; other shots were just repeated at random as cutaways. This is especially evident during the black mass scene, wherein all signs of von Blanc's and Libert's nudity is carefully removed, thus depriving the sequence of its full impact; while the original scene is elegant and provocative, the recut version feels choppy in the extreme.

Throughout the '80s, as the Franco cult grew, fans started to clamor for the release of the original director's cut, but the fact of the matter was simple: it had not been properly preserved. As the home video boom and the grey market scene continued to grow by leaps and bounds, the earlier "sexy" edit eventually surfaced on video, as well. Enterprising grey market vendors, looking to woo customers with the promise of something new and exclusive, took it upon themselves to splice the two versions together, incorporating every second of the sexy footage as well as the zombie footage to create a sort of "VIRGIN REDUX" version. It, however, was every bit as misguided as any of the earlier bastardized versions. In the 1990s, Redemption in the UK sought to recreate the director's cut in the best way possible: they utilized the original **UNE VIERGE** edit finalized by Eurociné in 1973. The end result, as Franco would later testify, represented about 80% of what he originally had in mind. It's quite likely that some scenes were chopped out by Lesœur and his editors during the tinkering process, but fortunately the film is so dreamy and ethereal anyway that it really doesn't become very noticeable. Without the additions of those godforsaken sex and zombie scenes (it's just as well that Lesœur didn't combine the two to create a sort of "NIGHT OF THE FUCKING DEAD"!), the surviving material takes on a life of its own and emerges as one of Franco's most delicate and satisfying projects. True, we will never be able to experience the film precisely as

Top and Center: Britt Nichols as Carmencé *[left]* and Linda Hastreiter as the blind girl in one of **A VIRGIN AMONG THE LIVING DEAD**'s more disturbing sequences: Christina (off-camera) watches in fascinated horror as the former slices the latter with a pair of scissors then drinks blood from her breast. **Above:** From **CHRISTINE, PRINCESS OF EROTICISM** Christina and a black phallus up the erotic ante!

he intended it back in 1971, but for what it is, the version of **A VIRGIN AMONG THE LIVING DEAD** which survives and is preserved on DVD and Blu-ray is pretty much what he had in mind. For fans of the outré and the bizarre, it really is one of the most distinctive EuroCult films of the glorious '70s.

THIS ISSUE IS RESPECTFULLY DEDICATED
TO THE LATE, GREAT
GERMÁN ROBLES (1929-2015)

A MONSTER IS LOOSE!—in TOKYO

Part 2 of a *MONSTER!* Testimonial to the Man Who Introduced *"Kaijū"* to America

by Stephen R. Bissette

Context is everything.

For our purposes here in Monster!, *the chronology central to this two-part article (see* M! *#22 for Part 1) is as follows:*

Lafcadio Hearn, Charles E. Tuttle and Reiko Chiba Tuttle, Gojira, Joseph E. Levine, Anne Cleveland, Kyu Sakamoto, Greg Shoemaker, and—at long last, the focus of this two-part article—Vernon Grant.

After disrupting the television news broadcast, the kaijū *finds his way into every nook and cranny of Tokyo society and day-to-day life.*

From interrupting a three-animal chase (dog chasing cat chasing mouse) to derailing a duel with samurai swords, the kaijū *pops from place to place, convincing those in denial that they are wrong and that monsters do indeed exist...*

The best evidence remains Vernon Grant's *A Monster is Loose!—in Tokyo* (1972, Charles E. Tuttle Company) was *not* a hit.

There seems to have been one, and only one, printing of *A Monster is Loose!*, and the book has never been reprinted to date. It is quite a rare book today, difficult to find and expensive when it does surface via the collector's market, though no doubt there are affordable copies still tucked away in used bookshops here and there, and it may turn up in the occasional flea market, antique shop, or estate sale for a song.

Still, *A Monster is Loose!—in Tokyo* originally was sold internationally. Charles E. Tuttle's publishing offices were in Rutland, VT and in Tokyo, with sales representatives in Zurich, London, Melbourne, and Edmonton (as listed on the book's indicia page), and the book was sold in book stores. As *Monster!* co-editor Tim Paxton noted in his editorial in *M!* #22, it was "something special that had caught my eye on a shelf at our local bookstore. It was a paperback book. What grabbed my attention were two words on the red spine: 'Monster' and 'Tuttle.'...What was it?"

It was the first English-language book to try to bring the word *kaijū* into the American marketplace as a sales point, defined for the reader on the very first illustrated page of the book (facing the indicia page). On page 3 (facing the indicia page), Vernon Grant had his *kaijū* crashing up through two panels, one sporting the definition for the English word "monster", the second panel showcasing the Japanese anglicized word and Japanese characters 怪獣 for "*kaijū*".

Thus, that first page in and of itself was historic.

In some ways, the kaijū *is quite unlike any ever seen in Japan before: he dances, he plays golf, and at one point, the* kaijū *even has a sword fight with a policeman...*

As for Vernon Grant, the first hurdle one must cross in researching and accessing Vernon's cartooning work is that he is not *"the"* Vernon Grant most Americans have known and loved as an artist for most of the 20th Century.

That Vernon Grant—*"the"*, or (for the purposes of this article) *"the Other"* Vernon Grant—was one Vernon Simeon Plemion Grant (April 26, 1902-July 9, 1990), illustrator extraordinaire arguably best-known as the creator of Snap! Crackle! and Pop!, the mascots of Kellogg's Rice Krispies cereal. Vernon Simeon Plemion Grant's distinctive artwork graced all manner of magazines—*Judge, Collier's, Ladies' Home Journal, Life*, etc.—and corporate branding and advertising for Kellogg's, Hershey's, General Electric, Gillette, etc. "That" Vernon Grant initially made his mark (while still a student at the Art Institute of Chicago) performing in vaudeville with his "how to draw" chalk talks, graduating to the big-time with his Santa Claus cover art for newsstand magazines and especially his work for Kellogg's cereals in the 1930s. Grant became Kellogg's international ambassador, circling the globe promoting their products during the Depression years and with the USO throughout WWII, all the while juggling freelance work for various companies with his popular children's book illustration gigs (which were often one-and-the-same; half of his original edition children's books and chapbooks were actually mail offer items from companies like Kellogg's, the Junket Rennett Custard Company, and Wright Silver Cream). Before retiring from the commercial art field in 1985, "the" Vernon Grant was among America's most influential popular artists.

However, "our" Vernon Grant—he-who-introduced-*kaijū*-to-America—was less-renowned, and inhabited a narrower niche in cartooning history.

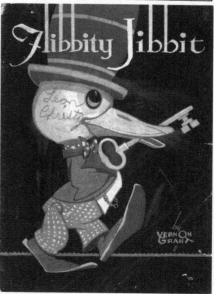

Top: "Our" Vernon Grant's history-making title page to *A Monster Is Loose!—In Tokyo* (1972). **Bottom:** Cover art for "the" Vernon Grant's children's chapbook *Flibbity Jibbit* (Junket Brand Foods, Little Falls, New York, 1943), scanned from the SpiderBaby Archives (note previous owner's handwritten name on the cover)

This is not a qualitative judgment, it's just a fact. "The" Vernon Grant is the artist your Google search will most readily turn up; "our" Vernon Grant will require you to dig a little deeper, as shall we...

———————

Unlike the daikaijū-eiga *mon-stars, this* kaijū *doesn't deliberately destroy the city: he is just trying to elude the authorities and enjoy himself. The* kaijū *innocently shows up amid Tokyo street activities and events, inevitably causing chaos, but he does manage to sneak into a volleyball game and enjoy the sights.*

He tags along with sightseeing tours initially unnoticed; bringing up the rear of a dancing troupe, he inadvertently calls attention to himself, prompting the instructor to chastise his clumsiness ("You must put more teeth into your dancing!"); Defiant student protestors ("The school is a monster! The system is a monster! We must crush all monsters!!!...") flee, their loud leader cowering behind the riot police lines...

———————

ADVENTURES OF POINT-MAN PALMER

IN VIETNAM

BETSY GRANT

Cartoons and Writings by Vernon Grant

Cover to the one-and-only biography of "our" Vernon Grant: *Adventures of Point-Man Palmer in Vietnam: Cartoons and Writings by Vernon Grant*, by Betsy Grant (Little Creek Press, 2014). It's available on Amazon, and is highly recommended!

"Our" Vernon Grant was an African-American artist, athlete, and soldier—hereafter, the *only* Vernon Grant I'll be referring to—born Vernon Ethelbert Grant on February 14, 1935 in Cambridge, MA. He graduated from Rindge Technical High School in 1952, studied for a year at the Vesper George School of Art, and worked at Houghton Mifflin Publishing's shipping department during this period (1956-57). Grant voluntarily joined the U.S. Army in 1958, completing his Basic Training at Fort Dix, NJ. According to his 1975 résumé, Grant was "commissioned a second lieutenant of Infantry 18 December 1961. Rose to grade of Captain. Discharged 7 January 1968 to begin university studies on 8 January 1968."[1] Grant served in Japan from February 1964 to June 1966 ("as the Chief, U.S. Army Element and Comptroller for the Far East Network... *[and as]* Deputy Information Officer and Information Officer..."), then in Vietnam from December 1966-December 1967, during President Johnson's escalation of the war ("...as Assistant Information Officer and Commanding Officer, 15th Public Information Detachment of the 25th Infantry Division...*[and as]* Commanding Officer of the 1st Signal Brigade Security Force-194th Military Police Company of the 1st Signal Brigade..."). He was discharged January 7, 1968 to begin studies the very next day at Sophia University in Tokyo, Japan, where he earned his BA. He continued at Sophia University's International Division Graduate program, which is what he was primarily occupied with (as well as writing book and movie reviews for the English-language *Mainichi Daily News*) at the time *A Monster is Loose!* was completed and published.

Prior to the publication of *A Monster is Loose!*, Vernon Grant had already made comics history by self-publishing not one, but two, Vietnam War cartoon volumes—arguably the first of their kind, specifically Vietnam War cartoon books by a U.S. soldier who had served in Vietnam—*Stand-By One!...* (1969) and *Adventures of Point-Man Palmer and His Girlfriend "Invisible Peppermint": Vietnam* (1969). Grant followed with *Point-Man Palmer and His Girlfriend "Invisible Peppermint": Vietnam to Tokyo* (1970). He subsequently moved back to Cambridge, MA in 1973 with fellow Sophia University graduate and wife-to-be Betsy Reese (they were married in 1978). Grant continued his cartooning career by self-publishing *The Love Rangers* (7 issues, 1977-88), an ambitious science-fiction/fantasy series which earned critical and fan attention from the *Boston Phoenix* and the comics community (*The Comics Buyers' Guide*, *The Comics Journal*, etc.).

———————
1   "Vernon Grant Resume of 1975", *Adventures of Point-Man Palmer in Vietnam: Cartoons and Writings by Vernon Grant* by Betsy Grant (2014, Little Creek Press), p.152-153.

Why, then, has history been thus far so unkind to Grant's legacy?

Thankfully, that is beginning to change.

Google search for "Vernon Grant" today, and unlike two years ago, you will find "our" Vernon Grant visible online for the first time ever...

In other ways, the kaijū *is in-synch with the breed of* daikaijū *more familiar to Westerners. Cornered by Tokyo police, he breathes fire from his maw; in accord with the new wave in 1970s* daikaijū-eiga *movies, the president of a corporate polluter chuckling on the phone in his office ("...dump it all in the ocean—I don't care if people call me a monster...") is confronted by the* kaijū *carrying a protest sign that reads "Stop Pollution."*

At one point a boy claims to recognize the kaijū *when it hides itself in a toy shop ("Yeah, I saw your picture on T.V."), but the* kaijū *handily devours a toy action figure of the monster-fighting "Super-Good-Man", just as Ultraman's monstrous foes hoped to do episode after episode...*

The fact that Vernon Grant has a greater web presence of late is thanks entirely to his wife and widow Betsy Grant, who has done much over the past few years to keep Vernon's work visible and accessible. Almost all we know about Vernon now comes from Betsy's first reprint volume of Vernon's work, *Adventures of Point-Man Palmer in Vietnam: Cartoons and Writings by Vernon Grant* (2014, Little Creek Press), an ideal introduction to Vernon's comics creations that also serves as the first biography of the man. Betsy followed that with a reprint edition of Grant's seminal *Stand-By One!* (October 2015, Little Creek Press). That both books are an act of love should be self-evident, and that more will follow is to be dearly hoped for and fully supported.

Until the publication of Betsy's biographical collection, I had only two of Vernon's original publications in my library: *Stand-By One!* (1969, self-published) and *A Monster is Loose!—in Tokyo* (1972, Charles E. Tuttle Company). The former was in my collection for decades, since I collect comics and comics-related publications by soldier artists; the latter I only acquired (at a dear price) last year, thanks to my friend and *Monster!* co-editor/designer Tim Paxton's ceaseless and boundless love for the book, which I'd never seen. Tim's love for the book prompted my years-long search for a copy, which was satisfied in 2014 and prompted my writing this article.

Without being aware the article was written by the same man, I'd also read and reread a terrific article entitled "Samurai Superstrips" by "Vern" (not Vernon) Grant published in *The Comics Journal* #94 (October 1984). The article confidently expressed Grant's profound love for Kazuo Koike and Goseki Kojima's *manga* series 子連れ狼 / *Kozure Ōkami / Lone Wolf and Cub* (28 volumes, originally serialized in Weekly 漫画アクション / *Weekly Manga Action*, September 1970-April 1976), analyzing what made the series such a hit in Japan and articulating what set it apart from all other *manga* to date:

"Several unusual factors had combined in a jell of genius to produce the greatest reader response ever recorded by the competition-heavy Japanese industry. What were these factors? How did they come into being? What are the forces which sustain them as interest in the adventure strip grows daily? A study of the above elements illuminates one of the most fascinating success stories of comic art. It offers guidelines to artists and writers in their efforts to produce meaningful material of high demand for readers and viewers—material to be applauded by critics, honored by educators, and appreciated by fellow craftsmen." [2]

Significantly, this article was a reprint. As noted

2 "Vern" Grant, "Samurai Superstrips," *The Comics Journal* #94 (October 1984, Fantagraphics Inc.), p.91.

Vernon Grant's first cartoon book, and one of the first such books of the Vietnam War era by a soldier creator: *Stand-By One!* (self-published, 1969), reprinted in October 2015 by Little Creek Press (available for $9.95 plus shipping at *http://www.amazon.com/Stand-By-One-Betsy-Grant/dp/194258606X* or *signed/personalized by Betsy Grant at http://bvgrantstudio. com/Page_3_2.html*)

at the end of the essay, *"The above article originally appeared as a three-part series in November 1972 issues of the English-language* Mainichi Daily News, *published in Japan."*[3]

This means that Grant was most likely the first to recognize and critically review *Kozure Ōkami* in the English language—a little over two years into *Kozure Ōkami*'s original serialization, the very year the first film adaptation was released in Japan (**LONE WOLF AND CUB: SWORD OF VENGEANCE** [子連れ狼 子を貸し腕貸しつかまつる / *Kozure Ōkami: Kowokashi udekashi tsukamatsuru*, April 1972]), one year before that film was dubbed and released in America, eight years before the compilation feature **SHOGUN ASSASSIN** (子連れ狼 / *Kozure Ōkami*, 1980) became an

3 *Ibid.,* p.94.

The Poetry Of Manga: Translated page from Kazuo Koike's and Goseki Kojima's manga series *Lone Wolf and Cub* (子連れ狼 / *Kozure Ōkami* [28 volumes]; originally serialized in Weekly 漫画アクション / *Weekly Manga Action*, September 1970-April 1976)

unexpected hit in America, and fifteen years before the first English-language translation/publication of *Kozure Ōkami* in America (*Lone Wolf and Cub*, 45 issues, 1987-91, incomplete), a full 28 years before its *complete* American serialization (*Lone Wolf and Cub*, 28 volumes, Dark Horse Comics, 2000-02). By the time Grant's article had been reprinted in *The Comics Journal*, Grant was well into his run with the self-published *The Love Rangers*, though no mention of his creator status accompanied the article in *TCJ*.

Vernon Grant was way ahead of his fellow American cartoonists and comics-loving fellows, though nobody seemed to notice at the time, and I've never seen any proper attention given to Grant's pioneer status in this regard.

I do recall a fellow cartoonist showing me copies of Grant's *The Love Rangers* back in the mid-1980s—shortly after the reprint of Grant's article on *Kozure Ōkami* in *The Comics Journal*, though none of us made the connection—but I never managed to track down copies for myself.

I once showed my late friend Mark "Sparky" Whitcomb my copy of *Stand-By One!*, mentioning

how much Grant's cartooning reminded me of Mark's drawing style. Sparky was initially taken aback—"actually, I think this looks kind of crude", he balked—until I pointed out the book had been published in 1969, and how much Bhob Stewart had praised Grant's later work. I wish I'd had a

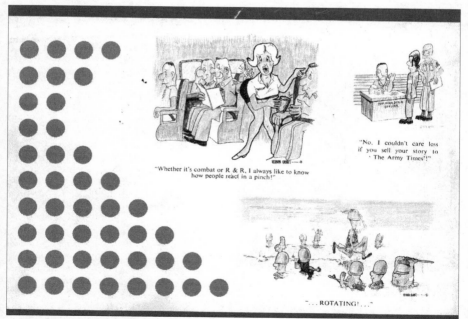

Compare Bill Mauldin's classic WWII military cartooning when he was in his early 20s *[top]* (circa 1943, from the military newspaper *Stars and Stripes*, when Mauldin was serving in the U.S. Army as sergeant of the 45th Division's press corps) with Vernon Grant's when he was in his 30s, while and just after serving in Vietnam and Japan *[bottom]* (back cover to *Stand-By One* [self-published, 1969])

Top: Cover art and interior page from Anne Cleveland's "evergreen" seller *It's Better With Your Shoes Off* (Charles E. Tuttle Company, 1955). **Bottom:** Sexy-but-sanitary *sentō* fun in Vernon Grant's *A Monster isLoose!—in Tokyo* (same publisher, 1972)

understandable. *A Monster is Loose!* was a livelier concoction, exercising a more inventive approach to the comics page and sequential narrative and gag cartooning, but Grant's cartooning chops weren't up there with, say, Bill Mauldin's or (as cited in Part 1) Anne Cleveland's.

I cite Bill Mauldin here because, like Mauldin, Grant's initial published offerings were concerned with military service and combat in the 20th Century, a venerable tradition among cartoonists dating back to WW1. I cite Anne Cleveland because she was the writer/cartoonist responsible for Charles E. Tuttle's most successful cartoon book, *It's Better With Shoes Off* (1955, kept in print via multiple printings until at least 1969 in both hardcover and paperback editions), and Tuttle was Vernon Grant's publisher for *A Monster is Loose!*

While I'm loath to compare elements of style, a candid assessment of Vernon Grant's work is necessary to this analysis. Mind you, I absolutely *love* Vernon Grant's cartooning and cartoon books—but affection isn't the issue here. Assessing the relative historical disregard for Grant's work *is*. Unfair as it may seem to compare any relative neophyte cartoonist's work to that of Bill Mauldin and Anne Cleveland, the comparisons are instructive. Grant was, whether he liked it or not, placing himself in the competitive marketplace with Mauldin and Cleveland. Grant did so consciously in his "About the Artist..." biography on the indicia page of *Stand-By One!...*, writing of himself, *"His incisive renderings coupled with his infantry background has made him one of the most important military cartoonists in print."* Hence, Grant invited the comparison with Bill Mauldin (one of WWII's most celebrated soldier-cartoonists). The comparison with Anne Cleveland wasn't a conscious act or invitation, but sharing a publisher (Charles E. Tuttle Company) begs the question, and comparing *A Monster is Loose!* with Tuttle's (perhaps) bestselling cartoon book was perhaps something the publisher did at some point.

Vernon Grant's line was relatively spare and often crude, rarely seductive to the eye; his line weight (rendered with pen, with heavier lines—primarily outlines of figures or characters to make them stand out from the sketchy backgrounds—indicating Vernon going back over his lines with his pen to lend them weight) was light and playful, lacking the aggressive confidence of Mauldin's brushwork or the sensuous flow of Cleveland's. While Grant's cartooning was attentive to detail, he didn't demonstrate the observational drawing skills of Mauldin or Cleveland; his work looked amateurish by compare. Grant's figures didn't have the gravity

copy of *A Monster is Loose!* at that time; Sparky would have loved it. Grant's *kaijū* character and the antic sexuality of *A Monster is Loose!* would have amused Sparky to no end, and bore even greater similarities with Sparky's own cartooning.

In hindsight, I can see why Sparky was initially taken aback. Seeing only *Stand-By One!* and his other military comics, a harsh assessment might be or convincing body language of Mauldin's or Cleveland's, either; Grant's figures were hard-won and expressive, but often ill-proportioned and stiff. Grant's cartooning was a labor of love, but the labor showed (i.e., his figures were labored), lacking the sloppy male urgency of Mauldin's brush-and-ink figures or always-eye-pleasing, always insightful energetic grace of Cleveland's (an aspect of Cleveland's work that was self-evident even in her first published work in Cleveland and fellow student cartoonist Jean Anderson's *Vassar*, 1938, Vassar Cooperative Bookshop).

That duly noted, one must also take into consideration the conditions under which Grant was cartooning prior to 1972. Vernon Grant's earliest published cartooning was for the *Mainichi Daily News* and the military newspaper *Pacific Stars and Stripes* ("A Grant Time in Japan", "Grant's Heroes", and "Grant's Grunts"), comics work completed for publication against tight deadlines while he was serving in Japan as a Captain in the U.S. Army (1966-69). Grant's cartooning did improve over time, benefitting also from Grant's ongoing reading of *manga* and logging long hours on the drawing boards.

Which leads me to the critical issue here: weighing Grant's work in the context of the likes of Mauldin and Cleveland *completely* misses the point.

Yes, there were and remain key contextual and thematic associations, but by 1969-70 Grant was working on another level altogether.

He was, in fact, the first American cartoonist consciously incorporating the influence of *manga* into his own work.

Don't take my word for it. Vernon Grant himself said so back in 1972: "Japanese illustrators are the greatest action artists I've ever seen," Grant told *Pacific Star & Stripes* staff writer CPO Tom Gsell. "In my monster book I tried to apply composition angles unused by American cartoonists... angles I learned here in Japan" (Grant to Gsell, "Monsters, Too: Cartoonist is Loose—in Tokyo," *Pacific Stars & Stripes*, April 22, 1972; ellipses were part of the original article text).

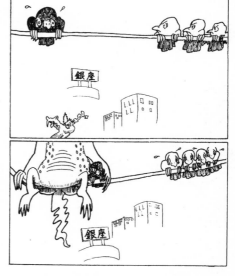

Further confirmation came from the late great Bhob Stewart. During a marathon late-1990s phone conversation (spread over two months of frequent back-and-forth calls) with Bhob Stewart, Bhob asked me if I'd ever heard of Vernon Grant.

When I said I had *Stand-By One!* in my collection, Bhob talked of his long-time friendship with Grant, Grant's love of *manga*, how deeply it shaped Grant's own comics creations, and he encouraged

Top: The exchange of business cards, or *meishi* (名刺), has its own formal etiquette, which the *kaijū* observes in *A Monster is Loose!* **Above:** An alien in his own right in a land known for xenophobia, the *kaijū* lends a loving cuddle to an outcast

Vernon Grant, *Love Rangers* art: this image was provided by Betsy Grant to my friend Jon B. Cooke for his excellent zine *Comic Book Creator* (#8, Spring 2015, TwoMorrows Publishing). I suspect the artwork scanned was wrapped in plastic, given the visual artifacts

me to track down more of his work. "You two really should meet some day, too," Bhob said, before riffing off in another direction on another subject altogether. Years later I stumbled upon Bhob's affectionate reference to Vernon's historical importance and his comics work in *The Comics Journal*, and kicked myself for never connecting the dots in time. Bhob's testimonial was, in fact, in the very same issue of *TCJ* that "Vern" Grant's article "Samurai Superstrips" had appeared.

In the context of reviewing Frederik L. Schodt's seminal book *Manga! Manga! The World of Japanese Comics* (1983, Kodansha International), Stewart wrote:

"...While extensive, Schodt's bibliography makes no mention of the 1972 articles on Japanese comics for the Mainichi Daily News *by American artist (*Love Rangers*) Vernon Grant, although Schodt's section titled 'Reading and the Structure of Narrative Comics,' on the Japanese graphic narrative structure, restates several analytical points originally offered by Grant in a 1972* Mainichi *piece, 'Talented Cartoonist Uses Film Techniques.' In a paragraph on American comics artists influenced by Japanese comics, Schodt once again ignores Grant, who has written and drawn over 150 pages of his Japanese-influenced* Love Rangers *in continuing stories spread over five digest-sized comics... Schodt cites Wendy Pini and Frank Miller, yet Grant who has read numerous Japanese com-*

ics in the original Japanese, may well be the only American artist at work on material that incorporates the Japanese sensibility on all levels of story, style, structure, page design, and novelistic length. Various problems of production, promotion, and self-distribution haven't slowed Grant's output. He continues to turn out his science-fictional tales of 'cosmic philosophy' that sometimes read as if Carl Barks were living in Tokyo."[4]

Coming from a seasoned comics aficionado and Carl Barks devotee like Stewart, no higher praise was possible.

By any measure, there is clear growth in Grant's cartooning skills between 1969 and 1972. *A Monster is Loose!* definitely demonstrated the maturation of his skills, and a conscious incorporation of *manga* techniques *no other American cartoonist was manifesting.*

No wonder Grant was not (superficially) working at a level that would have satisfied mainstream American cartooning or comic book editors or art directors; he was *working ahead of the curve.*

Grant was, in his way, as much of a pioneer underground cartoonist as many of those involved in the underground comix movement.

4   Bhob Stewart, "Miles of Manga: Japan's Dream Mechanism," *The Comics Journal* #94 (October 1984, Fantagraphics Inc.), pg. 69.

The kaijū *is a bit of a lech, too, appearing in a couple's conjugal bed ("It's a Monster!" "Heh, heh—yes m'dear, it is rather lar–?") and sneakily patting a woman's derriere while waiting for an elevator door to open. Toward the end of his Tokyo adventure (in the book's longest narrative/gag sequence), the* kaijū *is pulled into a* sentō *and savors a full bathing and massage session with a lovely* yuna *named Haruko-san...*

Steamy early 1960s eroticism in the *sentō*/bath sequences of the Japanese/US coproduction **THE MANSTER** (双頭の殺人鬼 / *Sôtô no Satsujinki*, a.k.a. **THE SPLIT**, 1959/62)

As Tim Paxton noted in his *Monster! #22* editorial, *A Monster is Loose!* was *"full of cartoony sex. Everything from the monster's encounters with women and their underwear (the days of the week thing had me scratching my head for years) to patting them on their shapely butt with his tail... But what really sent my preteen brain to boiling was the extended adventure that the monster had in a Turkish bathhouse... when other kids were sneaking peeks at their older brothers' collection of girlie magazines, I was fantasizing about being in a bathhouse with a sexy Japanese lady."*[5] Weird, eh? Don't be judgmental. Japanese Turkish baths (a *sentō*) and *yuna* (湯女, female bathing attendants) played a vital role in the sexual awakening of more folks than just Tim; I can honestly say the fusion of monsters and Turkish baths isn't entirely unique,

5   Tim Paxton, "Editorializing", *Monster! #22* (October 2015, Wildside Publishing/Kronos Productions), p. 3, quoted with permission.

either. I've had friends tell me how titillating and shocking the *yuna*/bath opening sequence of the Japanese/US coproduction **THE MANSTER** (双頭の殺人鬼 / *Sôtô no Satsujinki*, a.k.a. **THE SPLIT,** 1959/62) was for them at a formative age. *A Monster is Loose!* provided a much more playful introduction to that particular erotic turf.

Clearly, aspects of the *kaijū's* experience are caricatures of Grant's own experiences and perceptions as a soldier serving in Japan in the 1960s and his student life from 1968-72; how many incidents in *A Monster is Loose!* might

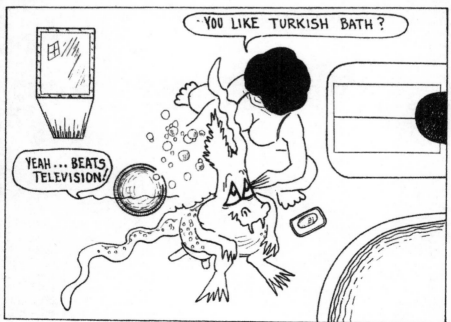

be exaggerations of real-life events, nobody can say. Though she first met Vernon after the publication of *A Monster is Loose!*, Betsy Grant has written about Vernon Grant's situation at the time in which *A Monster is Loose!* was created and published.

"Before I met him, [Vernon] *always had a very active social life. In fact, I felt very fortunate that some other woman had not scooped him up before we met and got married. Before we met in 1972, he had a Japanese girlfriend. As he said to Jason Thompson in a* Pulp Magazine *interview (May 12, 2001), 'I was going with a Japanese girl over there at the time whose father was the third highest-ranking person at one of the major ministries, and she had use of his card, his* meshi, *which allowed us to travel around. I would guess I've been in some places that foreigners would never get to see in a lifetime.'...*"[6]

6 Betsy Grant, *Adventures of Point-Man Palmer in Vietnam: Cartoons and Writings by Vernon Grant* by Betsy Grant (2014, Little Creek Press), p.57.

Betsy shares some particulars about what went into the book:

"*...shortly before he met me at Sophia University, he produced* A Monster is Loose!*—in Tokyo... Vernon had become deeply involved in reading Japanese comics and knew the great interest the Japanese had in monsters. Vernon thought there were some 350 monsters portrayed in comic books in Japan in 1977. In* [a 1977 interview with the] Cambridge Chronicle... *Vernon said, 'The television stations have monster funerals when they have to kill off a favorite.'...In an article done by the* Pacific Stars and Stripes *in 1972, Vernon said, said, 'Translating life into humor is the biggest thing with me.' ... The interviewer lauds 'Grant's tongue in cheek tongue-lashing of our human foibles' in the book...*"[7]

As Betsy Grant writes, *A Monster is Loose!* "*is full of stories of Japanese life, and foreigners' experiences therein, as represented by the*

7 *Ibid.*, p.54.

 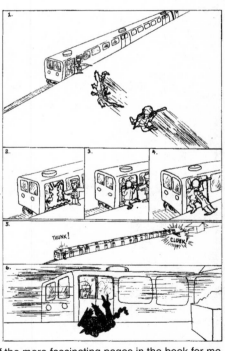

Tim Paxton notes, "This *[above left]* was one of the more fascinating pages in the book for me as a kid... I had never heard of someone being ignored because he was peeing on the side of a building." Not quite a cultural awakening, but a social "grace" uncommon over here in the States. Tim adds: "When I visited Japan in 2009, I never experienced the sardine-packing technique of the Japanese subway system, which is still in style today as much as it was in 1972... I never saw a subway pusher (押し屋 / *oshiya*) at work *[above right]*, nor made it to any Turkish bath houses..."

Left: Vernon Grant gag featuring the popular autumn/early winter Japanese snack *Yakiimo* a.k.a. *Yaki imo* (焼き芋・やきいも), a baked sweet potato, emphasizes the *kaijū*'s status as an outsider (*gaijin*). **Above:** Cover art to Grant's *A Monster is Loose!—in Tokyo* (Charles E. Tuttle Company, 1972), the one-and-only edition to date

Monster." The same was true of Anne Cleveland's *It's Better With Your Shoes Off*, which was entirely about a foreigner's experience of life in Japan; they really are companion cartoon books in more than just having the same publisher. Grant just took the cultural issues further, to more outrageous and comedic extremes, by making his outsider a *kaijū*. Grant's conscious use of the *kaijū* as his surrogate "self"—an obvious outsider constantly confronted by his *being* an outsider— is reflected in Betsy's recall of their outsider (*gaijin*) status in Japan:

"...I first had to learn to adjust to being a gaijin... *When I lived in Japan in the early 1970s, it seemed that anyone who was not racially Japanese was a* gaijin. *This was not an issue when I was with my Japanese friends I had first met at the University of Wisconsin in Madison who treated me as an individual. However, when I was on the trains or walking around the city I often heard Japanese people exclaiming* gaijin... *as I approached. I even remember seeing a young mother and father point me out to their toddler, teaching him I was a* gaijin. *It was my first time to have an awareness of what it meant to*

be identified by race.... When I was with Vernon, we were on the same footing, both foreigners. He helped me learn to adjust to being under the microscope out in public, being seen primarily as a gaijin, *and to accept it as part of my life in this new place...."* [8]

In this, *A Monster is Loose!* proved itself more than it appeared to be to the casual bookshop browser—making sense, too, of Tuttle's decision to publish Grant's book.

It was, in its way, quite a prescient piece of work, anticipating the coming wave of Western readers eager to engage with Japanese culture far more than any previous generation—

—and Grant, more than anyone in 1972, understood the fundamental role that *kaijū* would play.

Given the publication last year of *Adventures of Point-Man Palmer in Vietnam: Cartoons and*

8   *Ibid.*, pp.55-56. Betsy also notes, *"People have asked me how it felt to be a racially mixed couple in Japan... Amongst the students at Sophia University, there were white, black and Asian students from America, Japan, and Europe and all over the world, as well as many mixed couples. It was a very comfortable place to be."* (p.56).

Writings by Vernon Grant by Betsy Grant and Betsy's reprint edition this year of *Stand-By One!*, there's hope for the long-overdue reprint edition of *A Monster is Loose!—in Tokyo* in the not-too-distant future.

So, raise a toast, *Monster!* readers:

Make no mistake: *A Monster is Loose!* was and remains a seminal work. Vernon Grant's intention was to entertain and amuse readers, certainly, but he was also out to teach Americans about Japanese monster culture. "Monster are so big over here," Grant told Tom Gsell back in 1972, while Grant was still living in Tokyo. "Most foreigners who study Japan overlook this massive industry. They study traditional culture while missing the most

persuasive folk arts" (Grant to Gsell, "Monsters, Too: Cartoonist is Loose—in Tokyo," *Pacific Stars & Stripes*, April 22, 1972). As I noted at the beginning of Part 1 of this article, even American monster magazines were dragging their feet in 1972; only Greg Shoemaker and his fanzine *Japanese Fantasy Film Journal* were on the same page as Vernon Grant, at that time.

In oh so many ways, Vernon Grant was a cartoonist and a man ahead of his time.

So, raise a toast, *Monster!* readers:

Here's to Vernon Grant, the trail-blazing *gaijin* who tried to teach America about *kaijū*.

Part 2 of this article is lovingly dedicated to Betsy Grant.

Visit Betsy Grant's website dedicated to the memory and work of her late husband Vernon at http://bvgrantstudio.com/ *and visit her on Facebook at* Bvgrant Studio—*and please, tell her* Monster! *sent you.*

Article ©2015 Stephen R. Bissette, all rights reserved. Quotes from Betsy Grant, Vernon Grant are quoted here with permission of Betsy Grant, and related articles, book titles, and websites cited are the property of their original authors, quoted here for educational purposes; Vernon Grant's *A Monster is Loose!—in Tokyo* excerpts and artwork are ©1972, 2015 Betsy Grant, all other Vernon Grant artwork © their respective original year of publication, ©2015 Betsy Grant, reprinted here with permission of Betsy Grant. This one's also for Tim Paxton, exclusive to *Monster!*

Resources:

Vernon Grant (and Charles Tuttle):
http://bvgrantstudio.com/
Facebook: *Bvgrant Studio*
https://en.wikipedia.org/wiki/Vernon_Grant
http://www.independent.co.uk/news/people/obituary-charles-e-tuttle-1483336.html

Articles:
Betsy Grant, "Graphic Novel Pioneer: The Art of Vernon Grant," *Comic Book Creator* #8 (Spring 2015, TwoMorrows Publishing) , pp. 12-14.
Tom Gsell, "Monsters, Too: Cartoonist is Loose—in Tokyo," *Pacific Stars & Stripes*, April 22, 1972 (page number unknown; clipping provided by Betsy Grant)
Bhob Stewart, "Miles of Manga: Japan's Dream Mechanism," *The Comics Journal* #94 (October 1984, Fantagraphics Inc.), pg. 68-69.

Books:
Adventures of Point-Man Palmer in Vietnam: Cartoons and Writings by Vernon Grant by Betsy Grant (2014, Little Creek Press)
Stand-By One!... by Vernon Grant (first edition: 1969, self-published by Vernon Grant; second edition: October 2015, Little Creek Press)
A Monster is Loose!—in Tokyo by Vernon Grant (1972, Charles E. Tuttle Company)

"The Other" Vernon Grant:
https://en.wikipedia.org/wiki/Vernon_Simeon_Plemion_Grant

Books:
Beyond Snap! Crackle! Pop! The Story of American Illustrator Vernon Grant by Linda Williams (2014)

.... THE POLICE ARE CONDUCTING A THOROUGH SEARCH FOR THE MONSTER!.... MEANWHILE CITIZENS SHOULD REMAIN ON THEIR TOES.

SIDEBAR:
An interview with Betsy Grant

SRB: *Betsy, you've mounted an impressive promotional effort to get your late husband Vernon Grant's work out there for a new generation. It's obviously a labor of love. Have you worked in marketing before?*

BETSY GRANT: It truly is a labor of love. I love promoting his work. I was very successful selling health club memberships from 1978 through 2005, and it sure is fun now selling something Vernon did and the book I wrote. My Great Grandfather was H.H. Bennett, the landscape photographer of Wisconsin Dells who was the major force in promoting Wisconsin Dells to become the tourist destination it is today. So I inherited my marketing ability from him—but also learned a lot from my father, Oliver Reese, and from watching Vernon, who did all self-publishing.

SRB: *The website you've created to archive and promote Vernon's work is quite impressive—*

BG: It was Bhob Stewart who developed Vernon's Wikipedia Page in 2007. He did it, and then told me about it after. I was thrilled, as I had had no webpage at all before I met Bhob. I later developed a webpage on Go Daddy, with links to the Wikipedia page, with the help of a friend. Lately, when I have needed help, they have been excellent, solving my problems at all hours of the day and night. *[You should]* send *[your readers]* to my Facebook page at Bvgrant studio, for users of Facebook. I really put a whole lot more info on my Facebook page, lots more photos and comments, so they will know more about me and my books on there.

SRB: *Bhob Stewart was such a key figure for many of us growing up—for me, as a horror movie fan, Bhob was one of the most distinctive writers for the newsstand monster magazine* Castle of Frankenstein. *Once I became a working professional cartoonist and eventually a comics scholar, Bhob was one of my favorite comics historians and authors, a real role model. Do you know how and/or when Vernon first met Bhob Stewart? When did you first meet Bhob?*

BG: I do not know exactly when they met, but I think it must have been not too long after we moved back from Tokyo, which was in 1973. My feeling is he met Bhob at Million Year Picnic, as the late

Vernon Grant proudly showing off his then-new book *A Monster is Loose!—in Tokyo*, from *Pacific Stars & Stripes*, April 22, 1972 (photo by Staff Sgt. Don Gunn)

Jerry Weist, former owner of Million Year Picnic, was a roommate with Bhob in Somerville, MA. Bhob told me a story about Jerry. He had come home, and immediately felt sleepy, and lay down to sleep. Very fortunately for him, Jerry came home soon after, realized there was a major gas leak, and saved his life! So Vernon and Bhob must have spent hours and hours talking about comics, in coffee shops and perhaps at Bhob's place. Bhob said he had only been to our place once, and marveled at how many pairs of running shoes we had in the entrance way to our apartment. At some point Bhob moved to NYC, but they still kept in touch. I have a Christmas card from Bhob when he worked for Mad magazine, with Alfred E. Newman, dressed as Superman, gleefully smashing the glass of the Daily Planet building. Inside it says, "What! – Me Merry? Have a smashing holiday!" Vernon always talked about how helpful Bhob was to him.

When we did our will in 1996, Vernon wrote that Bhob Stewart was to be contacted when he died. It took some effort, but I found him through TwoMorrows Publishing Company, and talked to a woman there about how I wanted to contact him, and she sent Bhob my email and message. That was in February of 2007. It was the beginning of a great friendship. He was an incredible mentor and friend to me. I only met him in person once in Cambridge, which was great to finally see him in person, I think sometime in 2010. He was being driven around by a good friend, as his vision did not allow driving any more. If he was helping me on some project, we might email a few times a day, but it was almost daily contact with him until he passed in 2014. We also talked a lot on the phone, and more so when he went into the nursing home in Plymouth, which I think was in 2011 or 2012. What a fascinating man, with knowledge of some many things! I remember one day I called him and he cheerily said, "What do you want to hear about today?" He would tell me about other authors, gave me much information on cartoonists and art, copyright issues, movies of all eras, and music. Did he *love* jazz!—and he would send me links to so many fascinating things. He urged me to write, and would edit what I did. He also urged me to do a web site and do Facebook, and to publish Vernon's work.

One of my favorite conversations was when he told me about a play he had acted in. He went into the character of a cabbie driving someone to a mental hospital. He could do it all. And it was when he passed, and his good friend Brad Verter contacted me along with many of his friends of his passing that I learned what a prolific mentor he had been to so many artists and writers. So many people are in his debt for the advice he gave freely, even while he was in the nursing home. He was an incredible man. They had two memorial gatherings for him, one at Columbia in New York, and in Boston at The New England School of Art and Design at Suffolk University, where he taught for so many years. And his connections and friendships have continued to help me to this day. I think that he and Vernon are both smiling down on me.

SRB: Given the years in which he was creating and for the most part self-publishing his comics creations, Vernon was actually an underground cartoonist, in the aspect of not working in or for the mainstream newsstand comics publishing arena, and in terms of creating and self-publishing very personal comics. Was Vernon aware of the underground comix movement?

BG: Vernon credits me with teaching him about Underground comics, which he had never seen before. I brought some with me to Japan in 1972 (Vernon had then been living abroad, with no trips back to the US for a number of years, since at least 1968, so he had had no chance to see these American comics in Japan). So he first saw them in 1972. He loved them! Especially the *Fabulous Furry Freak Brothers*.

SRB: I first saw Vernon's work when I lucked into a copy of Stand-By One!...—

BG: Where did you buy *Stand-By One*? Were you or someone else stationed in Asia?

SRB: My older brother Rick was stationed in Thailand and served as a pilot during the Vietnam

"...GENIUS, SHEER GENIUS!..."

This is the Vernon Grant cartoon Betsy Grant refers to on the next page ("...joke of soldier skating on water...") in the interview; from *Stand-By One!* (1969/2015)

War, so I was always looking for comics by soldiers—growing up in a military family, I'd been collecting cartoon books written and drawn by soldiers most of my life. I think it was a military book dealer who sold me my copy of Vernon's first printing of Stand-By One!..., *if memory serves. I found that copy back in 1973, the year I graduated from high school.*

BG: How did you come to buy *Adventures of Point-Man Palmer*, and why did you buy it?

SRB: *That's thanks to Tim Paxton, a long-time friend who co-edits and handles all the design and production on* Monster! *Tim alerted me to the existence of* A Monster is Loose!—*in Tokyo sometime back in 2010 or so. I searched for a copy restlessly after that, primarily in online book dealing venues, and would also search for anything else by Vernon. I finally found a copy of* A Monster is Loose! *early in 2014, and started work on this article, but I kept doing online searches for Vernon's books, hoping to stumble upon back issues of* Love Rangers, *if nothing else. At some point this year [2015] one of those searches brought up your book,* Adventures of Point-Man Palmer, *and I ordered a copy without hesitation.*

Betsy, you've read my articles at this point. Are there any key points I've missed about Vernon's work?

BG: I want to make the point that although it is of interest and important to analyze Vernon's artistic style, I think a huge part of the value of what he did was his sense of humor—that sells what he did, and keeps reselling it. I know Vernon admired and liked Bill Mauldin—he collected many of his books. But my personal feeling is Bill Mauldin and his humor is darker, and not as obviously funny to civilians as Vernon's cartoons and stories are. My first attachment below (joke of soldier skating on water) I will add to this email will show perfectly his amazing quirky sense of humor that I have seen many civilians and veterans alike laugh at.

Another thing of significance of what Vernon did was also how he often showed how well he understood life and human nature—which makes it great fun for people to see his work. A really good example of this is the scene [in *A Monster is Loose!*] of the Monster suddenly becoming "invisible" by doing what just about every red-blooded Japanese man does on his way home from work, after a few too many drinks—peeing on the wall. And when the Japanese men do that, everyone learns to ignore them (a culture shock, for sure, for us American women—but I learned to ignore it, too).

SRB: *It's obvious the* kaijū *character in* A Monster is Loose! *was a self-parody of and for Vernon, with some autobiographical elements informing that character. Are there aspects of the* kaijū *character only those who knew Vernon personally would readily recognize?*

BG: His Monster face is very definitely Vernon's face and expressions. I do not think I realized this until the last few years. With his brow furrowed in this picture attached of Vernon in Vietnam, I think he looks exactly like the Monster. So I think he got a kick out of thinking of himself as the Monster, at times, too. It was his alter ego, getting a chance to gently needle people about their actions and thoughts in the story line of *A Monster is Loose!*

SRB: *I'm asking this as someone who has self-published upon occasion: Now that you're self-publishing, via Little Creek Press, do you think you've had a little taste of what Vernon did for so long, self-publishing his own work? Do you feel a greater affinity for what he worked so hard at for all those years?*

BG: Yes, I certainly do. He spent hours talking to people and sending letters to his friends and contacts in the comic book and fanzine world. I spend hours on phone and sending emails now, and studying the internet. He had to do much extra work as we had no personal computer then. He would use our typewriter and then have to walk into Central Square in Cambridge, MA to make copies of everything he did. However, a big advantage he had over me was that he was the artist—and would also spend time drawing fun cartoons about what he was selling. My advantages are that I have been able to build on many relationships he created in the comic world, and in Cambridge, MA—and using computers and the internet definitely speed up my marketing efforts. However, I still spend hours, as he did, establishing and continuing relationships to create the success I have had. And in the long run, I still have to pick up the phone, or sit down at my keyboard, and "cold call" people and television and media people to bring attention to Vernon's work and our books. I think he did very well in his efforts. It is one thing to be a talented artist, but another to then have to become a salesperson, too. It is not easy to do. I know his personality and having been a communications officer in the Army really helped him.

SRB: *Will there be a reprint collection of Vernon's* Love Rangers *comics coming in the near future?*

BG: I am considering it, as well as a reprint of *A Monster is Loose!–in Tokyo,* but have not decided yet. Please watch my website and Facebook page for my updates, and thank you so much for your

encouragement to do so, as well as for this interview and your great two-part article about Vernon!

SRB: *Our deepest thanks to you, Betsy, too. Thanks so much for making time for this conversation, and good luck with all your future endeavors.*

———

This email conversation was conducted between November 20-22, 2015—well after the completion of this two-part article—and the final ms. was proofed by Betsy Grant on November 23, 2015. A *Monster!*-sized thanks to Betsy Grant! *[Thanking you kindly, Betsy Grant!* ☺ *– TP, SF, BH & TS]*

Captain Grant in Saigon Compound, 1967

FLYING
MONSTERS ATTACK
NEW YORK!

by Dawn Dabell

If you think pigeons make a mess of historical landmarks, just wait till you see what **THE GIANT CLAW** does to the Empire State Building!

*I wanted to tackle some flying monster movies for my latest reviews, so I cast around for a few ideas. Two movies which quickly stood out as ideal candidates were **THE GIANT CLAW** (1957) and **Q: THE WINGED SERPENT** (1982). Both movies feature remarkable flying creatures intent on wreaking havoc. I toyed with the idea of including **THE FLYING SERPENT** (1946, USA, D: "Sherman Scott"/Sam Newfield) too, but the more I thought about it, the more I realized that **CLAW** and **Q** go better together. Both are low-budget cult favorites with humor (not always intentional!) going for them; both follow a similar story structure; and both are linked by the fact that the flying monster at the heart of each is on its way to terrorize The Big Apple!*

85

WINGED MONSTER FROM 17,000,000 B. C. ATTACKS!

SEE
Atom-Age
Science
Against
Ice-Age
Flying
Killer!

THE GIANT CLAW

starring **JEFF MORROW · MARA CORDAY**

Written by SAMUEL NEWMAN and PAUL GANGELIN
Technical Effects Created by RALPH HAMMERAS and GEORGE TEAGUE · Produced by SAM KATZMAN
Directed by FRED F. SEARS · A CLOVER Production · A COLUMBIA PICTURE

THE GIANT CLAW
USA, 1957. D: Fred F. Sears

When a film becomes famous (or perhaps I should say *in*famous) for its unintentionally hilarious titular monster, sci-fi and horror fans invariably rush to bump it up their "must-see" list. Is there a better case in point than **THE GIANT CLAW**?

On paper, the film seems promising enough: a giant alien bird terrorizes everything in its path... a handsome hero and a beautiful lady mathematician try their best to thwart the rampaging massacre... fighter pilots try without joy to shoot the bird down... and everything ends with a climactic showdown in New York! The film clearly has a lot going for it. The plot is sound and the cast consists of some fairly respectable actors with a strong back-catalogue of credits. Okay, it's evident right from the start that the film is not going to be making it onto the "required viewing schedule" for anyone on the Oscars committee. Nevertheless, it is certainly fun from the word go! Within moments, we see a large shadow racing across the sky, and one character utters words which get used a lot as the film progresses: "It's as *BIG* as a *battleship*!!" Just in case we forget how big the monster is, we are reminded over and over (and over...and over...) throughout the film: "Something, he didn't know what, but something as *big as a battleship* had just flown over and past him"; "I said it looked *like* a battleship, not that it *was* a battleship"; "Once more a frantic pilot radios in a report on a UFO. A bird. A bird as *big as a battleship*!"

Electronics engineer Mitch MacAfee (Jeff Morrow) reports sighting a strange, large UFO during a test flight. Air Force planes are scrambled to investigate further, but cannot find any evidence of his sighting. They see nothing, and their radars remain blank. Dismissing his claims as fool's talk, his superiors quickly put ideas of a UFO out of their minds. Later, a few planes go missing and, during a flight to New York, MacAfee and attractive mathematician Sally Caldwell (Mara Corday, of **THE BLACK SCORPION** [1957, USA, D: Edward Ludwig]) find their aircraft under attack from a flying

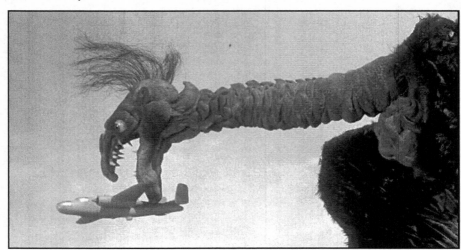

A B-25 Mitchell bomber is no more than buzzard bait for **THE GIANT CLAW**!

assailant. Eventually, they learn that the menace in the skies is an extraterrestrial bird—undetectable by radar, fiercely aggressive, as "big as a battleship"... and heading straight for NYC!

Two years prior to this, Morrow had starred in one of the most-loved '50s sci-fi films, **THIS ISLAND EARTH** (1955, USA, D: Joseph Newman). That film is regarded as something of a classic nowadays, and is a highpoint in Morrow's filmography. It may come as a surprise to see an actor of his stature appearing here, in a film viewed by critics and audiences as something of a joke. In fairness to Morrow, his performance is most professional. Viewers might be laughing their asses off at the events on screen, but Morrow seems to be taking it all very seriously, as if he's starring in a very different film from the one we are watching. Not once does he come across as insincere or embarrassed, and his onscreen chemistry with leading lady Corday is very authentic. Their witty banter is actually quite charming. Seeing him trying to woo her while the hilarious killer bird brings terror to the world is just one more lovable ingredient in the whole wacky confection.

Mara Corday is decent as the female lead and love interest. She doesn't come across as a woman in distress who needs saving by the heroic leading man; instead she is spunky and intelligent, able to hold her own against her male counterparts. (Admittedly she does submit to some of Morrow's pick-up lines on a few occasions, but who wouldn't fall for those hysterically corny lines?!) Throughout the '50s, Corday appeared in a number of men's magazines, and even went on to become "Playmate of the Month" in *Playboy*'s 1958 October issue. It's hardly surprising she was so popular among the male audience at the time: she was a classically beautiful woman with curves in all the right places. Even female audience members can feel that they'd like to be in the shoes of this attractive, intelligent and strong woman helping to save the world!

It's evident from the final product that it wasn't all plain sailing behind the scenes! Stop-motion maestro Ray Harryhausen was originally sought to create the monstrous bird—he had previously provided animation effects for another Fred F. Sears film, **EARTH VS. THE FLYING SAUCERS** (1956, USA)—but budgetary constraints meant they couldn't afford to hire him this time. Instead, the studio took their project to a low-budget Mexican special effects company. Sadly, what the Mexicans created was far from scary and far from convincing; the end result is more a cutesy marionette bird with a lovably goofy face. Ironically, this notoriously lame puppet—and its utter failure to scare audiences in the slightest—resulted in a film which has become something of a

Bird-Brained: It known as **THE GIANT CLAW** looks positively *insane* in this shot!

must-see for seekers of "so-bad-it's-good" cinema. The film's monster looks like an oversized emu, with big boggly eyes and a large shiny beak. It does not instill in the audience one iota of terror—it is actually regarded by viewers as cute and adorable, especially when its head bobs up and down on a clearly visible wire to the accompaniment of a loud "squawking" noise.

Italian poster for **THE GIANT CLAW** (art unsigned). The ad-line translates to *"A Monster from Another Planet Attacks the Earth"*, and the title in English is "THE MONSTER OF THE SKIES"

Top to Bottom: The flying feather-duster gets a bird's eye view of its victims, who die laughing before it has a chance to eat 'em alive. (And since when do birds have *teeth*, anyway?!) As expected, **THE GIANT CLAW** becomes a dead duck in time for the final fade

The stars of the film were mortified by the "monster" when they finally saw it. While at the premier of **THE GIANT CLAW**, Jeff Morrow, seeing the film for the first time, became incredibly embarrassed at the audience reaction every time the extraterrestrial bird came onscreen. Viewers were laughing hysterically, and Morrow slid further and further into his seat in shame. He claimed he was so embarrassed that when the film finished he sneaked out of the auditorium so no one would spot him!

In Morrow's (and the other's) defense, none of them had seen the giant bird until the screening, so didn't know what they were in for. They were obviously shocked to see it on the big screen. According to Corday, in an interview with Tom Weaver, producer Sam Katzman had previously told her: "Boy, this is gonna be something! I'm spending most of the budget on the special effects!" It's therefore completely understandable they would be shocked upon seeing the bird for the first time. She went on to tell Weaver, "When we made the movie and we were supposedly looking at the giant bird, I was envisioning something really horrifying. And when I saw the movie, I couldn't believe it! It was incredible!" She then goes on to relay how dreadful she thought the movie was!

As another way of cutting costs, stock footage was used, including scenes from the aforementioned **EARTH VS. THE FLYING SAUCERS**. In the final scenes, when the giant bird attacks New York, the same footage of people running through the streets is reused time after time. It's possible to spot the same people running down the same stretch of street again and again as the film cuts to the supposedly panic-stricken citizens fleeing for their lives. Britain's *Radio Times* declared **THE GIANT CLAW** was "bad enough to be funny"… and they're *not* wrong!

The effects in the film are frequently laughable. In one scene, the bird swoops down and snatches a train in its beak, but it's pitifully obvious it is just a model train. Then there are the hilarious scenes where parachutists get gobbled-up by the giant menace while descending though the air. The film may have been rolled out as a serious sci-fi movie, but in actuality **THE GIANT CLAW** is a *HOOT*! Delivering unintentional chuckles galore, it completely deserves its reputation as a cult classic. This is a film which should be seen by sci-fi fans the world over—it's a blast for all the *wrong* reasons.

Q: THE WINGED SERPENT
USA, 1982. D: Larry Cohen

There are some "monster" movies which almost all horror fans seem to love…and **Q** is one of them. The film receives nothing but the highest levels of praise in most discerning circles. What makes this '80s horror film worthy of such high regard? And does it really live up to its reputation?

As well as being an obvious homage to the B-movies of the '50s, the film also injects enough levels of humor, violence and gore to appeal to a modern-day audience. We see the gruesome remains of a body that was skinned as part of a ritualistic sacrifice; there are a number of decapitated bodies scattered throughout the film. Adults are also treated to a gloriously voyeuristic scene of a young woman applying sun cream to her boobies while readying herself for a spot of topless sunbathing, all in exaggerated close-up. A scene no doubt appreciated by many a male viewer, although for the remainder of the film there is no further nudity.

A giant flying serpent has been spotted in the sky over New York. The police are initially skeptical, but then a series of deaths occur on various rooftops around the city, and it quickly becomes apparent that the monster is not only real, but it's also *devouring* people! A seedy ex-con-turned-piano-playing-bum (Michael Moriarty) discovers the nesting place of the deadly serpent after hiding out in the aftermath of a botched diamond heist. But rather than handing his knowledge of the beast's whereabouts over to the cops, he uses it to try to demand a fortune in money to reveal what he knows. Detectives Shephard (David "Kwai Chang Caine" Carradine) and Powell (Richard "Shaft" Roundtree) are investigating a series of Aztec-style ritual murders around the city, and conclude that the flying serpent may be Quetzalcoatl, an Aztec deity, summoned to bring great devastation upon the Big Apple.

The film boasts a respectable cast, nicely headed by B-movie regular Carradine. As one expects from Carradine, he puts in a decent enough effort as the officer trying to solve the mystery of the ritual killings. In numerous exploitation films of this kind,

This interesting juxtaposition of similar shots from **THE GIANT CLAW** *[top]* and **Q: THE WINGED SERPENT** *[above]* shows the two films' respective winged monsters flapping past the NYC skyline, albeit a quarter-century apart

"Q" IS HERE!

It's name is Quetzalcoatl... just call it "Q"... that's all you'll have time to say before it tears you apart!

MICHAEL MORIARTY · CANDY CLARK · DAVID CARRADINE · RICHARD ROUNDTREE
in a LARRY COHEN FILM "Q"
SAMUEL Z. ARKOFF presents a LARCO PRODUCTION
music by ROBERT O. RAGLAND production executive PETER SABISTON written produced and directed by LARRY COHEN
released by UNITED FILM DISTRIBUTION COMPANY

US poster (art by Boris Vallejo)

he could always be relied upon to do solid work. When Michael Moriarty's character first appears onscreen, many viewers may find him a little on the annoying side. However, as the film progresses his performance actually becomes a highlight. Moriarty is quirky, funny and extremely convincing in his portrayal of the nervous criminal who will go to any extreme for his moment of fame; a character who shows little remorse for others and demands money and absolution for his crimes in return for exposing the creature's lair. Roundtree as Powell, the other officer on the murder case, and Candy

Q looks awful cheerful while going on a killing rampage against heavily-armed NYPD blues...

Clark as Moriarty's hard-done-by girlfriend Joan are also worthy of a mention.

Director Larry Cohen is famous for his horror and B-movie output, especially films such as **IT'S ALIVE** (1974), **IT LIVES AGAIN** (1978) and **THE STUFF** (1985, all USA). **Q** was not only directed by Cohen, he is also credited as writer too. A look at Cohen's CV makes it obvious he is a man of many talents, boasting over 20 director and producer credits and more than 80 writing credits to his name. And of these, **Q: THE WINGED SERPENT** is regarded as one of his very best horror/fantasy films. *[See* Monster! *#21 (pp.77-100) for an article about Cohen by Steve Bissette – ed.]*

The theatrical posters for the film's release showcase some fantastic artwork (by acclaimed fantasy illustrator Boris Vallejo), featuring the Aztec God Quetzalcoatl on top of the Chrysler building. This wonderful image, plus the terrific tagline *"Its name is Quetzalcoatl... just call it 'Q'... that's all you'll have time to say before it tears you apart!"* had audiences flocking to theaters to see Cohen's latest blood-curdler.

There are a couple of things about the film which don't quite work, which I should perhaps mention now. The first being the number of different subplots taking place throughout the narrative: we have a crime which goes wrong, a winged serpent swooping down on members of the public, and a police hunt for a ritualistic murderer. Any of these plot threads could quite easily have formed the basis for individual films, but here they are all mashed together into the one story. It's all just a little over-busy. Another weakness comes in the form of the monster itself, which just doesn't hold-up too well even for 1982. Cohen opted to use stop-motion animation, making the creature look a little clunky and dated for a film of this era. Although Quetzalcoatl is a menacing creature, killing anything in its wake, it looks too cute to be truly scary. In one scene, Quetzalcoatl's egg is riddled with bullets, causing a baby Q to hatch which is then shot by the armed police. The creature would probably have audiences cooing *"Awwwww!"* as they witness its adorable face appearing through the bullet-holes in its egg, before being blown to pieces.

Luckily we don't see Q onscreen too often during the course of the film, so the un-persuasiveness of the monster is not too damaging overall. In fact, in some ways it's rather charming...

Back in the '90s, **Q: THE WINGED SERPENT** was aired in the UK as part of the much-loved *Moviedrome* series. It followed Lewis Teague's **ALLIGATOR** (1980, USA) as part of a Sunday night double-bill, and was adorned with an informative introduction by filmmaker Alex Cox, who always began with a short talk about the film about to be screened. In his short intro, Cox refers to the chaotic filming schedule of **Q**, pointing out Cohen's total lack of regard for rules when shooting scenes in the streets of New York. Rather than applying for the correct permits, Cohen instead chose to run through the city streets just capturing footage. Some of these scenes would no doubt have caused obstruction to pedestrians and commuters alike. To quote Cox: "Cohen is a true guerrilla filmmaker. He doesn't bother with permits or permissions or anything like that. Finish the first draft, gather up whatever character actors are to hand, and get out there and *shoot*! Several times the production of **Q** was halted by police, who thought the hail of gunfire coming from the upper floors of Manhattan skyscrapers was genuine!"

Keep Watching The Skies! David Carradine opens up on the airborne menace in this Anglo-titled German lobby card for **Q**

Although no one would deny that the special effects are under-par, the film still receives mainly glowing reviews from the critics. The *Radio Times* declared it a "hugely enjoyable cult horror thriller, imaginatively written and directed: by turns scary, funny and impressive." And *Time Out* went as far as to say, "…we have no hesitation in awarding Oscars all round." And no cult film would be complete without a quote from a cult movie book— *Videohound's Cult Flicks and Trash Pics* sums it up perfectly: "A cult of admirers surround this goony monster flick about dragon-like Aztec god Quetzalcoatl, summoned to modern Manhattan by gory human sacrifices, and hungry for rooftop sunbathers and construction teams. Direction and special effects are pretty ragged, but witty script helps the cast shine, especially Moriarty as a lowlife crook who's found the beast's hidden nest."

Q: THE WINGED SERPENT is certainly worth watching. For fans of horror and fantasy films it has plenty of gore, just enough tension and some wonderfully eccentric performances from the cast members. In the *Moviedrome* introduction, it was described as "a combination of a slasher movie and King Kong!" I can't think of a better way to describe it! Ignore the flaws, and *go see it!*

Mortally wounded by gunfire, Q alights atop a skyscraper whose roof reminds her of a tiered pre-Hispanic pyramid

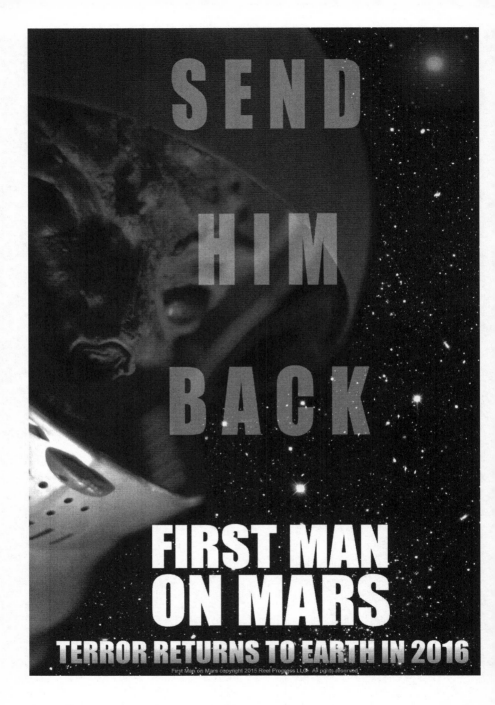

SEND HIM BACK

FIRST MAN ON MARS

TERROR RETURNS TO EARTH IN 2016

First Man on Mars copyright 2015 Reel Progress LLC. All rights reserved.

A mock satricial poster for **FIRST MAN ON MARS** (coming in 2016)

HOW TO MAKE A MONSTER

by Mike T. Lyddon

Part 2: "Lights, Camera, Disaster! The Best-Laid Plans..."

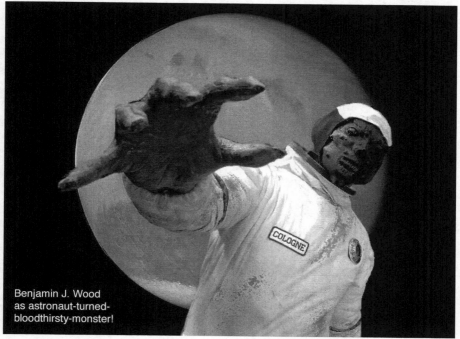

Benjamin J. Wood
as astronaut-turned-
bloodthirsty-monster!

The first chunk of production on **FIRST MAN ON MARS** (2016, USA) happened over an eight-day stretch in May of this year. A good portion of the film takes place in the swamps and marshes near the fictional town of Black Bayou, Louisiana, and most of the scenes were shot in these swampy exteriors. The film concerns the first astronaut ever to set foot on Mars, only to become infected by Martian spores. He eventually returns to earth but the command module plummets deep into the swamps of Black Bayou during the height of Hurricane Katrina when massive communications failures made it impossible to track the spacecraft. So our intrepid spaceman-turned-monster prowls the swamps and marshes, munching on the occasional human who crosses its path. Some hapless rednecks trigger the beacon on the command module, which alerts scientists who venture into Black Bayou to search for the astronaut and module. The month of May in the deep south is warm and humid, typically 80 to 90 degrees, but preferable to shooting in the

"hell" months of July, August and September when you can have many 100° / 100% humidity days in a row. Back in 1993 when we made **CUT UP** (1994, USA) in New Orleans, we made the mistake of shooting in July. If you're shooting for sound, you can't have the air conditioner running, so there were a few interior scenes where the set reached 120 degrees, and the cast/crew damn near *melted*! After that I never shot a film in the south in the summer. Day One, all was going smoothly and we were well into the first scene, when the Aaton Super 16mm camera our cinematographer John Woods was using suffered "catastrophic" mechanical failure. John and First AC Jon-Claude Harris attempted to remedy the problem, but to no avail. This is a prime example of things going south, no matter what you do. A month or two before, John had taken the camera in for servicing, and he shot test footage which checked-out fine. Fortunately, there is an "image equivalency" between Super 16mm film and HD video in the digital realm, so my plan all

Top to Bottom: Sam Cobean and Joey Harmon as the nerdy scientists; the Martian miniature sequence, featuring a Mars rover; Marcelle Shaneyfelt as Dr. Martine Munro; and girls with guns! (Candace McAdams *[at left]* and Kelly Murtagh)

along was to simultaneously shoot on film with HD back-up. In a worst case scenario, this would allow me to use a shot—or even an entire scene—from the digital files, and this method proved useful on more than one occasion.

Then came disaster number two…an actor meltdown. The cast this day consisted of talented newcomer Marcelle Shaneyfelt as Dr. Martine Munro, Kirk Jordan as Sheriff Dick Ruffman, Jeffrey Estiverne as Deputy Jordy Sample and seasoned actor Sam Cobean as "Scientist Number 2". But another actor on set started displaying strange behavior early in the day which I initially chocked up to first-day jitters, but it eventually got to the point where he couldn't even repeat a short, simple line fed to him off-screen. We concluded he was either off his meds, on too many meds or on some kind of hallucinogen. He was soon replaced by actor Joey Harmon with the help of Sam Cobean (Sam also ended up recording some wonderfully bizarre Theremin music for the soundtrack), and this turned out to be a very wise decision indeed. The comedic chemistry between Cobean and Harmon playing the goofy, nerdy scientists added yet another dimension to the film.

After Day One, we had to switch to my trusty old Canon Scoopic, which had been modified to "Ultra 16" (very similar to Super 16 in format). Because of its relatively light weight (9lbs) and the ease of loading film rolls, the Scoopic was originally popular for RNG ("run and gun") news gathering and sporting events. However, there were two distinct drawbacks to the Scoopic: It is an MOS (without sound) camera, because it is too loud for recording location sound and it only accepts 100-foot rolls of film, unlike the Aaton, which handles 400-foot rolls, giving you about 11 minutes of uninterrupted shooting per roll. So, for the remainder of the shoot, after a 10-to-12-hour day on set, I found myself at 1 a.m. in my bathroom in total darkness cutting 400-foot rolls of film down to 100-foot rolls, to be used in the Scoopic for the next morning's shoot. *Not* what I had planned, but—hey—the show must go on!

One day later a storm came which wiped out a full day of shooting on top of the half day we'd already lost, so in the first three days we were already behind a day-and-a-half.

Fortunately, the next three days were interiors that went off without a hitch and led us into the final stretch of exteriors, which consisted of the monster, girls, guns and a creepy old fishing boat...

There were a total of six different actors who ended

up playing the role of Astronaut Eli Cologne/The Monster, but Benjamin J. Wood played the creature in most of the key scenes. At 6' 4", he towered over most of the other actors, and upon donning costume designer Rubi Lyddon's amazing custom astronaut suit, he gave a monster-worthy performance under some very harsh conditions.

Candace McAdams and Kelly Murtagh did an outstanding job portraying the models from "*Bullets and Bimbos*" magazine, an over-the-top fictional publication in the vein of *Guns 'N Ammo*. Gavin Ferrara and Brian Lanigan gave hilarious performances as Kletus and Ramone de la Fleur, two rednecks who have an unfortunate encounter with our mutant spaceman.

Over the next three weeks we shot the remaining seven days of live-action scenes, including a tricky yet very rewarding sequence where a girl fishing (perfectly portrayed by actress Tressler Burton) encounters the astro-monster, with rather unpleasant "musical" results. This turned out to be the longest scene in the film, clocking-in at just over six minutes and involving three different locations. J.C. Harris and myself took over cinematography chores for the remainder of the live-action scenes, which included one very funny vignette with one of my favorite actors, Rusty Jackson, Jr. Rusty and I go way back to the short film days in New Orleans before the aforementioned **CUT UP** and **ZOMBIE! VS. MARDI GRAS** (1999, USA), and his character, Coroner Fritz Leiber, replaced the original character name of Fred Sadismo in the **FIRST MAN ON MARS** predecessor, my short subject *Mutilation Maniacs* (1981, USA). In the first scene he does a '70s-style PSA called "Mars: It's Kind of Dangerous", wherein the affable-yet-creepy coroner dishes on the angry red planet and offers an ominous word of warning.

After wrapping the live portion of the film, I continued editing, bringing the actors in for ADR ("automated dialog replacement") and setting up the stop-motion animation for a Martian dream sequence, which ended up taking about two months to prep and shoot. I designed and created the two stop-motion figures and built the miniature sets to match the live-action green screen shots we'd done earlier.

During this time, most of the cast and crew got together for a rough cut screening of the film, which was a rousing success, and just the catalyst I needed to launch headlong into the tedium of the animation. I think doing stop-motion is great, but at some point when you've been inside a room for eight hours animating and you accidentally bump the set and have to shoot the shot all over, it can get frustrating. At press time I am finishing editing the animation sequences for inclusion into the entire movie. Then it's another month-or-so of sound editing and tweaking before the finished film ships off to the first round of prospective distributors.

In retrospect, I am proud of the fact that even with a minuscule budget I was able to pay the cast and crew something (hint: especially on a feature, you *should* pay your cast and crew something), and there were no injuries during a shoot that was inherently dangerous (our bayous have no shortage of alligators and venomous snakes).

I hope to return to these hallowed pages of *Monster!* in 2016 with tidings of distribution and success on our micro-budget creature feature—**FIRST MAN ON MARS!**

Astronaut Eli Cologne (Roy "Rusty" Jackson, Jr.) enters a mysterious Martian cave

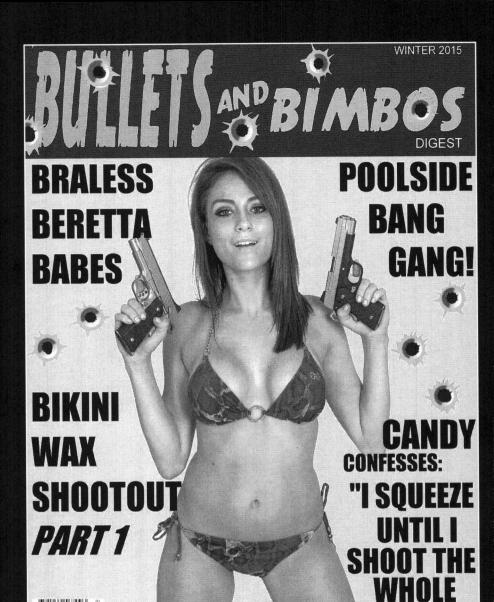

BULLETS AND BIMBOS

DIGEST

BRALESS BERETTA BABES

POOLSIDE BANG GANG!

BIKINI WAX SHOOTOUT
PART 1

CANDY
CONFESSES:
"I SQUEEZE UNTIL I SHOOT THE WHOLE LOAD!"

(Note: Our coffee-and-copy boy Mongo McGilli-cutty wracked his brain to come up with a caption for this here pic, but all his ideas were much too tastelessly lowbrow to use, so we decided to let our readers come up with a more tasteful one of their own instead)

WHEN *FAMOUS MONSTERS* GAVE IN TO THE FORCE:
STAR WARS & THE END OF THE CLASSIC MONSTER MAGAZINE

By John Harrison

When monster movies took a back seat to **STAR WARS**, we knew it was the end!

When the long-running and highly-influential *Famous Monsters of Filmland* celebrated their 20th Anniversary milestone with their 142nd issue (published in April 1978), guess who enigmatic publisher James Warren and editor Forrest J. Ackerman made their cover star for that historic issue? Bela Lugosi? Lon Chaney, Sr.? Boris Karloff? Christopher Lee? Guess again! For all the horror greats that had been featured in the magazine since it first hit the stands on a cold day in February 1958, the character that was chosen to grace the cover of that 20th

Anniversary special was none other than that most famous of monsters...Darth Vader. Many long-term readers and die-hard monster fans were justifiably outraged, disappointed or simply puzzled by the choice, but none of them should have been too surprised. George Lucas' **STAR WARS** (1977, USA) had been not only the box-office sensation of the previous year, but was becoming an unexpected international cultural phenomenon, and had already graced the front cover of *Famous Monsters* three times previous to its anniversary issue.

Rick Baker *[far right]* and crew, with some of their FX shop's creations for **SW**'s famed "Cantina" sequence

Of course, *FM* wasn't the only genre magazine giving over space to coverage of **SW**. The movie was all over the newsstands throughout much of 1977 and '78. But other magazines—at least the ones that were already around well before the movie was even released—balanced out their coverage of the film. Fred Clarke's *Cinefantastique* did a terrific double-issue devoted to the movie, then moved on. England's *House of Hammer* featured a **STAR WARS** photo cover on its sixteenth issue, before getting back to the horror business at hand. Even *Starlog*, a publication specifically geared more towards a sci-fi/space adventure readership than the monster/horror crowd, only featured the movie on its cover twice during the film's initial theatrical run.

In comparison, of the 13 issues of *FM* published between September 1977 and January of 1979, six had full **SW** covers, while two others bore *Battlestar Galactica* (1978-79, USA) covers, one a **CLOSE ENCOUNTERS OF THE THIRD KIND** (1977, USA) cover, and another a photo of an alien from Don Dohler's low-budget sci-fi flick **THE ALIEN FACTOR** (1978, USA). Three other issues featured the **STAR WARS** name prominently on the cover (even interior ads for new **SW** toys were getting front cover headlines!). Under the *Famous Monsters* banner, Warren also published the **STAR WARS SPECTACULAR**, a special 50-page one-shot magazine devoted to the movie, which appeared in late 1977.

I had only discovered the magazine not long before the film was released, so while I was disappointed to start seeing so much science-fiction and fantasy in the magazine, I remained a devoted reader who would excitedly snap up each issue as soon as it hit the stands over here (at the time, it would usually take about three months for overseas publications to reach Australian shores). There were, after all, still monster-related articles inside the magazine, though at the time I didn't realize that many of these were simply reprints from earlier issues, something which would have no doubt caused the older readers even more dismay. And of course, I loved to drool over those pages of cool goodies offered by Warren's mail-order division, Captain Company (although even there, ads for Aurora monster kits and 8mm horror films became outnumbered by ads for anything and everything with the **SW** logo or characters on it).

Did **STAR WARS** belong in *Famous Monsters*? It certainly deserved and warranted some coverage within its pages. *FM* often covered fantasy and science-fiction cinema, and aliens and invaders from Mars form a big and vital part of the classic monster movie oeuvre (and a Bill Selby painting of Robby the Robot from **FORBIDDEN PLANET** [1956, USA] had graced the cover of #133). **SW** shared a similar sense of adventure and fantasy as, say, a classic Ray Harryhausen production from the 1950s or '60s, and it featured a lineup of some pretty strange and imaginatively bizarre forms of alien life, many of them created by young makeup genius Rick Baker and featured in the famous Mos Eisley Cantina sequence, where the "scum and villainy" of the galaxy go to drink and ply their dirty trades. And the seven-foot-tall furball Wookie, Chewbacca (played by lanky British actor Peter Mayhew), had something of a classic werewolf angle to his design, though he was a lot nicer and more loveable than most cinematic wolfmen (as long as you were on his side!).

What grated the long-term readers of *Famous Monsters* the most was not the fact that it had covered **SW**, but the way in which the magazine sold itself out so completely to the movie, to the point where it could be mistaken for an official **STAR WARS**₍®©₎ fan magazine, with articles and related content taking up to 50% of an issue. Other magazines had come along in the wake of **SW** to exploit its success and the renewed interest in sci-fi cinema; American titles like *Science Fantasy Film Classics*, *Fantastic Films*, and *Starburst* in the UK. Hell, there was even the official *Star Wars Poster Magazine* to give fans their fix. The "Monster Kids" of the late 'Seventies wanted to see *monsters* on the cover of their favorite magazine, not cute wise-cracking 'droids!

The dominance which **STAR WARS** exerted over *Famous Monsters* says some interesting things about the magazine's demographic and the motivations of its publisher. While *FM* is rightfully considered an influential magazine which played a pivotal part in the explosion in monster movie fandom during the late 'Fifties and early 'Sixties, its simplistic writing and reliance on Forry Ackerman's juvenile puns kept the magazine's appeal squarely in the younger age bracket. Warren no doubt went where the money was, and putting **STAR WARS** on the cover issue after issue no doubt helped spike the magazine's short-term sales, as did the multitude of **SW** products advertised within its pages (a **STAR WARS** competition, announced in issue #147, required readers to spend at least $15 on **SW** merchandise from the magazine to be eligible to enter—a tidy sum for a kid in 1978!).

The first issue of *Famous Monsters* to feature **STAR WARS** on the cover was #137, the 1977 Yearbook, cover-dated September of that year (*"Best Issue Ever!"*). Whoever wrote the ten-page article/review of the movie for this issue obviously didn't see the opening of the film, or never read the publicity material properly, as the article starts off with: "Thousands of years in the future."—when we all know that **STAR WARS** takes place "A long time ago, in a galaxy far, far away..."! The movie was back on the front cover for the next two issues as well, with diehard readers having to wait until issue #140 before a genuine monster finally graced *FM*'s cover again (in the form of Maelo Cintron's lush painting of Glenn Strange as the Frankenstein Monster), although the respite was short-lived, with a photo cover from Spielberg's **CE3K** appearing on #141, before Darth was back yet again for the 20th Anniversary special. We could forgive (heck, I even *welcomed*) the cover articles

Top: *Yeesh!* The boring grid-like photo montage cover for *FM* #137 (September 1977). **Above:** Maelo Cintron's fine art cover for *FM* #140 (January 1978) reminded readers of how sweet things used to be...*sigh*

devoted to Ridley Scott's **ALIEN** (1979, USA/UK) which came along in 1979, since that movie was a genuine space horror with one of the most effective and terrifying alien critters to come from the stars in some time.

Top: ☺ Basil Gogos' painted cover art for *FM* #147 (September 1978). **Above:** ☹ The utter eyesore cover to *FM* #151 (March 1979)

But truth be told, it wasn't just **STAR WARS** and the sci-fi craze it generated that contributed to the end of *Famous Monsters of Filmland* as a classic monster magazine. Where it had once featured some of the most stunning cover art ever seen on a genre magazine (contributed by the likes of Basil Gogos and Ken Kelly), by the late '70s it was resorting

more and more to cheap-looking photo covers which completely lacked the class of their earlier issues. A cut-out photograph of Christopher Reeve as Superman, against a bland black backdrop, was a bit of a comedown from a beautiful Gogos painting of the Creature from the Black Lagoon or Kelly's stunning cover art of The Fly (though Gogos did contribute a terrific painting of a Tusken Raider, one of the Sand People from **STAR WARS**, for the cover of #147).

The cover of issue #151—featuring a cut-out montage of photos of Superman, a Cylon from *Battlestar Galactica*, Gollum from Ralph Bakshi's animated version of **LORD OF THE RINGS** (1978, USA), and a bunch of Kenner **STAR WARS** action figures and vehicles (part of the aforementioned competition)—probably ranks as the *WORST* cover ever to grace *Famous Monsters* in its original 191-issue run. Certainly it is my least favorite. A continued reliance on reprint articles and the arrival of *Fangoria* magazine in 1979—which laid on a lot more horror and gore than *FM* ever would, and in full gaudy color to boot—also helped to contribute to *FM*'s decrease in relevance and popularity.

Famous Monsters tried to keep in touch, offering some color pages for a brief period, and even putting Jason Voorhees on the cover of an issue (#163) when the first **FRIDAY THE 13TH** movie was released in 1980, while a photo of the killer from Joe D'Amato's infamous sleaze-and-gore classic **ANTHROPOPHAGUS** (*Antropophagus*, a.k.a. **THE GRIM REAPER**, 1980, Italy [see *Monster!* #10, p.15]) shared the front cover of issue #180 with Karloff's Frankenstein Monster. Some typically stunning Gogos portraits from Hitchcock's **PSYCHO** (1960, USA), **THE MUTATIONS** (1974) and **THE GORGON** (1964, both UK) would still grace the odd cover during the magazine's final couple of years, but for the most part *FM* would stick to emphasizing fantasy over horror, with covers and articles devoted to Superman, Flash Gordon, Indiana Jones and movies like **STAR TREK: THE MOTION PICTURE** and Disney's **THE BLACK HOLE** (both 1979, USA), Roger Corman's **BATTLE BEYOND THE STARS** (1980, USA), 007's **MOONRAKER** (1979, UK) and even comedienne Lily Tomlin's spoof **THE INCREDIBLE SHRINKING WOMAN** (1981, USA). The release of the first **SW** sequel, **THE EMPIRE STRIKES BACK** (1980, USA) accounted for another three front covers in a row.

When Warren Publishing finally hit the skids in early 1983—the victim of flagging sales,

a mystery illness that struck Jim Warren, and Ackerman's resignation as editor—*Famous Monsters* #192 was in the works, which was, in a somewhat fitting indication of what the magazine had finally become, to have been yet another **STAR WARS** issue, featuring a cover painting by Bill Selby depicting the cantina sequence from the first movie. Much of the issue was completed and pasted-up prior to Warren folding, ending up in liquidation, like most of the company's other assets.[1] In 2012, Philip Kim, current publisher of the revamped *Famous Monsters*, finally published issue #192 as a "25th Anniversary Collector's Edition", including Selby's cantina cover.

Hence, a quarter of a century after the original run of the magazine ended, *Famous Monsters* was still living on the characters created by George Lucas in 1977, populating that galaxy far, far away…

1 For an inside account of the final days of *FM* and Warren Publishing, it is worth seeking out Randy Palmer's terrific article "The Rise and Fall of *Famous Monsters of Filmland*", which appeared in issue #9 of Richard Klemenson's long-running zine *Little Shoppe of Horrors* (a scan of the article is archived online at *www.littleshoppeofhorrors.com*).

Top & Center: Bill Selby at work on his **SW** "Cantina" scene painting, along with the finished work. **Above:** As it appeared on the cover of *FM* #192 (February 1983, but not published until 2012)

THE BIG KHOONI

A "Bloody" Basketful of Hindi Horrors

as reported by Tim Paxton

For me, as a collector, Indian films are equal parts fun *and* frustration. I began amassing my collection starting in the late '90s, and have taken a few things to heart when perusing the length and breadth of online catalogs, which are the only places where I have ever purchased VCDs or DVDs. When sitting down and reviewing such companies, you need to have a lot of patience and a keen eye, as their sites can be of unfathomable length and very *little* breadth. There can be a hundred pages of movie titles, with little or no information to go on. Typically, a site lists nothing more than a film's title, date, director, musical director (yes, that *is* all-important), and stars. If you're lucky, a brief description may be available, although more than likely just a genre will be listed (i.e., action, horror, obscure, mythology, comedy, etc.) and maybe cross-references to other titles. Even better, there could be an image of the DVD/VCD cover—granted, most of them are sized very small, little more than thumbnails—so you can get a good look at that insane artwork (which is typically too good to be true!). If the VCDs or DVDs in question are Hindi, they are more than likely to have their titles Romanized; which means that the Hindi will be transliterated into "English", so to speak. For the most part, the same can be said of other subcontinental languages, although some of their VCDs or DVDs will be in Tamil, Telugu, Malayalam or whatever, rather than being Romanized. That said, for the Hindi titles, there are certain words that have become well-associated with Bollywood horror films. Well, at least the cheapjack ones I like to watch...

...and *write* about, although a recent posting on Facebook would say that what I review in *Monster!* has been somewhat "repetitive". There are a lot of movies made in India every year, but as far as cheap monster movies are concerned, there can *never* be enough (and there rarely are!).

Anyways...

Back in *Weng's Chop* #1, I made a short list of the top Romanized Hindi "horror words", and since then I have been able to add a few more. Some of the words on that list include: *raat* ("night"), *laash* ("corpse"), *panja* ("claws" or "clutching hands"), *maut* ("death"), *naga/nagin/nag* ("cobra deity"), *bhoot* ("evil ghost"), *aatma* ("spirit"), *tantrik* ("wizard" or "religious man"; typically depicted as a bad fella for these sort of films), *cheekh* ("scream"), *dushman* ("killer"), *bhayanak* ("terrible"), *shaitan* ("devil" or "Satan"), *pysaai/pyaasa* ("spirit" or "nymph"), *chudail* ("witch"), *haiwan* ("killer"), and *khooni* ("bloody" or "killer"). Please note that the spellings of these words can fluctuate wildly, most likely a word like *nagin* can alternately be spelled *naagin* or even *nāga*, with an added accent to emphasis that long "a". There are quite a few combinations of these words which are used in tandem with more common ones to create terribly spooky-sounding film titles. Some examples are **EK RAAT SHAITAN KE SAATH** (2004, D: B K Malhotra), **PYAASA HAIWAN** (2003, D: Kanti Shah), **SHAITANI AATMA** (1998, D:

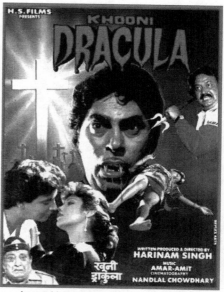

An exciting and dramatic poster for the insanity known as **KHOONI DRACULA**

103

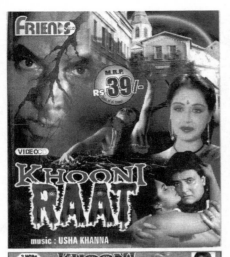

Harinam Singh), **SHAITAN TANTRIK** (1999, D: Wajid Sheikh), **PYASI CHUDAIL** (1998, D: Rafi), and **BHAYANAK BHOOTANI** (the Hindi-dubbed retitle of A.G. Baby's Telugu-language production **ADIVARAM AMAVASYA** [ఆదివారం అమావాస్య, 2000]).

Nowadays, Indian horror films have shied away from the classic trigger words and have concentrated on more obscure or "Western"-sounding titles like **CLICK, 1920: THE EVIL RETURN, HELP, PIZZA** (yes, *pizza*!), **MUMBAI 125KM 3D, ALONE, ADVENTURE OF HAUNTED HOUSE,** and **HORROR STORY**. These bolder-sounding titles are less archaic and leave the likes of *khooni, raat, laash, panja,* and *dushman* in the proverbial dust, although the ever popular *bhoot* (and its variants *bhootani, bhootan, bhut,* and *bhootni*) are still in use, possibly because of the ancient word's deep psychological roots in most all of the languages of the subcontinent, if not much of the Indo-European languages still around to this day.[1]

Just for the sake of this article alone, I have picked a very popular "add-on" word: *khooni*.

Chronologically speaking, there have been earlier films with the operative word *khooni* in their title than the ones I will review here. Not too much is known about them, as they no longer exist and/or if they do, then nothing much if at all has been written about their plots. An example of such a "lost" title is **KHOONI** from 1946. Little has been recorded about it, other than that the film was directed by K.L. Kahan. Authors Ashish Rajadhyaksha and Paul Willemen mention **KHOONI** by title and director alone in their essential *Encyclopaedia of Indian Cinema* (p.515), as they do a dozen other films. They include the tantalizing-sounding **KHOONI LAASH** (*"Bloody*

---

1   *Bhūta* is a Sanskrit term that carries the connotations of "past" and "being" and, because it is descended from "one of the most widespread roots in Indo-European — namely, *bheu/bhu-*", has similar-sounding cognates in virtually every branch of that language family: e.g., Irish (*bha*), English (*be*), Latvian (*but*) and Persian (*budan*).

Never Judge An Indian VCD By Its Cover! The films within the colorful packaging provided by these three VCD manufacturers are not properly represented by their cover art. **Top & Center: KHOONI RAAT** (1991) and **KHOONI JALJALA** (2000) are "straight" crime-driven dramas with no supernatural overtones. **Bottom:** As for **KHOONI AANKHEN,** a 1988 Hindi retitling/redub of Baby's horror film **KARIMPOOCHA** (1981), it doesn't feature a baldheaded, fanged monster in any way, shape or form. The supernatural entity in the film is actually a demon-possessed jalopy—something which isn't even featured in the artwork at all

Corpse" [?], 1943, D: Abdur Rashid Kardar), but little else that sounds remotely horror-tinged. I strongly suspect I may be misunderstanding the content of **KHOONI LAASH** in hopes that it might be what I want it to be: the earliest known Indian horror film; however, this is probably just wishful thinking on my part. More than likely the film is merely a much more mundane murder mystery or a historical drama of some type. Most of the films therein seem to be historical or social dramas that utilize the word's rather broad definition to include "fatal", "fighting", and "killer" as part of their translation.

Kahan's **KHOONI** still has me fantasizing: what of its plot—who knows? I would love to believe it could be an early example of Indian horror with elements of the paranormal. There *are* earlier fantasy films made prior to the mysterious **KHOONI**, if you consider the genre of Mythologicals, as well as Devotionals, to be "fantasy" (one example has the child-god Krishna taming the snake demon in **SHRI KRISHNA JANMA** [1918, D: D.G. Phalke]). However, as cool as they may be—I have only seen a few thus far—mythologicals will not be the focus of this *Monster!* article.

At this time I should point out that horror films, as a social and cultural rule, are not seen as positive things in India. This was true in just about all countries around the world, other than for the USA and a smattering of others. True, monsters and horrible things happened in Indian cinema prior to the explosion of that genre in the 1980s. As stated above, they were always associated somehow with mythologicals as a way to keep the terror content to a minimum. The first supernaturally-tinged non-mythological/devotional production that I know of is Kamal Amrohi's **MAHAL**, from 1949. That film vaguely deals with reincarnation and features the "ghost" of a young woman. Other ghostly-themed films began to arise during the 1960s in Southern Indian cinema, but nothing too grisly. **NAGIN** (1976) and **JAANI DUSHMAN** (1979, both D: Rajkumar Kohli), as well as some other early Bollywood productions—such as those made by the Ramsay clan—pretty much wedged open the door for the genre to begin its entry into Indian theatres.

As far as *khooni*-titled monster movies are concerned, the three most noteworthy examples are **KHOONI MAHAL** (1987), **KHOONI MURDAA** (1990, both D: Mohan Bhakri), and **KHOONI PANJA** (1991, D: Vinod Talwar), all of which were covered extensively in *Monster!* #21 and #10, respectively. These gruesome creature features pretty much paved the way for the use of the titular keyword and its association with the horror genre, albe-

it only for a very brief period of time, so it comes as no surprise that any films with *khooni* in their titles produced prior to 1987 had nothing whatsoever to do with horror.

Horror films in India nowadays: really, there is very little difference than from a decade previous. It has only been that recently that the horror genre has shrugged off the Ramsays' corruptive influence.

Or *has* it…?

Indian "Scream Queen" actress Bipasha Basu, who starred in more than her share of horror films, including **RAAZ** (a.k.a. **SECRET**, 2002, D: Vikram Bhatt), **AATMA** (2013 D: Suparn Verma), **CREATURE 3D** (2014, D: Vikram Bhatt), and **ALONE** (2015, D: Bhushan Patel), believes that today's horror films treat previously taboo subject matters like the occult and religious horror differently than the genre has done in the past (which relegated them to being played in smaller venues to a more select audience). "Horror films evoke a certain kind of emotion," says Bipasha. "As a viewer, you will have an expression coupled with excitement. One can be scared, choked with emotion, cry or laugh, but one can never fall asleep while watching a crisp horror film."[2] (Yet another confusing soundbite trotted out by Bollywood which makes little to no sense!) Director Ram Gopal Varma legitimized Indian horror in 2002 with his film **BHOOT**, but very few directors thereafter managed to step up to the bar. RGV took the genre out of the sleaze-pit and made one heck of a film. I have yet to read an interview or talk to a director who can explain why Indian horror films are so almost universally bad, so Bipasha's explanation is just utter bullshit. But more on this in *Weng's Chop* #9, which will feature my lengthy essay on the most popular and enduring theme to be found in India's horror cinema: that of spiritual/demonic possession.

One more side-note and then on with the article proper: I was amused to read that the one horror film which gave RGV quite the fright was Bernard Rose's **CANDYMAN** (1992, USA). "I remember the first time I had seen the film in one part," he recalled in a 2012 news-bite. "I had switched it off in the first half-hour. Then I went to the mirror and said 'Candyman' four times. But couldn't get myself to say it the fifth time, because I got scared that—what if Candyman *really* comes?"[3] This helps explain a scene or two in his 1996 film **DEYYAM** (see *Monster!* #15 [p.93]), and is just a minor example indicating that even RGV can't help ripping-off

2 https://www.quora.com/Will-the-Indian-film-industry-ever-be-successful-in-producing-horror-films

3 http://movies.ndtv.com/bollywood/the-horror-film-that-scares-ram-gopal-varma-most-607983

KHOONI DRACULA
THEME SONG

In the middle of the night,
and chilling silence...
Who is the bloodthirsty one
hunting the beauties??

He is the servant of his master,
on whose signal he walks
Whomever it is
is indeed a terrible demon!

Save yourself from Dracula,
He strikes at nightfall
Save yourself from the killer's
teeth. He is bloodthirsty!

Killer Dracula, killer Dracula
[Repeat]

When he goes prowling in the
middle of the night
[Repeat]

Nobody can catch him as he
hunts innocent virgin beauties

Watch out, save yourself, run....
Killer Dracula, killer Dracula....!

Hollywood, just like almost every other Indian director around.

I had wrongly believed that the 1991 film **KHOONI RAAT** (D: J D Lawrence) was a horror film, although this was an understandable misassumption on my part, as I bought the VCD set, and its sleeve artwork had that crummy "Grade C" look about it, plus the cast included Javed Khan, who was not a stranger to low-budget monster movies. Instead however, like those earlier titles I mentioned, this one was less of a translation to "Bloody Night", but rather leaned more towards meaning "Terrible [or Fatal] Night". Gyanendra Choudhry's similarly-named 2004 film was more what I was searching for, although it was nightmarish on a whole other level that what I was hoping for. But more on that one when we get to it.

Another misunderstanding is **KHOONI ANKHEN**, which is the 1988 Hindi release retitling of Malayalam-language director A.E. Baby's 1981 film **KARIMPOOCHA**. Although it is not an "official" *khooni* film, it is a doozy of a supernatural thriller from one of the unsung masters of South Asian cinema. The Indian film industry may have tied with Italy in the '70s and '80s when it came to being the unofficial—is there *any other* kind?—rip-off capital of the world. It's sad to note that one of the most interesting Malayalam directors, Baby, had wasted his time adapting popular Hollywood horrors for Indian consumption. Had this ghost-car film not been made two years before John Carpenter's **CHRISTINE** (1983, USA), there would be a strong case for plagiarism. As it stands, **KARIMPOOCHA**'s closest American relative is George Bowers' **THE HEARSE** (1980), with a smattering of John Irvin's **GHOST STORY** (1981) tossed in the mix for good measure.

Moving right along, we run smack-dab into Harinam Singh's 1992 **KHOONI DRACULA**...

It's hard to believe that this film[4] is from the early '90s (various internet sources cite 1992 as its year of production/release, but the official Censor Certificate dates it 1993), as it has that definite "early 2000s" feel to it. But so as not to muddy the waters more than they are already, I'll stick with what I know.

Would you like to watch a film even cheaper and more perverse than any that Kanti Shah has ever made? Then any one of Singh's films will fit the bill! The main themes in Singh's overall oeuvre boil

---

4 Not to be confused with Singh's later **SHAITANI DRACULA** (2006) or the equally strange **DRACULA** (1999, D: Bhooshan Lal), or even Saleem Suma's **SON OF DRACULA** (2000 [no relation to either the 1943 or 1974 films of same name, needless to say!]). These are titles which I shall eventually cover in the pages of *Monster!* when their time rolls around.

down to what is so typical of any Indian horror film of the day: rape, murder, and a vengeful *bhoot* (typically of the female variety). Although **KHOONI DRACULA** doesn't feature any wronged woman, there is a lot of debased female flesh on display. Better directors have used these tropes and created classics (re: pretty much any Ramsay film in the monster genre), but Singh's approach is far more base. *All* of his films have the look and feel of a fever dream. Not much within them makes sense, and the way that they are presented emphasizes their nightmarish qualities. Most of his films contain recycled or cannibalized elements: music, stock footage, actual scenes lifted from bigger-budget films, and so forth. By the time his career ended in 2006 with **SHAITAN DRACULA**, his budget was way *beyond* tight, and he was even recycling his *own* past products (it seems that cut-and-paste was by then a budgetary art that Singh had really perfected).

KHOONI DRACULA opens with a flash of lightning—probably the most oft-used bit of stock footage seen in Indian cinema!—and trees wildly twisting in a stormy wind (again, popular stock footage). The camera then pans downward, and we see a prone figure on the ground. We can safely assume it's Dracula, due to him/it being a monstrous thing with long black hair and a rubbery Halloween mask for a face. His "master" (unknown) hands the monster a slip of paper which proves to be a list of the names (and I assume addresses) of young virgins—female ones, natch!—whereupon the creature grunts and rises from the ground. A series of additional lightning flashes, then Dracula dons a mangy-but-fancy wide-brimmed top hat to go with his ratty cape and the rest of his fashionably black garb. Cut to a leggy brunette getting ready for bed, and Dracula, transforming from the Halloween-masked horror to a mustachioed man, albeit still dressed wearing his drab attire.

Dracula (played by director Singh himself) enters the woman's bathroom as she steps out of the shower.[5] He takes off his hat and approaches her, his eyes all lustfully aglow with a red glare. She is under his spell and the vampire runs his hands all over her supple body and lowers her to her bed. A bolt of lightning strikes her house, then Dracula takes a bite out of her neck and gobbles her blood. *Cut to the opening credits!*

The vampire strikes numerous times, dressed to kill either in his monstrous self or in human form. This creature even has his own theme song, and it's one of the best things about the film. Although it was never released as a 45 rpm single as far as I can tell, it

KHOONI DRACULA was made in 1993, a year after Coppola's **BRAM STOKER'S DRACULA**, and I could totally see Singh opting to dress his Dracula in a fancy top hat and cape like the one Gary Oldman donned. However, what really struck me were the (random?) similarities between **KHOONI DRACULA** and Mario Bava's **BARON BLOOD** (1972). But more about that in the next issue of *Monster!*

could have been a top-ten Bollywood pop tune called "Khooni Dracula". This finger-snapping ditty is typically played in the film while the beast is stalking and feasting on women. The song is a jaunty one as it warns people that "Nobody can catch him as he hunts virgin innocent beauties" (see sidebar on the preceding page; with thanks to Omar Ali Khan for the translation). Yes, local young ladies are dropping like flies, and the police are powerless to stop the vampire responsible. We see Dracula rise from his "tomb"

---

5   No doubt a scene that was one of the many nudie inserts for the film, as she steps from the shower in a bathing suit and a towel wrap.

KHOONI DRACULA is without a doubt the most stylish of any Indian horror film, no matter the decade. Take for instance, the incredible wardrobe of the lead monster. Dracula wears an outrageously tall, beat-up top hat, mangy cape and ratty black wig while stalking his victims. And let's not forget that amazing rubber Halloween mask, which is Dracula's "actual" face! All of his fashion sense does nothing for his fans, and by the end of the film he gets skewered by a holy trident then his body is tossed on a bonfire for the late-night weenie roast

(which is a patch of dirt in the local charnel grounds) and stroll through a gate which magically opens for him. As usual he is decked out in his cape and top hat.[6] His appearance is either that of the floppy rubber vampire mask—with (and sometimes without) a big red splotch between his eyes, and (again, only *sometimes*) sporting a third eye in his forehead—or else that of the dapper-mustachioed Singh with overly large plastic teeth. At the drop of a top hat, Dracula attacks ladies when they're bathing or taking a shower (fully-clothed, of course!), draped on the couch reading a book (he sneaks up on them from behind), or in a swimming pool (where the monster rises out of the water only to be slashed by the screaming maiden before she is munched on). He is positively insatiable in his appetite for virgins' blood!

It's up to a gaggle of "kids" (a.k.a. your usual Bollywood "Scooby Gang") to finally track the monster down. They use one of their number, a sexy girl (*what else?!*), as bait. The ruse works, and Dracula shows up expecting a light dinner and a bit of a grabby snuggle, only to be ganged-up-on by the kids. He flees the scene, but the blood-drinking villain doesn't make it very far (it seems a tad unfair to have seven kids armed with weapons chasing a monster who is having a hard time seeing out through the eyeholes of his Halloween mask as he tries to flee!), and the hunters corner the creature in a jungle clearing. It panics as its enemies approach, armed to the teeth with clubs, sticks and *trishuls* (tridents, the holy symbol of the god Shiva, which are repeatedly seen in Indian horror movies, as regular viewers/readers will know). The monster has his forehead eyeball smashed and gets run-through with the *trishuls*. To be honest, it was hard to really see what was going on, as Singh went the unusual route of filming the climactic battle *in the dark*—as opposed to the usual day-for-night shots—with very little illumination. As naturalistic as this may be, it wasn't a good creative choice on his part (although it may have been done out of necessity, due to the minuscule budget). By the end, the monster lies mortally wounded on the ground covered with *his* own blood instead of others'. To finish the deed, the kids then cremate Dracula's remains in accordance with Hindu customs. Smart move: meaning no sequels!

---

6 The oversized hat reminds me of a Korean *gat*, which, made of horse hair and with a ridiculously wide brim, was traditional headgear worn by men in Korea during the 1600-1800s. Its exaggerated design was based upon certain European styles of the time. An XL top hat similar to the one that Dracula sported *was* popular with "gentlemen" in colonial India during the mid-late 1800s, however, I think its use in **KHOONI DRACULA** more than likely came about due to fact that Gary Oldman had worn a tall hat in Francis Ford Coppola's **BRAM STOKER'S DRACULA**, and, having presumably seen promotional materials for that film (which was released in late 1992), Singh rushed his own infinitely cheaper Drac flick into production.

Despite all the bad press that to this day plagues **KHOONI DRACULA** (even folks who are diehard Indian monster movie buffs hate this poor film), I found it pretty entertaining, and one of the closest adaptations of Bram Stoker's novel to come out of Bollywood. *Whaaaat?!* you ask incredulously. Yes, it's true: right after the equally bizarre **KHOONI DARINDA**, which I will cover a little later on, a few other adaptations were also produced. The Ramsays' vampire film **BANDH DARWAZA** (1990) was a better production all-round, and it is a beautiful film to watch on a technical and artistic level, but, if you want to charitably bestow some sort of merit upon it, Singh's **DRACULA** hewed closer to the well-trod source material. And unlike the Ramsay films, Singh didn't rip anyone else off (well, except for Bram Stoker's estate, anyway!). That, and Singh was probably the very first director to intentionally usher in this kind of cheap and lazy "devil-may-care" horror film. Mohan Bhakri made some micro-budget classics prior to 1993, but his films, no matter what they lacked financially, always at least exhibited some kind of directorial flair. Besides, Bhakri had monster-maker Srivanas Roy, and—well—Singh had the, uh…local Dollar General store (or equivalent) at his disposal.

Various film blogs, online stores, and "legit" movie databases have chronicled his work which, **KHOONI DRACULA** included, primarily consists of horror films: these encompass **GUMNAAM QATIL** (2001), and the unofficial *shaitani* quadrilogy, **SHAITANI BADLA** (1993), **SHAITANI AATMA** (1998), **SHAITANI DARINDA** (1999), and **SHAITANI DRACULA** (2006). The remaining titles in his filmography include the "sexy dramas" **JEB KATARI** (1997) and **DHANNO DHABE WALI** ([2004] without a doubt his most accomplished), as well as his bandit films, **BASANTI KI SHAADI HONEY-MOON GABBAR KA** (2002) and **RAMGARH KA DAKU** (1993?).

If I had more resources and time I would love to delve deeper into the wacky world of Harinam Singh, but as it turns out he is a tough character to track down. Singh is as common a last name as Smith is over here, and most Googling brings up the popular yogi who sort of shares the same name (Hari Nam Singh; teacher of meditation and healing in the Kundalini Yoga and Sat Nam Rasayan traditions). None of my sources in India want to even discuss this "Ed Wood of India" (a title I would dispute, as I find Wood's films brilliantly composed in spite of their puny budgets), as his output even embarrasses folks who are into the lowly work of the Shah Brothers and their ilk.

That said, *really* cheap horror films began to creep into the market post-1993. They were manufactured for smaller theaters which catered to less-sophisticated audiences. The Ramsays may have begun the process, but even their most inane titles looked like stellar productions when compared to **KHOON KI PYASI DAAYAN** (1998, D: B Santosh), or **CHANDAAL ATMA** (1999, D: S.R. Pratap), or

I had high hopes that the film would be as exciting as this lobby card for it…sadly, it wasn't

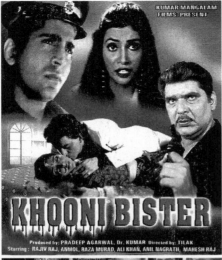

Home video artwork for Hindi "horror" films: you can't judge a book by its cover, and the same can be said of how the Indians enjoy dressing-up their films in hopes of higher retail returns. **KHOONI BISTER** *[top]* is a mystery/cop drama, not a horror film, although it is presented as one; and *[above]* is one of your typical 4-in-1 DVD set deals, which deliver the goods for a mere $1.99—but what you see is *not* always what you get!

QATIL CHANDALINI (1999, D: Rajan Lyallpuri), or **BHOOT HI BHOOT** (2000, D: Boss), or **JADOO TONA** (2001, D: Kishan Shah [not Ravikant Nagaich's same-titled and entertaining

1977 **EXORCIST** rip-off]), or **AAGEY MAUT PEECHE MAUT** (2001, D: A.T. Joy), or...

...Dilip Gulati's **KHOONI No. 1** (1999), which, while billed as a "horror" film, is actually an idiotic little comedy; this despite the opening sequence involving a man picking up a gorgeous hitchhiker and delivering her to the Hotel *Gumnaam* ("Anonymous" Hotel; harking back to the thriller **GUMNAAM** from 1966), where she eerily disappears like the famous "Vanishing Hitchhiker" of legend *[Filipino folklore/urban legend tells of a similar spooky thumb-tripper, known as "The White Lady" – SF]*. In **K#1**, we witness a ghostly floating disembodied head exploding from a mysterious doorway, a black housecat which screams like a cougar, a monster sequence "borrowed" (a.k.a. blatantly stolen!) from the Ramsays' **VEERANA** (1988), and an extended musical number involving a ghostly "Woman in White" performing a mournful ditty about lost love and her death or something or other.

WOW! Judging by that opener, I'm thinking this might actually turn out to be *good*... Later, a carful of kooky kids arrive at the hotel, and we're all set for some eerie hijinks...

Director Gulati made around fifteen films in his short career. All, like **KHOONI No. 1**, were exploitation productions that fell into three categories. First you have his jungle films, which were his earliest and most successful on both a financial and artistic level: **JUNGLE BEAUTY** (1991), **JUNGLE LOVE STORY** (1998), and **ZIMBO** (1999), his rip-off of the once-popular series starring titular Indian jungle man, who was himself a rip-off of ERB's Tarzan. Those films just cited, like most of the ones to follow, starred many of the same Grade C actors and actresses who populated other sleaze productions of the time: for instance, Joginder Shelley (any films with him in it are usually worth a watch just for his scene-chewing antics), plus Amrit Pal, Raza Murad (once an A-lister who then fell on hard times; sort of like the Joseph Cotten [etc.] of his day), Shakti Kapoor, Kiran Kumar (a perennial fave), Birbal, Anil Nagrath, Jai Thakur, Dharmendra (who was once one of the biggest stars of Indian cinema), and even Kanti Shah's bodacious wife Sapna danced for two sequences in **KHOONI KANGAN** (2000), a ghost film that—believe it or not!—got a bona fide DVD release in the USA, with English subtitles yet. In that film, the ghost of a murdered woman haunts her killers. The rest of Gulati's filmography included a few bandit films, another horror film where he would waste Sapna's talents once again in another minor role (i.e., his 2001 witch film, **MAIN HOON QATIL JAADUGARNI**), as well as two straightforward (and dreadful!) "comedies".

But what of **KHOONI No. 1**? As I mentioned above, the film begins with some potential. Somewhere after the first twenty minutes or so, though, I realized that unless something really drastic was going to happen (and soon!), I had been duped into buying another dud. The plot meanders from one jokey sequence to the next, involving a couple of thieves, undercover police officers, stolen goods, a murderer in a rubber monster mask, and a mysterious woman who may or may not be a *bhoot*. We are unlucky enough to have that floating head/cat yowl/**VAARENA**/woman-in-white singing while strolling through a cemetery composite scene repeated not twice but fully *five fucking times* throughout the film! And what was the point? Nothing about this sexy she-spook (who pops in and out of existence for no apparent reason, seemingly at random) is resolved by the time **K#1** ends. A similar opening sequence occurs in **KHOONI BISTER** (2001, D: Tilak Raj), a film that was sold as a horror film, but is in reality just another crime drama with a few weird sequences set in a cemetery. But no monster, and no ghost.

Yet another series of nightmarish repetitions is the *singularly* interesting element of our next film, and the only reason to bother mentioning it after **KHOONI No. 1**. The primary difference between Gyanendra Choudhry's **KHOONI RAAT** (2004) and our two previous entries is that the ghost which appears *is* an actual vengeful spirit, with a purpose. **KHOONI RAAT** is built upon yet another sequence involving a spectral "Woman in White". This time around, the order of events include a Bollywoodish James Bond theme playing while a car is being driven down a winding road, then we are introduced to a gorgeous *bhoot*-babe wandering through a boneyard. This revenge-bent female ghost subsequently kills a man, then another (and *another*, and so on…), and after each murderous assault there is a crash of lightning (ahhh, that classic stock footage again!), then the camera cuts to a man lying on the ground. He awakens from what appears to be a bad dream, only to get to his feet and walk out of the scene, shaking his head in disbelief. As may you be while watching these inexplicable scenes. What *is* going on here…?

The above-described sequence of events happens a total of *five* times; exactly the same order of scenes, with the same outcome…only the manner of death delivered to the skeezy male victims differs. (When will this madness stop?!) It's only when a holy man attempts to communicate with the bloodthirsty *bhoot* that we get the full picture. We learn that the killer is the justifiably resentful avenging restless spirit of a woman who was gang-raped and then beaten to death by five men; the same scumbags she killed-off throughout the course of the film. The *tantrik* announces that her actions were justified, whereupon

Top: VCD sleeve art for the cut-and-paste monstrosity known as **KHOONI RAAT** (2004). **Above: KHOONI ILAAKA** may not be a great film, but it does star a favorite actor of mine: the late and underappreciated Rami Reddy, who is featured prominently in this pressbook graphic, as well as in the one featured on the back of this issue too. Reddy typically played heavies in low-budget thrillers and horror films, although he did manage to get a comedic role from time to time

111

the ghostess is permitted to depart our realm in peace, her vengeance satisfied. **KHOONI No. 1** is a patchwork classic if there ever was one! At least after all of the preceding editing nonsense the killer turned out to be of supernatural origin rather than of the more boring flesh-and-blood mortal variety.

Next up we have **KHOONI ILAAKA: THE PROHIBITED AREA** (1999), a funky little monster flick from director Teetrat Singh and producer Jitendra Chawda. The latter cut his teeth working on two earlier Kanti Shah films, **LOHA** ([1997] action) and **MAUT** ([1998] horror), before jumping into the low-budget ring with this horror effort. **KHOONI ILAAKA** was produced with the Kanti Shah-associated production company Satya Sai Films. Essentially, **KI** should be lumped in with most of the crap made by the Shah Brothers (Kanti and Kishan; not to be confused with the Shaw Brothers!), except for the fact that, despite **KI**'s humble production values, Chawda does manage to make a purse out of a sow's ear. It doesn't hurt to have the extremely fit Sapna in a minor but sexy role, as well as the always enjoyable Rammy Reddy (a.k.a. Rami Reddy) chewing up the scenery as an evil *tantrik*, along with blue-eyed wonder Vinod Tripathi just being his usual crazy self.

On their way back from a jaunt, a man (Tripathi) and his wife Rosy (Jyoti Rana) have car trouble on a deserted stretch of road. When the vehicle refuses to start after it stalls, the two are attacked by a ghost in the guise of animated vines and a laughing human skull. Rosy is taken by the ghost, while her husband encounters a sexy "woman in white" spook (cue the usual mournful tune typically sung by such ghosts). This encounter *doesn't* end well! When the couple fail to return home, the missing man's brother (Raj Premi) and girlfriend (Shabnam) head out to look for them. Luckily for the searchers,

they encounter a friendly priest who tells them (in flashback) a sad tale of his battle with an evil *tantrik* (played by Reddy), who had used innocents to further his lust for power through black magic. He would also—natch!—round up sexy young ladies to satisfy his depraved lusts. But the *tantrik* is confronted by a pair of angry ruffians, one of whom is the local village *thakur* (which, roughly translated, means one of the rich landowner caste of India) who has had enough of the randy wizard's "amorous" antics. In hopes of putting a stop to his evil shenanigans—good luck to that!—the ruffians chop off the *tantrik*'s forearms, murder him, then dump his body in the nearby forest. Unluckily for the village, the powerful wizard returns from the dead for revenge, his body possessing a large Banyan tree, which grabs people in its boughs (often assisted by the *tantrik*'s own severed limbs) and kills them. The *thakur* is taken by the monstrous tree and becomes transformed into a fork-tongued demon, and together with another unfortunate soul they kidnap travelers so the *tantrik* can murder them and drain their life-force.

Despite the decidedly threadbare plot, Singh manages to keep the viewer engaged with numerous (*six!* Count 'em!) godawful dance numbers and some truly heinous comedy routines which help carry—or rather, cripple—the remainder of the film's plot. A rich merchant decides to build a hotel next to *Khooni Ilaaka*, the haunted forest where resides the evil-possessed Banyan tree. It isn't until the film's final fifteen minutes that things really begin to get hairy. The green-faced beast with forked tongue attacks our main characters (well, the *surviving* ones, anyway), and a plea is made to the deity Shiva. Their cries for help are heard by the god, who sends one of his priestly *sadhus* ("attendants") to confront and combat the wizard. In a spectacular pitched battle of

The Tops In Tantriks: Indian villains come in all shapes and sizes, and within the horror genre they are typically wizards with a grudge. Two of the most popular actors during the Golden Age of Hindi Horror to portray such *tantriks* were Rami Reddy *[left]* and Rajesh Vivek *[above]*

magic and mayhem (um, okay, that's a "slight" exaggeration) the swami is able to defeats the two monsters and the *tantrik* when the latter's pesky limbs are skewered by the priest's trusty *trishula*, whereupon the evil one explodes in a ball of flame. The End.

The main reason for watching this film is the afore-noted Rami Reddy, an actor known for his roles as evil *tantriks* and other such malignant characters. After the beetle-browed actor Rajesh Vivek (star of **VEERANA**, and other horror classics), Reddy was the go-to guy when Vivek was unavailable. Earlier in his career Reddy was typically cast as a thug or gangster, appearing in films by noted directors K. Raghavendra Rao and Ram Gopal Varma, before getting his break in Kodi Ramakrishna's angry goddess smash hit **AMMORU** in 1995 cast as—yep, you guessed it—an evil *tantrik*. Thanks to **AMMORU**, combined with his dark complexion and large, stocky build, it was a role which caused Reddy to thereafter be typecast, and one from which he has never managed to fully break free. Still, I guess he couldn't have gone hungry, as he did star in over a hundred films, all-told. For me, his most memorable movies are the fantasy-based ones. These include portraying wonderfully wicked wizards in Ram Narayanan's **JA DURGA SHAKTI / AMMORU THALLI** (2002) and Sanjeeva Rao's **NAGA PRATISTA** (2002), as well as—just for a rare change of pace—playing a kind-hearted Catholic priest battling an evil *bhoot* (in the bodacious shape of Sapna, who makes for one succulent succubus indeed) in Kanti Shah's **CHEEKH**, from 2004. Sadly, Reddy died due to complications arising from a chronic liver ailment in 2011 during the filming of Kodi Ramakrishna's still-unreleased goddess film **JAI BHADRAKALI**.

As for the rest of the cast in the present film, we again have the shapely Sapna (a.k.a. Sapna Tanveer, wife of Kanti Shah), who shows up halfway through **KHOONI ILAAKA** to add some spice with some sexy dances for three musical numbers, and does so very well. I had been hoping to see her in a more substantially expanded role here, rather than merely in an overly long comedic segment serving as the foil for some horrible impersonators, but what can you do. The sad thing is that she *can* act and handles her scenes well, be they action, drama or comedy (check out *Weng's Chop* #5 [pp.180-203] for my near-as-dammit to complete Kanti Shah and Sapna filmography). But with **KHOONI ILAAKA**, her thespian talents (other than for the more—*ahem*—obvious ones!) are totally wasted, sad to say.

Mediocre musical interludes aside, **KHOONI ILAAKA** still manages to surprise me each time I re-watch it. It has short passages of material which could have made for a truly awesome film as a

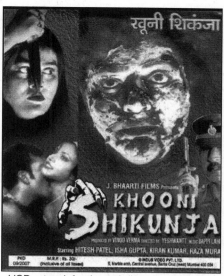

VCD artwork for the weirdly compelling flick
KHOONI SHIKUNJA

whole if a similar quality level had been maintained throughout. Producer-director Chawda was able to work some of the same kind of movie magic into his next project, **DAFAN** (2001), starring Amit Pachori, which was a definite improvement. It's interesting to note that, for some reason, **DAFAN** was one of the few films made under Kanti Shah & Co.'s umbrella that scored an English-subtitled DVD release. Just for the record, Chawda also directed three goofy action thrillers, **DACAIT** (2000), **EK LOOTERA** (2001) and **GANGOBAI** (2002). Until, like so many of his fellow filmmakers, he too eventually faded from the Indian indie scene, never to be heard from again...

Since the New Millennium dawned, there have already been numerous more "modern" horror films produced, but cheapjack productions nonetheless still somehow get made, too. Mind you, I am not complaining. It's these minor miracles that help keep the past glories alive. And what I mean is that, by the time Ram Gopal Varma's **BHOOT** was made in 2003, films like **KHOONI SHIKUNJA, KHOONI KAALA JADU, KHOONI KANGAN, KHOONI TANTRIK,** and **KHOONI SHAITAN** had managed to survive, even though, according to various box office sources, none of them made any kind of return on their producers' investments. These and the last stragglers in this article—**KHOONI, KHOONI PED** (and the aforementioned **KHOONI RAAT**)—were made at a time when, according to director Suparn Verma, "I was sick and tired of this genre being abused by clichés such as haunted villas, 200-year-old curses and the tacky presentation of the genre." His ghost story **AATMA** was only a slight variation on theme, albeit one of the more interesting films of 2013.

But merely turning your back on the "clichés" is not the answer. And neither is ripping-off other films to get the job done. At least most of these little indie horror flicks had some regional originality to them, and they are not simply the latest trendy Thai, Japanese, or English tale dressed up in a sari with additional musical numbers added just because it is expected. The "crappier" little films are thankfully not the pretentious, bloated, self-important and overindulgent productions made by boastful "Big Time" directors. They entertain despite their tired tropes that had to be dusted off each and every time they were re-trundled back out for the umpteenth time. I personally like the hoary vengeful "Woman in White" theme, which goes all the way back to the early 1960s. I also adore the *el cheapo* effects, and get a real kick out of seeing just how far these by-the-skin-of-their-teeth filmmakers can stretch their pitiful budgets. Most all of these films were box-office disasters when released, but at least they knew what they were making: crap cinema made for the lowest common denominator... which includes me! ☺

Next up we have two weird little monster movies (like that come as any surprise!)

KHOONI SHIKUNJA (2000, D: Yeshanti) is a quickly-made horror film starring some very familiar faces, including that of Anil Dhawan, who is a highly popular actor in all sorts of films, including **LAASH** (1998, D: K Mansukhlal) and the Ramsays' **AAKHRI CHEEKH** (1991; see *Monster!* #14, p.90). This time around we are treated to yet another one of those pesky vengeance-mad she-demons that stalks and slaughters the deserving dirtbags who raped and murdered her. She appears as a frightful boil-covered specter oozing blood and rage, either personally attacking an individual or possessing the body of an alluring young woman in order to carry out the deadly deed.

But then, just when you're thinking you've seen all this before, there comes an oddball plot-twist: it seems there is more to the story when it becomes clear that some money-hungry humans are behind the creation of the demoness, and they possess the means of controlling her/it for their own nefarious ends. The ghost-possessed young woman picks off the family members of a rich household as well as the men who raped and killed her. In one absurdly bizarre scene, she turns into a baby doll to attack and chomp on one of her rapists.

The film draws to a close as the creature, which has been possessing the body of a young man's girl-friend, turns on those who created her. She is destroyed when the god Shiva intervenes. Oh wait—the film doesn't end at the destruction of the demon. To flesh-out the running time to almost two hours, there's an additional six-minute fight sequence, complete with comedic bumbling, heroic fisticuffs, and a catfight. Silly stuff indeed!

This is as good place as any to mention that the Indian film industry as a rule produces films of a "multi-genre" nature, this in order to hopefully maximize their B.O. returns by catering to as many consumer demographics as possible all in one go. Most of you are already very aware of the musical numbers that pop up at seemingly random moments in most Indian films (but not *all*, as is sometimes believed). These at best toe-tapping splashes of color, dance and song are usually an alternate narrative to what can be typically a very plot-heavy film. Bollywood movie music is called, logically enough, *filmi* music, which means "of films" in Hindi.[7] Such moments of frenetic nuttiness ideally add to a film's overall surreal appeal. But the comedy bits that pop up out of nowhere can be soul-crushing stretches of sheer, dreadful tomfoolery. Whereas *filmi* carries the narrative, in virtually all of Indian cinema, the slapstick actions of "funny-looking" actors mugging for the camera or pulling faces put a stop to any of the forward momentum achieved. In the horror-drama genre, these sorts of interruptions can be devastating from a dra-

VCD sleeve art for the crazy **KHOONI TANTRIK**, featuring actors from the film as well as Indian actress Kiran Rathod and a demonic Deadite from Sam Raimi's 3rd *Evil Dead* entry—neither of which, by the way, are in the Bollywood film!

7 en.wikipedia.org/wiki/Bollywood#Bollywood_song_and_dance

A strange, fleshy goggle-eyed zombie creature pops up for a few minutes to terrorize folks in **KHOONI TANTRIK**

matic standpoint, at least to someone more used to moviemaking standards here in the Western hemisphere. Almost every Indian film has these would-be comedic episodes. As one director told me, "Here in India we make films that are typically 150 minutes long. Indian cine-goers get headaches after watching continuous horror scenes, so we insert comedy scenes as a way to balance-out the scary parts. These scenes are there to relax to audience." It's a formula that may work for them, but it makes me cringe!

There is very little to recommend about our next feature, **KHOONI KAALA JADU**. The film is typical of director R Mittal, a man who seemed to delight in crafting some really dull horror films, such as **BHAYAANAK PANJAA** (1996), **TOWER HOUSE** (1999), and **DAAK BANGLA** (2000 [*not* the 1987 Ramsay film of same name]), and loads of actioners and inane "sex" comedies. In **KKJ**, there is a sexy female ghost who is hot for revenge (what else?!), but by the year 2000, when this film was made, even that was getting to be old hat.

Director Teerat Singh attempted to liven-up the genre with his 2001film **KHOONI TANTRIK** (*"Killer* Tantrik"), although after watching the film I don't think he really achieved his goal. One wonders if Teerat Singh is anyway related to Harinam Singh, since they are both in the same business and seem to have dipped their cast crew from the same murky pond.[8] Once the credits began to roll, I realized that **KHOONI TANTRIK**'s questionable cinematography was by Saleem Suma, who worked on the above-discussed **KHOONI ILAAKA** and was the director of **SON OF DRACULA** (both 1999). Now, that latter film is *really* fucked-up; more about **SON OF DRACULA** in January's issue.

8   To be honest, the family name of Singh is one of the more common in India and Pakistan (especially among Sikhs of the Punjab), so I don't think so.

KT is a tale of two highly-religious brothers—twins, in fact—who dabble on the opposite sides of God, although they did once love one another. When the "good" brother, a devotee of the god Shiva, helps a young woman, he is assassinated by her disgruntled boyfriend. The *tantrik*'s "bad" brother, a dabbler in the dark arts of the goddess Kaali, takes matter into his own hands, and once again vengeance is the name of the game. First to die is his bro's assassin, then numerous other characters follow in succession as the film progresses. It takes over an hour before an honest-to-goodness monster shows up, but when it finally does raise its ugly mug, I was pleasantly surprised. Now, I'm not saying that this creature is a splendid example of how a Hindu horror should look. The zombie/demon appears out of nowhere and resembles a cheap rented gorilla costume (belted, with a hood) topped by a weird goggle-eyed, fleshy head with bucktooth fangs. It is clearly *not* the work of makeup FX men Srinivas Roy or Alok Dutt, but rather that of one Sunny Mukesh, who clearly didn't have two rupees to rub together for his monster budget. But it worked for me!

Those on the *tantrik*'s (s)hit-list hire their own holy man when the monster begins to become too much of a pest. The shaggy-haired swami (played to the frenzied hilt by the one-and-only Joginder Shelly) heads a gang of torch-toting villagers to track the monster down. Now comes one of the few tender moments seen in these sorts of screwed-up horror films: when the woman from the beginning of the film approaches the monster, it/he confesses that he is in fact the reanimated corpse of the good *tantrik*, who has returned to right various wrongs. She then lights the monster up with her torch, and it is consumed by the purifying flames (thus assuring his reincarnation, as a dirt burial isn't the proper way to put a Hindu spook to rest). The film ends shortly thereafter when the Joginder swami works up a wicked spell and a dead-

Kanti Shah Sexy Shockers: Pressbook artwork for **KHOONI SHAITAN** *[top]*, and the VCD cover for **KHOONI** *[above]*; the latter's layout features a demon from Lamberto Bava's **DEMONS** (1985)

by Shirke, a veteran actor of over 100 films, whose roles are typically villainous. He also played the fork-tongued demon in another of Teerat Singh's films, the above **KHOONI ILAAKA** from '99, as well as a being a regular in the Kanti Shah & Associates stable of cast and crew.

Speaking of which, trashmeister Kanti Shah entered the fray with two of minor classics from the most productive period of his career. First up is **KHOONI SHAITAN** from 2002, a film set in the sprawling *mahal* ("house", or "mansion") which the director has used as a shooting site for practically all of his monster movies. **KS** stars regulars Amit Pachori, Anil Nagrath, and Vinod Tripathi, along with the alluring Nitu and Tina (who seem to always be in various stages of undress throughout the film; must be an exploitation movie or something!). They are trapped in the mansion while a murderous monster (an extra-large actor in a gorilla suit) roars and rampages around the grounds. The film is full of the Shahs' usual verbose dialog, violent sexual situations, and has an ending that makes no sense whatsoever.

The film known simply as **KHOONI** (2004), on the other hand, is fairly entertaining as micro-budget thrillers from this time period go. A young horny wife cheats on her husband with a rocker-type dude in a spooky mansion. They are caught in the act by the cuckolded husband (Vinod Tripathi again), who is then murdered and buried in a graveyard not far from the estate. A shape-shifting zombie rises from the grave and all hell breaks loose for the rest of the film. Sapna arrives at the mansion to put things right—if anyone can do it, it's her!—and Shah regular Amit Pachori tags along as a police inspector. What more do ya want? Sex, mystery and zombie action! And no dance numbers to speak of! Now, that is *shocking*!

For more on the films of Kanti Shah and Sapna, may I suggest you get yourself a copy of *Weng's Chop #5*. Besides the usual incredible array of stuff therein, you get my coverage of over 100 of the Shahs' movies from the beginning of their careers to the eventual disintegration of the Indie Empire that Shah, his wife and brother built for themselves.

We now round-out this article with a couple of doozies which are fine examples of what makes these little flicks fun...even if they do make for decidedly *cheap* thrills indeed.

First, a little preview of our forthcoming project, the reboot/reincarnation of the long-dormant *Monster! International* megazine, which WE PROMISE is due to drop before the end of this year, and should be up around 300 pages in total of monster-stuffed madness. In it, in addition to oodles of other great material by our valued and talented stable of contributors, my

ly, creeping, impossibly *lo-o-o-o-ong* piece of magical rope overpowers the Deepak Shirke *tantrik*. This evil wizard is then dragged kicking and complaining all the way across the jungle to the feet of Joginder, who is more than happy to curse his defeated foe, who then drops dead with blood running out of this ears. *BAM!!!* Another one bites the dust. The End.

The identical twin *tantrik* brothers are both played

Monster! co-editor Steve F. and I have co-written a COLOSSAL *[note block caps!* ☺ *– SF.]* account of mummies in the movies, totaling upwards of 80,000 words (*GULP!*). It includes coverage of two rare Indian examples, **KHOONI PED** (खूनी पेड़ ["Murderous Tree"], 2003), one of the only Bollywood mummy movies that I know of besides Keshu Ramsay's truly strange **DAK BANGLA** (1985), which is also covered therein, too (but they're only the tip of the iceberg; or pyramid, I should say). It would seem that **KHOONI PED** was the last of its kind. By the time 2004 rolled around, what monster movies were being produced in India besides Kanti Shah's 2003 beastly **PYAASA HAIWAN**? Very few. By the time director Jagdish Gautam thought it advantageous to unleash his micro-budget mummy movie, the Ramsays had moved on into TV production (starting in the mid/late '90s) with their high ratings-getting TV series *Zee Horror Show* (1993-98), and RGV's **BHOOT** gave the theatrical spook genre a much-needed *bhoot* (pun intended) in the pants. Monster movies, never a huge draw with Indian audiences, have been dead in the cinema ever since (the two major attempts to re-institute flesh-and-blood monsters as going cinematic concerns were Wilson Louis' **KAALO** [2010; see *M!* #4, p.63] and Vikram Bhatt's **CREATURE 3D** [2014; see *M!* #10, p.11], both of which bombed badly).

Nevertheless, the present movie **KHOONI PED** opens as a young woman is being chased through a fog-shrouded forest by a giant swathed in sloppily-wrapped linen bandages. She is struck by the mummy and has her eyeball knocked out by the force of the blow. Then the monster closes in for the kill... but—wait—it is all just a dream, and our horrified heroine wakes up with a start. As is so typical of just about any mummy movie, here we have a group of college medical students who are studying the remains of a huge human corpse wrapped in oddly fresh-looking linen (and stored in a dingy "lab" inside a big cardboard box; a prop which is conveniently much cheaper to use than renting or building some expensive fancy sarcophagus instead). Meanwhile, a Kaali *tantrik* who is hanging around the campus grounds warns the students that there is a devil afoot. Of course, his words are ignored, and an accursed banyan tree—yes, yet another one!—begins strangling students with its roots and branches. But what of the mummy, you ask? He's coming, but not until (*GROAN!*) about 70 minutes into the film. Firstly the creature has to be brought to life, and the terrible tree uses the blood of two students to do just that. The pair are attacked by gnarled branches that choke them and drain them of their life essence, transferring it drop by drop into the mummy which, for whatever reason, now lies buried beneath the tree (ehh, did I *miss* something somewhere…?). Once the magical ichor has been absorbed, the monster (such as he—er, *it*—is) roars to life.

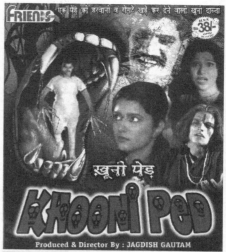

Produced & Director By : JAGDISH GAUTAM

Mummy Mayhem: VCD artwork *[top]* and two exciting scenes from **KHOONI PED**, wherein *[center]* a marauding mummified, mulleted murderer menaces numerous cast members before *[above]* being put down by a kindhearted *tantrik*

Now we finally get some action in the film! Most unfortunately, however, the oversized mummy is nothing like the wonderful monster that stalked its prey in the aforementioned **DAK BANGLA**. That creature was the creation of master monster-maker Srimivas Roy, and was truly hideous to behold. **KP**'s mummy, on the other hand, is basically just an XL actor wearing what looks like baggy white coveralls and wrapped in much-too-clean bandages. Once the wrappings come loose and fall from his head, we see that (double-*GROAN!!*) he's just a regular-looking guy with his face plastered in grey greasepaint, sporting a large "Persian" mustache and a funky mullet haircut that would make any American redneck green with envy. This mulleted mega-"mummy" is on a mission to feed the haunted tree human flesh and blood, and maybe—just maybe—the *tantrik* can stop it (d'ya think?). **KP** picks up steam in its last ten minutes when the mummy uses the power of the haunted tree to bring the dead back to life, causing some pasty-faced zombies to devour a few students while their fearless leader lumbers off in search of more prey. The beneficent *tantrik* intervenes, and, using his *trishula* and with the help of some "untainted" blood voluntarily donated by a pair of "good" students, he is able to destroy the marauding mummy-man. With the tree now no longer haunted, the holy man vanishes after a job well-done, and everything is hunky-dory once more.

Jagdish Gautam made a few other films prior to **KHOONI PED**. I was unable to track down any of his other horror titles besides that one, although I did find sets of lobby cards for both **DAAYEN** ([1997] with genre favorites Javed Kahn, Sripradha, Raza Murad, and Jagdeep) and **TANTRIK SHAKTKI** ([2003] with Kiran Kumar, Shakti Kapoor, and Grusha Kapoor). Judging by these lobbies, the films look just as cheap, dumb and outdated as **KHOONI PED** is. Perhaps unsurprisingly, Gautam has since vanished from the scene, presumably never to be seen nor heard from again.

While all of the better-known horror films by the trashmen of the 1990s/2000s are fun in their own peculiar fashion, I will end this article on an odd note with a relatively obscure late '80s film called **KHOONI DARINDA**...or was that a late *'70s* film? Or perhaps a composite product of the '60s, '70s *and* '80s? Yes,

Top to Bottom: KHOONI DARINDA is a cut-and-paste nightmare production, with all sorts of oddball sequences and edits which make it pretty much intelligible by the time you get to the end. But the principal footage shot by director Nazard Khan looks great, with its scientist hero, toothy villainous vampire and bloodsucking babes who sit seductively on the roofs of cars to entice victims into their, *um*...arms

I'm covering another one of "*those*" productions, like I did in issue #19 (p.4) with **NISHI TRISHNA** (1978?/1988? D: Parimal Bhattacharya). I must confess that I totally messed-up my account of this film in *M!* 19, wherein I mistook **KHOONI DARINDA** for a long-lost 1978 film called **SHAITAN MUJRIM**. From all accounts, the latter sounds like a wild film full of scientific wizardry, saucy sex and hip musical numbers, as well as boasting a horny vampire on top of it. In that film, a scientist is able to reanimate the dead by use of a special serum he develops; however, a severe side effect of this procedure is that the experimental living corpse has now become…a bloodsucking fiend!

I should have known something was up when I noticed that the list of assistant directors on the present film includes fully *five* (5) individuals. **KHOONI DARINDA** is most definitely a cut-and-paste/patchwork job cobbled-together in desperation. IMDb gives the film as a 1987 production, directed by its producer Dhirubhai Daxini, and not by Nazard Khan, who receives onscreen credit (one can only hope he was proud to put his name on it!). Given the state of the "finished" product, I can only assume that Khan was responsible for the initial work and, for some reason, Daxini later played "film doctor" (Monte Hellman he ain't!) by attempting to knit all the various sequences together in hopes that an at least quasi-cohesive plot might be the end result. But where did its original source materials come from? There are a lot of flashbacks to a lab set, assorted vampire attacks, plus musical and comedy numbers which are all rendered in various weird duotones of pink, yellow, blue, magenta and so forth. There are two brief scenes in full (albeit washed-out) color wherein Dev Kumar plays the lusty monster, as seen in the original **SHAITAN MUJRIM**.[9] Much of the film looks old, outdat-

ed and is jumbled confusingly into a disjointed whole, with mismatching stock, characters coming and going with no rhyme or reason, and much random use of stock footage from the previous film. But one of the most telling aspects is its soundtrack; not the musical numbers themselves, but the actual audio recorded for the film. Much of **KHOONI DARINDA** is either actual soundstage capture with incredible amounts of tape hiss and background noise (even directional cues from off-camera!) to be heard, or else the background score is played over top of parts where the actors should properly be heard speaking their lines, with little or no post-dub work done (other than with the playback singers for the filmi sequences). It all seems so slapdash and sloppy, hurried off in such a way as to get the film out the door and into the theaters as fast as possible; but one can't imagine that any meager profits to be had from this massive mess could have been worth the effort (such little of it as was expended).

The main "inspiration" for **KHOONI DARINDA** seems to have been Terence Fisher's **DRACULA** (a.k.a. **HORROR OF DRACULA**, 1958, UK [see M! #13, p.25]). Unlike the Ramsays' **BANDH DARWAZA**, which some unschooled critics claim is a rip-off of the same Hammer production, Khan (who must've handled the principal shots in the film) definitely borrowed heavily from Fisher's film. From the first scene where our hero meets a vampirized "bride", as well as when the vampire lord descends the haunted mahal's main staircase to strike her away from their mutual human prey, to various other sequences throughout, the proceedings literally reek of Hammer's **DRACULA '58**. Had the film remained intact and been properly finished, I guarantee you it would have been much more re-

9 A film which itself was inspired by the 1967 Pakistani vampire movie **ZINDA LAASH**…but more about *that* next issue of *Monster!*

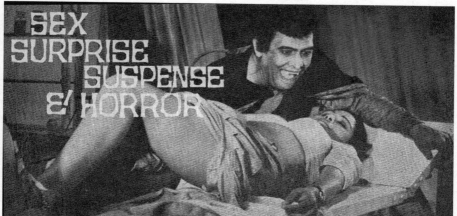

SEX SURPRISE SUSPENSE & HORROR

Detail from the pressbook for **SHAITAN MUJRIM**, a lost horror film from 1977 which was the prequel to **KHOONI DARINDA**, and from all accounts made a lot more sense

Top to Bottom: What **KHOONI DARINDA** *could* have been (but isn't) will always be a mystery. Granted, grand larceny was committed for certain scenes—Terence Fisher would have had a fit!—but there are also some very original, very cool sequences to be had. Take, for instance, when our hero resorts to drawing a Hindu religious symbol on his palm to destroy the vampire...a tactic which popped up decades later in the 2012 Ramsay horror film **NEIGHBOURS: THEY ARE VAMPIRES**

membered than it is(n't). As it stands today—it's available for viewing on YouTube or Dailymotion—it is a horrible mess! And in a way, this muddled mishmash of a movie provides a fitting prelude to those later productions I covered above; primarily Gyanendra Choudhry's bat-shit insane **KHOONI RAAT**, and also so some degree **KHOONI DRACULA**, as well as some of Singh's later projects, too.

It's hard to recommend a film that is so much of a Frankenstein Monster-like stitch-job. However, since **KHOONI DARINDA** is only available to view on the internet (I have yet to discover if it was ever even released to DVD or VCD, let alone on VHS or Beta), I think anyone interested should give it a summary run-through. Of note are the scenes involving the vampire himself, with his big, wolfish grin, his vampire brides—especially the scenes where they run after cars down vacant roads and then and sit on the hoods/roofs to entice their victims!—and at the very end when the leading man has an extended battle with the monster. For that amazing climax, the vicious vampire beats our hero bloody until the latter falls to the floor. As the monster closes in for the kill, the human uses his own blood to draw the symbol "om" on his palm, which he then uses to blast the vampire, whereupon the creature collapses, lines of "powerful energy" illuminating his writhing frame, then promptly fades into a skeleton. The special effects used for this final scene are some of the cheapest and oldest on the books: basically, the holy fire is nothing more than crudely animated lines that must've been scratched into the emulsion of each frame (something I used to do when I made 8mm monster movies as a kid). The result is weirdly surrealistic, and hence effective in its own primitive way.

The indie Indian films of yesteryear are sadly long-gone, although there are still lowercase grade c films being made, but most of these newer productions are just as uninspired as their predecessors were. The plotlines have been updated slightly, but there are still *tantriks* and ghosts, the possessed and their exorcists, and nosy, noisy gangs of "kids" getting into all sorts of trouble with the supernatural. And they are every bit as cheap, if not more-so. Some recent low-budget examples include **AA INTLO** (Telugu, 2009, D: Chinna), **PIZZA** (Tamil, 2012, D: Karthik Subbaraj), Hemant Madhukar's **MUMBAI 125 KM 3D** (Hindi, 2014), Ram Gopal Varma's super-cheap **ICE CREAM** (Telugu, 2014), **MACHHLI JAL RANI HAI** (2014, D: Debaloy Dey), and **6-5=2** (Kannada, 2013, D: K S Ashoka).

But monster movies?

Nope. *Forget it!*

I really miss that...

MONSTER! #23 MOVIE CHECKLIST

MONSTER! Public Service posting: Title availability of films reviewed or mentioned in this issue of MONSTER!

Information dug up and presented by Steve Fenton and Tim Paxton.

The Fine Print: Unless otherwise noted, all Blu-rays and DVDs listed in this section are in the NTSC Region A/Region 1 format and widescreen, as well as coming complete with English dialogue (i.e., were either originally shot in that language, or else dubbed/subbed into it). If there are any deviations from the norm, such as full-frame format, discs from different regions or foreign-language dialogue (etc.), it shall be duly noted under the headings of the individual entries below. We also include whatever related—and sometimes even totally unrelated!—ephemera/trivia which takes our fancy, and will hopefully take yours too.

AMITYVILLE II: THE POSSESSION (1982) *[p.19]* – US DVD tagline: *"If These Walls Could Talk...They Would SHRIEK!"* UK DVD tagline: *"Don't forget to check under the bed..."* Like the rest of the *AH* series, this the first sequel is currently available via any number of sources in most of the usual formats (barring Blu-ray as yet, apparently), both new and old. As far as online VOD outlets go, it can be either rented or purchased as an Amazon Instant Video, in both HD or SD quality modes. Coming complete with a number of extras, the British PAL Region 0 DVD edition issued by Sanctuary Visual Entertainment seems to be about the most optimal version of **A2TP** presently available. It can be ordered online through the video retail site Flesh Wound Imports (*fleshwoundpictures. com*), who are also offering Sanctuary's special 2-disc 3D Collector's Edition of the franchise's second sequel, **AMITYVILLE 3-D** (1983, USA, D: Richard Fleischer). The present title was put out on domestic DVD by MGM Home Entertainment in 2005; their Spartan zilch-extras edition at least came complete with a widescreen or fullscreen option (which one would *you* choose?!). It was first (?) issued on British PAL Region 2 DVD by Castle Home Video in 1999. Under the Czech title **AMITYVILLE POSEDLOST** (*"Amityville Obsession"*), it was released on DVD in the Czech Republic by Magic Box, in English with a native dialogue (*"Česky"*) option. Similarly, for its release in Italy by Pulp Video as part of their "Cult Collection" (under the shortened Anglo title **AMITYVILLE POSSESSION**), the film came with both English and Italian audio track options. Further back in time, **A2TP** was first put out on North American Betamax/VHS cassette by Thorn EMI Video, and reissued in the same formats by Embassy Home Entertainment/Nelson Entertainment in 1987 (back cover blurb: *"Home, Sweet Home... A framework for fright with no room for the timid!"*). Its '80s UK PAL VHS release was by Warner Bros./Weintraub Entertainment Group, and it was released in Japan during the same period on NTSC VHS by Thorn EMI/King Video, in its original English version,

Vinegar Syndrome's 2013 double feature DVD

with Japanese subs. In his homeland if a lot less-so here in N. America other than by "those in the know", well-above-average Italian director Damiano Damiani (1922-2013) is better-known for his more upscale/socially conscious Eurocrime action dramas starring the likes of spaghetti cinema big guns Franco Nero or Giuliano Gemma. The present film makes for an interesting departure from his usual milieux/material, and it remains one of the few films in Damiani's canon ever to receive major theatrical/ video distribution on this side of The Big Soup.

BLOOD THIRST (1971) *[p.24]* – Ad-hype: *"Sinister! Inhuman! What Was the Thing That Came Out of the Eerie Blackness of Night... To Satisfy its Blood Thirst!"* By far this film's optimal video version thus far—their nice clean and sharp transfer print presented in its original widescreen theatrical

Horror

Screen Power

Sie kehren
zurück...

FRIEDHOF der ZOMBIES

000132
82 Min

Screen
Power

FRIEDHOF
DER ZOMBIES

2000 German VHS jacket for
CEMETERY OF TERROR

aspect ratio of 1.66:1—was released in 2013 by Vinegar Syndrome (VS) as a double-bill DVD in their "Drive-In Collection", for which the co-feature was another Filipino-shot horror, the bland-but-not-entirely-without-its-charms quest-for-eternal-life schlocker **THE THIRSTY DEAD** (1974, D: Terry

Its star Gerrit "Bud the Chud" Graham gives
the appropriate reaction to **C.H.U.D. II**!

Becker). Back in 1994, Something Weird Video put **BT** out on VHS tape, and began issuing it on DVD-R in 2001. It was subsequently released on domestic DVD by BCI Eclipse (in 2003), Alpha Video Distributors (2004) and Retromedia Entertainment (2008), but all those scritchy-scratchy full-frame versions paled in comparison to VS's pristine edition, which is in about the nicest condition you could expect for a movie approaching 50 years old (especially one of such obscure and lowly origins whose original elements likely weren't taken care of particularly well in the interim).

CEMETERY OF TERROR (1985) *[p.26]* – The year after its production in '86, this film was put out under its original Mexican title **CEMENTERIO DEL TERROR** on US Hispanic Beta/VHS cassette by Video Mex International of Tarzana, CA. It also aired on the Telelatino channel at some point during the '90s, so maybe you might have taped it off there. Although poor "Gringo" Moore our reviewer only got to see the untranslated *español* version for his review (not that he reckons he missed too many—if any—subtleties of plot, mind you), under the Anglo title given here the film was released on domestic dual layer DVD in 2006 by BCI Eclipse/Deimos Entertainment of CA in a double-bill edition (under the joint heading "Crypt of Terror, Vol. 2") together with same director Rubén Galindo, Jr.'s **GRAVE ROBBERS** (*Ladrones de tumbas*, 1990, Mexico), which covers highly similar territory indeed (back cover copy for **GR**: *"Four teenagers on a camping trip decide to rob a nearby graveyard. They stumble across an ornate grave and tomb housing the corpse of an executed Satanist from the days of the Inquisition... Soon the deceased Satanist zombie, armed with a massive battle-axe, rises from the grave to claim his treasure"*). Both films on the Deimos disc are presented in their original Spanish (with English subs), and both come in their original full-frame theatrical aspect ratio. That said, Deimos' website (*www.deimosdvd.com*) seems to no longer be operative, so presumably the company either went out of business, or else moved house (?). As of this writing, a number of copies of the afore-noted, presumably limited edition double feature DVD were up for grabs on eBay, ranging from about $20 to $25. In the year 2000, under the title **FRIEDHOF DER ZOMBIES** (*"Cemetery of the Zombies"*), **COT** was issued on VHS tape in Germany in an *Ungekürzte Fassung* ("uncut version") by the Screen Power Home Entertainment label, yet another company (formerly @ *www.screen-power.de*) which now appears to be defunct (i.e., *kapüt*).

C.H.U.D. (1984) *[p.33]* – Now here's a movie that has turned into quite the mini cult phenom in the more than 30 years since it first emerged from deep below ground into the light of a projector bulb; but it's not just worth remembering because it co-stars future comedic superstar Daniel Stern. Even many people who may not have seen it (nor would even want to) are familiar with its odd if seemingly vulgarly blunt and to-the-point acronymic name, which conjures up who-knows-what sorts of slithering, slimy nastiness in the hearer's mind at the sound of it. As for its video history, Media Home Entertainment released it on Betamax/VHS way back in 1985, and that same year it was released north of the border in the same formats by Canada's Astral Video and on American laserdisc by Image Entertainment. During the same period, it was put out in the same tape formats (albeit in PAL rather than NTSC) by Medusa Home Video of the UK. It was subsequently released on American tape by both Video Treasures (in 1989) and Starmaker Video (1991). After Anchor Bay issued it on VHS in 1997, it was first put out on domestic DVD by the same label in 2001 (@ a 1.77:1 aspect ratio), and their edition (which they reissued in 2008) featured audio commentary by director Douglas Cheek, screenwriter Shepard Abbott and lead actors Stern, John Heard and Christopher Curry. Besides this, the only other special features were a theatrical trailer and still gallery. More recently in 2011, Image—who had first issued it in a digital disc format (i.e., LD) back in the mid-'80s—put it out on Blu-ray/DVD as part of their "Midnight Madness" series. For its German release as **C.H.U.D. – PANIK IN MANHATTAN**, there is no sign of any monsters on the cover artwork, which is instead dominated by a painted illustration of a pair of shapely gams in red high-heel shoes. Earlier this year, composers Martin Cooper's and David A. Hughes' soundtrack was issued as a 12" vinyl record album by Waxwork Records (*www.waxworkrecords.com*). Totaling 31 tracks in all, split over two sides (tagged "Tunnel A" and "Tunnel B"), track titles include the likes of "1-900-CHUD", "I C.H.U.D. NY", "M.U.T.A.T.E.", "D.E.C.A.P.I.T.A.T.E.", "Street Meat", "Sewer Chewers", "Blood Shower!" and, last but by no means least, "This Ain't No Disco" (damn straight!). Stylin' **C.H.U.D.** tees bearing the film's original "monster-raising-manhole-cover" poster design—screen-printed in white and yellow on jet-black fabric—can be gotten at the Rotten Cotton website (*www.rottencotton.com*). As mentioned by Eric M. in his fondly favorable review, shirts are also available from the site Red Bubble (@ *http://www.redbubble.com/people/hydraalpha*). As for other franchise-related merch/tie-ins, coming with a hefty price tag of $300.00, sculptor James Groman's "Custom Ganmetal Celsius" dwarf C.H.U.D. statuette was first unveiled in 2010 at LA's Toy Art Gallery (T.A.G.), but those of a more frugal bent might want to pick up Retroband's much

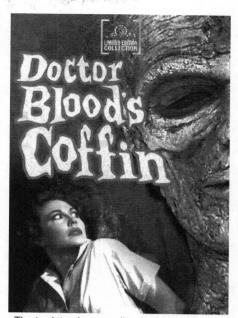

The to-date nicest quality version of this film that's been made available

cheaper made-in-Texas 1980s-style C.H.U.D. action figure (for "Ages 4 and up"), a more correctly-proportioned toy which comes with limitedly poseable limbs and even a miniature plastic sewer lid on which the film's title—albeit curiously sans periods—is embossed. Stiff, crudely clunky and no-frills, it basically looks a lot like one of those old mass-produced "Made in Hong Kong" **STAR WARS** figures from Kenner. Oh yeah, for those who want it—whoever and wherever ye may be!—the much-maligned sequel **C.H.U.D. II** ([1988, USA, D: David Irving] sometimes subtitled **BUD THE CHUD**, which better emphasizes the fact that it's a "comedy" [note quotes]) was put out on Beta/VHS tape by Vestron Video in 1989, who also released it on laserdisc. In 2012 it was "finally" made available on Region 1 DVD from Lions Gate…consider yourself warned! To end this entry on an indirectly related note of trivia, there's even a movies/TV shows-still-in-production (etc.) news website called CHUD.com (*www.chud.com*), which has little or nothing directly to do with the movie from which it obviously took its name, their acronym instead standing for "Cinematic Happenings Under Development". Well, you learn something new every day.

DOCTOR BLOOD'S COFFIN (1961) *[p.7]* – Released on R1 DVD by Alpha Video in 2002 and by Cheezy Flicks in 2005, cropped, and a little soft (visually on a par with the YouTube version). In 2011

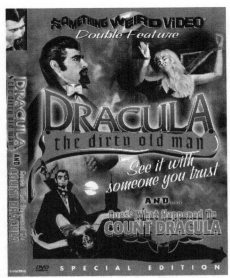

SWV's double DVD of no-budget Drac dregs

there was the "MGM Limited Edition Collection" release on DVD-R, a better image in the correct aspect ratio, and the best DVD version to date. Another DVD-R followed in 2014, from Mr. Fat-W Video, and there was another discount DVD release of unknown vintage from the Canadian company Front Row Entertainment. The 2014 R2 release from Final Cut Entertainment seems to be poor quality, judging by reviews on Amazon UK. No news of a Blu-ray release at this time. **DR. BLOOD** has also been known to turn up on TCM and Svengoolie's show. ~ **Jolyon Yates**

DRACULA, THE DIRTY OLD MAN (1969) *[p.17]* – Released on DVD in 2002 by Something Weird Video/Chiller Theatre as the main feature

Columbia's 1960s US Super 8 box

alongside Laurence Merrick's **GUESS WHAT HAPPENED TO COUNT DRACULA?** (ad-line: *"See it with someone you trust!"*), this "double feature" includes a fairly colorful, fullscreen print, but, as expected, it still contains the customary scratches and minor damage inherent in such bottom-of-the-barrel obscurities. As per usual for SWV, this disc also features an assortment of trailers, short subjects and still galleries, which are sometimes even better than the films themselves. A plethora of "blood-soaked" trailers include Robert Hartford-Davies' **BLOODSUCKERS** (a.k.a. **INCENSE FOR THE DAMNED**, 1970, UK); Andy Milligan's eerie **THE BODY BENEATH** (1970, USA/UK); the US Box Office International trailer for Jean Rollin's **CAGED VIRGINS** (*Requiem pour un vampire*, 1971, France); Harry Kümel's **DAUGHTERS OF DARKNESS** (*Les lèvres rouges*, 1971, Belgium/France/Germany [see *Weng's Chop* #8, p.160]); Jorge Grau's **THE LEGEND OF BLOOD CASTLE** (*Ceremonia sangrienta*, 1973, Spain/Italy); Herschell Gordon Lewis' tedious **A TASTE OF BLOOD** (1967, USA), Renato Polselli's **THE VAMPIRE AND THE BALLERINA** (*L'amante del vampiro*, 1960, Italy [see *Monster!* #15, pp.74+107]), and a K. Gordon Murray "combo" trailer for Fernando Méndez's **THE VAMPIRE'S COFFIN** (*El ataúd del vampiro*, 1958, Mexico), starring the recently-deceased Germán Robles (R.I.P., Count Lavud/ Duval! ☹), and Rafael Portillo's **THE ROBOT VS. THE AZTEC MUMMY** (*La momia azteca del robot humano*, 1957, Mexico). In keeping with the vampire theme, the short subjects turn out to be abbreviated versions of a couple of vampire-themed porn flicks—or "adult-fanged featurettes"—from the Sexy 'Seventies. First up is **DRACULA AND THE DIRTY OLD WITCH**, which actually turns out to be a condensed version of Duncan Stewart's **THE BRIDE'S INITIATION** (1976, USA) featuring Carol Connors and a frequently-nude-and-heavily-made-up Dracula (Marc Brock) searching for his perfect partner. The second featurette is a condensed version of Modunk Phreezer's (?!) **SEX AND THE SINGLE VAMPIRE** (1970, USA), which has John Holmes as Count Spatula! A "Ghastly Gallery of Ghoulish Comic Cover-Art" with drive-in radio-spots round out the extras on this jam-packed DVD. Oh yeah, before I forget, for you Easter Egg hunters, look for a snippet from Antonio Teritoni's **COUNT EROTICO VAMPIRE** (1971, USA), yet another '70s vampire-themed horror porn. ~ **Dennis Capicik**

THE GIANT CLAW (1957) *[p.86]* – Original theatrical ad-lines: *"Bird-Monster Goes Berserk!"* ... *"Winged Monster from 17,000,000 B.C. Attacks!"* First made available for private home viewing circa the 1960s in a 200ft (approx. 8 min.) Super 8 millimeter cut-down reel from Columbia Pictures. At the height of the 'Eighties home video boom (in 1989), inevitably hyped as a "Campy Cult Classic" it was released on domestic videocassette by GoodTimes; although their version came in the dreaded LP ("long-play") mode, we were happy to have it nonetheless, as the price was right (i.e., dirt-cheap). For our money nowadays, your best bet is picking this up on DVD in Sony/Columbia Pictures' great economical 2007 fourfer set simply entitled *Sam Katzman*, part of their essential "Icons of Horror Collection". In addition to being presented in its proper original theatrical aspect ratio—same goes for the other films included therein, which come in either 1.85:1 or 1.33.1—the film is quadruple-billed with three other must-have Katzman-produced titles from the nifty 'Fifties: Edward L. Cahn's pair of stylistically-worlds-apart zombie flicks, **CREATURE WITH THE ATOM BRAIN** (1955) and **ZOMBIES OF MORA TAU** (1957)—the former more topical to its times, the latter more "old school" in style—as well as **CLAW** director Fred F. Sears' lesser-seen and long-little-known Atomic Age lycanthropy gem **THE WEREWOLF** (1956, all USA), starring Steven Ritch in an affecting, pathos-laden performance as man-made-wolfman against his will by scientific (i.e., nuclear) means. With a pair of films per DVD, this 2-disc box set comes in twin slim-line clamshell boxes enclosed within a sleek, smooth-sliding cardboard slipcase, with attractively designed packaging that includes original promotional materials for each film printed on both sides of the paper insert jacket. As **LA GARRA GIGANTE**, the present film is also available as a Spanish-language edition (with English option) in the Columbia Essential Classics line. And now for some trivia of related interest: An excerpt of a primitively-produced if enthusiastic amateur dimensional animation short entitled *Godzilla vs. The Giant Claw* can be viewed on YouTube at the link "Stop Motion Godzilla 2014 vs The Giant Claw Part 1" (@ *https://www.youtube.com/watch?v=rDdPQVv4lmc*), which evidently competed as an entry in G-Fest XXII's video contest, apparently winning its creator Michael Aguilar the Ray Harryhausen Award. In our opinion, the Claw puppet looks great, but the Big G one is decidedly—*er*—iffy, but gotta give 'em points for trying. Also on YT, *The Beast from 20,000 Fathoms vs. The Giant Claw* is a short, crudely-cobbled-together mash-up of original theatrical trailers for the two films mentioned in its title. For a clip of a video game featuring **CLAW**'s goofy goggle-eyed turkey monster rendered in Atari-style digital cartoon form, key in the link title "Angry Video Game Nerd Adventures! The Giant Claw!" at the same site. Yes indeed, it definitely appears as though this film's pricelessly zonked-out giant alien birdie has become firmly ensconced in popular

Fine Feathered Fiend: The crude-but-lovable puppet turkey seen in the fan-made sto-mo short *Godzilla vs. The Giant Claw* (2014)

culture, which is a good thing, so far as we here at *M!* are concerned. Hell, there are probably at least three different garage bands calling themselves The Giant Claws somewhere across the globe, too…

GRYPHON (2007) *[p.42]* – Under the title **ATTACK OF THE GRYPHON**, this was released on domestic DVD by Sony Pictures Home Entertainment, *sans* any special features. It was also released in other Anglo markets under that same extended title.

GUESS WHAT HAPPENED TO COUNT DRACULA? (1971) *[p.16]* – Released on DVD in 2002 by Something Weird Video as the second half of a "double feature" with **DRACULA, THE DIRTY OLD MAN** (see separate entry above). Presented fullscreen, the print used for this DVD is a little on the dark side and contains the usual scratches and splices—especially at reel changes—but, thankfully, retains many of Robert Caramico's garish color schemes quite well. See the **DTDOM** entry for more info on this disc and its many extras. ~ **Dennis Capicik**

ICE SPIDERS (2007) *[p.43]* – On domestic DVD from Sony Pictures Home Entertainment, or buyable/rentable as an Amazon insta-vid in HD or SD. Incidentally, it's a little-known fact outside Canada that this film's director Tibor Takács served as producer on a number of seminal early (circa 1977-'78) underground Torontonian punk rock records, including The Viletones' young, loud'n'snotty first 7" 45 rpm EP "Screaming Fist b/w Possibilities / Rebel" (on Vile Records; also released in a 12" version), as well as a lesser-known 33⅓ rpm seven-incher/four-songer (i.e., "I Want To Be a Yank / Can Stress Kill? b/w [I'm Not Your] Stepping Stone / Living Inside My Head", on Brainco Records) by obscure TO "Dadaist" arty-punkers The Cardboard Brains, amongst others. Howzat for trivia you can actually use to look hip at parties?!

THE IMMORTAL VOYAGE OF CAPTAIN DRAKE (2009) *[p.44]* – This Sci Fi Original presently seems to be available on disc just about everywhere else on the planet but here in North America. Go figure. Them what wants it knows where to get it, as it isn't very hard to find. For instance, it's available on Region 0 DVD in Germany as **DIE UNGLAUBLICHE REISE DES SIR FRANCIS DRAKE** (*"The Incredible Journey of Captain Drake"*), and on Blu-ray in the same country for some reason under a different title (**DER KÖNIG DER PIRATEN** / *"The Pirate King"*), evidently as a belated cash-in on Depp's hopefully long-since-scuppered *Pirates of the Caribbean* franchise. Both those cited versions come complete with English audio tracks, for those who need (or want) 'em.

THE INVASION OF THE DEAD (1973) *[p.36]* – Back in *Monster!* #20 (p.28), Les "Gringo" Moore previously gave his two pesos' worth about this film under its alternate Spanish title

Anglo-titled Dutch video box for
THE INVASION OF THE DEAD

BLUE DEMON Y ZÓVEK EN LA INVASIÓN DE LOS MUERTOS, but for this issue Jeff Goodhartz has given us his take on an English fan-subbed version contained on a "grey market" DVD-R of the film which can be obtained online at Video Screams (*videoscreams.com*). Under its original Mexican title **LA INVASIÓN DE LOS MUERTOS**, the film has been issued on NTSC Regions 1 & 4 (Latin-American import) DVD by Televisa as part of their "Collección Mexico en Pantalla" series (*"Cine Inolvidable"*), in Spanish without any English; copies of same are available at Mercado Libre (*www.mercadolibre.com.mx*). As of this writing, the same site was also offering copies of **LIDLM** in conjunction with **LOS ENDEMONIADOS DEL RING** (*"Demons of the Ring"*, 1966, Mexico), a double feature (*"2 en 1"*) edition released by Televisa in 2011 as part of their "Joyas del Cine Mexicano" line. Directed by the prolific Alfredo B. Crevenna of **SANTO CONTRA LA MAGIA NEGRA** (see separate entry below), despite its promising title **ENDEMONIADOS** is a monsterless masked Mexi-wrestling flick co-starring "Karloff" Lagarde, Armando Silvestre and Jorge Rivero (*Santo* series regular Fernando Osés also puts in another of many Mexploitation appearances therein). The film's "demons" are purely figurative rather than literal (e.g., Lagarde plays a *luchador* whose ring name is Satan; for the sake of ironic symbolic contrast, René "Copetes" Guajardo appears as another wrestler called Ángel). As for our present title, it was released on Beta/VHS in the Netherlands by Phoenix Home Video sometime in the '80s under the alternate Anglo title **INVASION OF DEATH**. (Incidentally, back in the vid info listings to *M!* #20, due to its Anglo title we suggested that said tape might have been of British origin, but we were wrong. We also made the suggestion that an English-dubbed export print might exist, but evidently we were wrong about that "fact" too. You can't win 'em all, as they say!) Under its Spanish title, there are at least four evidently identical copies of this film uploaded at different links on YT, all struck from what appears to have been that aforesaid Dutch VHS copy (in the original Spanish, with Dutch subs). For more backstory about this intriguingly enigmatic cinematic crazy quilt, visit the Cool Ass Cinema website (@ *http://www.coolasscinema.com/2014_08_11_archive.html*).

THE INVASION OF THE ZOMBIES (1961) *[p.12]* – Under its original title **SANTO CONTRA LOS ZOMBIES**, this is purchasable at the Mexican retail site Mercado Libre (*mercadolibre.com.mx*) as a Regions 1 & 4 DVD from Virtual Digital, in Spanish with English/French soft-subs options. It's also been released—in Spanish only?—as part of the "Colección Grandes Clásicos" series (label unknown). It was formerly viewable VOD on Amazon via Veranda Entertainment under its Spanish title, but is currently unavailable at said site. Founded by future Hollywood-based movie director Julian Grant (who later made *RoboCop* TV movies) circa 1990, the short-lived Toronto offshoot of Sinister Cinema (Grant officially licensed the brand-name from the American company) released a number of Sinister USA's already-extant titles in Canada for a roughly two-year period before calling it quits due to insufficient sales. One of their initial two-dozen-or-so releases was **TIOTZ**, which, like other Canadian SC tape releases, came in an illustrated cardboard slip-cover (in this case featuring a detail of a poster from a different Santo movie). Their transfer, struck from the same master seen on the version offered in the US SC's catalogue, was an old TV copy of K. Gordon Murray's English-dubbed print. Unfortunately, a "duping error"—Grant used to dub "made-to-order" copies himself in the basement of his home in TO—caused a whole lengthy section of the present film to be double-printed, resulting in a way-overextended, roughly 2-hour total running time. Like all the other Canuck SC releases, the tape is now hard to come by. A copy of KGM's Anglo dub was also put out on domestic VHS by Something Weird Video (SWV) in 1994. Several uploads of the Spanish version are on YouTube.

KHOONI flicks *[pp.103-120]* – Kanti Shah's **KHOONI SHAITAN** (2002) *[p.116]* is out on Video Compact Disc (VCD) from Ultra Video, and has also been comped as part of a classic "3-in-1" DVD which also includes two more Shah horrors, **PYASI BHOOTNI** and **PYAASA HAIWAN** (both 2003). **KHOONI TANTRIK** (2001) *[p.115]* can be had on VCD via Friends Video. All these following titles can likewise be acquired in the same format: **KHOONI DRACULA** *[p.106]* ([1992] Time Video; OOP?), **KHOONI RAAT** *[p.106]* ([2004] Kamal Video; OOP), **KHOONI** *[p.116]* ([2004] Friends Video), **KHOONI ILAAKA** *[p.112]* and **KHOONI No. 1** *[p.110]* (both [1999] Priya Video), **KHOONI PED** *[p.117]* ([2003] Friends Video [FVCD 220]) and **KHOONI SHIKUNJA** *[p.114]* ([2000] Indus Video). None of these discs cited so far come with English subtitles, and all but **KHOONI No. 1** and **KHOONI RAAT** are available to stream gratis on the internet via YouTube, etc. (at the present time, the ultra-obscure **KHOONI DARINDA** *[p.119]* is available solely on the 'net). One film that does have English subs is **RISE OF THE ZOMBIE**— not **RISE OF THE ZOMBIES**, Nicky Lyon's 2012 American film, but rather the 2013 Luke Kenny/ Devaki Singh-directed film *[p.4]* of singular rather than pluralized title—which is available on Indian DVD from Times Music (and is also streaming

Sinister Cinema presents

INVASION of the ZOMBIES

starring SANTO

WRESTLING

THE OFFICIAL HOLLYWEIRD SEAL OF APPROVAL ™

1961, B&W, 85 mins
(aka: Santo Against the Zombies, El Santo Contra Los Zombies)
Prod: Fernando Oses   Dir & Scr: Benito Alazraki   Stars: Santo, Lorena Velazquez, Armando Silvestre
"*Hilarious wrestling sequel!*"

The short-lived Toronto wing of Sinister Cinema's ultra-rare 1990 VHS

VOD on Amazon). Another one with English subs is Krishna D.K.'s and Raj Nidimoru's zombie opus **GO GOA GONE** (2013) *[p.2]*, which can be obtained on DVD through Eros International (UK) and Eros Entertainment (USA), as well as from the same company in India, too (that Eros version also comes with English). Most—if not all—the above titles are/were acquirable via Induna (*www.induna. com*). Another online retail resource you might wanna try your luck at is WebMall India (WMI [@ *www.webmallindia.com*]).

LA HORDE (2009) *[p.39]* – A quote taken from *Empire*'s review of the film, which was included on the front cover of the British DVD release: "*The DIE HARD of Zombie Flicks.*" An exceedingly dark, bleak and über-ultra-megaviolent zompocalypse flick in the Extreme Horror category, which really stands out from the rest of the—um— horde. As the one-and-only Chas. Balun might well have said of it, "This sick puppy really delivers the gore groceries in gut-crunching style!" It's funny how, whatever era they originate from, foreign

127

movies dubbed into English (and undoubtedly vice versa) always have such a hollow, artificial ring to their audio tracks; same goes for that to the dubbed domestic version of the present title, known as **THE HORDE**, in which some pretty— and sometimes even highly—intense scenes are somewhat undermined by questionable rewritten/ rerecorded dialogue (e.g., as when Eriq Ebouaney as *mucho macho* Nigerian alpha male Adewale yells, "Grab the rod! ...Go on, stick it in! *Stick it in!!*" or when Doudou Masta as his trigger-happy psycho kid brother Bola shrieks hysterically, "They *ate* the Czech! *The Czech!* They ate the fucking Czech!"; however, in that latter case, the voice actor's pronunciation of Czech is such that it sounds like he's actually saying "chick" instead... guess you had to be there). Indeed, it sometimes makes you wonder whether the Anglo voice-dubbers might have been taking the piss out of the material somewhat, when it isn't really appropriate, considering the grim and decidedly non-camp context. Then again, they might just be inadvertent side effects of the post-synching process. After all, trying to fit translated words of similar meanings to the movements of actors' mouths speaking a different language while retaining the integrity of the original script is obviously problematic at the best of times, so, all things considered, most of the dub-job isn't really all that bad...but give us the subbed version any day. Ideally enough, I (i.e., SF) re-watched this film the same night that episode three of *Ash vs Evil Dead* aired (the one entitled "Books from Beyond", in which the freaky

Video Mutation: El cheapo domestic full-frame DVD release, with the wrong cover art!

blue demon Eligos makes its initial memorable appearance). In his review of **LA HORDE**, Andy Ross fittingly compares Jean-Pierre Martins, who plays cop hero Ouessem (redubbed "Wes" in the English version), to *ED*'s Bruce Campbell, and at times the French actor does indeed evoke a burlier, rougher, mustached and far grimmer—indeed, entirely humorless—version of the American actor, which was presumably why the former was cast as protagonist here. As **THE HORDE**, the film was released on domestic Blu-ray and DVD in 2010 by IFC Films as part of their Midnight line; thankfully their edition includes the original French-dialogue version with an English soft-subs option, as well as the dubbed version. In the UK, the film was issued under the same Anglo title by Momentum Pictures Home Entertainment, but evidently their disc only contained the English dub (?). The US edition comes with a number of special features, while the UK one doesn't (?). Hopscotch Films issued the film on digital disc in Australia and New Zealand. More recently (2011), Alliance Canada put it out on Region 1 Canadian Blu-ray.

MAGGIE (2015) *[p.55]* – Available in both disc formats from Lionsgate, this can currently be streamed VOD via such online sources as Amazon *et al.* In Australia/New Zealand, it's out on disc from Sony Pictures/StudioCanal, and in the UK from Universal Home Entertainment.

MISS ZOMBIE (2013) *[p.57]* – This bleak and despairing B&W Nipponese horror movie has been put out on domestic Japanese DVD by Amuse Soft, but whether their edition comes with English subs or not, who knows? Like Bri H. (who mail-ordered it on Korean disc; check the Asian retail site Zoom Movie [@ *www.zoommovie.com*]) says in his review, watch for it on Netflix when it surfaces on these shores. It's bound to be up for grabs online elsewhere too.

MUTANT (1984) *[p.30]* – VHS ad-line: *"The Undead Are Tomb Stoned!"* This has been released on domestic DVD by Liberation Cult Entertainment as the second feature in their "Mutants and Monsters Double Feature", paired-up with Greydon Clark's howler mutated-killer-kitty-on-the-loose schlocker **UNINVITED** (1988, USA); both films are presented full-frame in that edition (?). There is a nice widescreen version of this movie floating around (label unknown), but BEWARE the RiffTrax edition of same, which makes *MST3K* seem like the height of wit by comparison, and that's sure saying something. In 2005, this was put out on ultra-cheapo dollar-store DVD by Miracle Pictures/PMC Corp., in a full-frame version that looked about as good as an old VHS copy (which was probably where they got their "master" from); and not only that, but the disc's cover art used a shot of the toothy, drooling monster from **FORBIDDEN WORLD** (1982, USA, D: Allan Holzman), one of whose alternate titles was **MUTANT**, hence the apparent mix-up (or perhaps it was fully intended to deceive potential buyers into believing there was an **ALIEN**esque monster in it?). The present film was released on British Beta/VHS cassette during the '80s by EV/CBS Video, and in Norway during the same decade by HVC/Scandiafilm A.S. in its original English-language version, with Norwegian subtitles.

NIGHT CLAWS (2012) *[p.22]* – Available on domestic DVD from Midnight Releasing, this movie can also be streamed VOD in either HD or SD on Amazon, priced accordingly. It's also been put out on Blu-ray in Germany under the title **NIGHT CLAWS – DIE NACHT DER BESTIE** (*"Night of the Beast"*, natch), which comes with both English and German audio options.

Q: THE WINGED SERPENT (1982) *[p.88]* – Ad-line: *"Q – You'll Just Have Time To SCREAM Its Name..."* On original theatrical posters—rated "M" for mature audiences—for its 1980s (June '83) Australian release by Roadshow Productions, it was touted as *"The highest flying 'Monster Movie' of all time! ...It's Bloody Goreful!"* Formerly (circa the '80s/'90s) available on domestic Beta/VHS cassette from MCA/Universal Home Video and in the UK during the same period on PAL cassette from Hokushin (for which a critic's cover quote from Britain's *The Standard* newspaper described the film as *"...JAWS with wings"*), Q was later put out on laserdisc stateside by Elite Entertainment in a "Letterboxed Edition", first issued on domestic DVD by Anchor Bay in 1998, then later still (2003) by Blue Underground in the same format. Much more recently (2013), it was rereleased in a snazzy Blu-ray edition by Shout! Factory—its optimum incarnation thus far—and can also be rented or purchased in an SD-only version as an Amazon insta-vid (for $2.99 or $9.99). Down Under in Australia, it was released on DVD by Umbrella Entertainment (box copy: *"Larry Cohen's Cult Monster Movie Classic"*). That edition features both an audio commentary by Cohen, plus *Confessions of a Low Budget Maverick*, a 25-minute on-camera interview with the filmmaker; those same special features have appeared elsewhere on other disc editions of the movie. In the UK, Arrow Films issued it on PAL Region 2 DVD as part of their specialized Arrowdrome Horror line (*"Step Into The Cult Arena!"*), including such extras as an insert booklet penned by Brit film scholar Stephen Thrower (formerly of the Eurocentric '90s zine *Eyeball*). It was released on '80s SECAM-format Beta/VHS in Germany by AllVideo under its anglicized

domestic West German theatrical title **AMERICAN MONSTER**, although, despite its Anglo retitle, All's tape edition only came dubbed into German. During the same period, it was released on Nordic videocassette by the Mayco A.S. label of Oslo *sans* "Q" as simply **THE WINGED SERPENT** (ad-line: *"Det flyvende monster"*), in its original English with Norwegian subs.

RE-KILL (2015) *[p.53]* – Tagline: *"We Are The Endangered Species."* As part of the "8 Films To Die For" After Dark Horrorfest imprint, this is on DVD from Twentieth Century Fox Home Entertainment, as are the other seven films in the package (including **UNNATURAL** [2015, USA, D: Hank Braxton], about a genetically-mutated polar bear!), which were released last month, and can all also be streamed VOD online. The present film is out on DVD in Australia from Transmission Films.

SANTO CONTRA LA MAGIA NEGRA (1973) *[p.46]* – This title was formerly available (*circa* the '80s/'90s) on Hispanic N. American Beta/VHS cassette from Mexcinema Video Corporation, in its original Spanish language *sans* English translation. **SCLMN** is currently available on Mexican DVD (label unknown) from Mercado Libre's website (*www.mercadolibre.com.mx*), again in Spanish-only form, and there is a copy of same on YouTube of pretty decent picture quality; animal rights activists might wanna skip over the part where the black billy-goat gets sacrificed for real, however (dare I say "Trigger Warning"?). The film was at some point issued on domestic bootleg video under the bullshit if more catchily exploitative modified Anglo title **"SANTO VS. BLACK MAGIC WOMAN"**.

A VIRGIN AMONG THE LIVING DEAD (1973) *[p.59]* – US/UK (& etc.) videotape blurb: *"A Ghoulish Journey Through the Very Center/Centre of Hell!"* We could probably write another 10,000 words or more just on the confusing video history of this film in all its various incarnations over the years, but instead we'll just stick to the bare essentials so we can get this ish off to the printers and into your grubby maulers ASAP... It is most familiar/valuable to North American VHS collectors in its mid-'80s Wizard/Lightning Video "big box" incarnation, which came in the now iconically familiar and gloriously colorful painted cover art by prolific Italian illustrator Spataro, which had only the scantest relation to the actual film itself, but sure looked fancy. In 1993, Edde Entertainment/T-Z Video issued it under the grossly misleading title **ZOMBIE 4** (!), albeit clearly subtitled **A VIRGIN AMONG THE LIVING DEAD** (*"Enter the World of Undead Horror... Jess Franco's Cult Masterpiece"*); not one of the several zombies

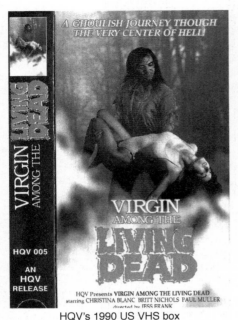

A GHOULISH JOURNEY THOUGH THE VERY CENTER OF HELL!

VIRGIN AMONG THE LIVING DEAD

VIRGIN AMONG THE LIVING DEAD

HQV 005

AN HQV RELEASE

HQV Presents VIRGIN AMONG THE LIVING DEAD
starring CHRISTINA BLANC BRITT NICHOLS PAUL MULLER
directed by JESS FRANK

HQV's 1990 US VHS box

depicted on the packaging for this release actually appears in the movie, which was later also put out on VHS by Sinister Cinema (in 2001), as well as by Cinefear (year indeterminate). It was released on British PAL Beta/VHS cassette by Careyvision Ltd. (#CHV 1014) in 1985 under the banner heading "Horror Theatre". Under the slightly shortened title **VIRGIN AMONG THE LIVING DEAD**, it was reissued on American tape by HQV in 1990, complete with misleading photographic cover art depicting a stitch-mouthed, longhaired zombie "Goth"/headbanger dude (picture a scarier-looking version of Misfit Glenn Danzig) cradling a swooning leotarded brunette babe in his arms. And speaking of misleading box art, the monster-filled cut'n'paste cover to VideoScope's English-dubbed/Spanish-subbed '80s Latin-American (Argentina, etc.) VHS edition, retitled **TESTAMENTO DIABÓLICO**, really took the cookie, incorporating pasted-on cut-outs of bestial brute-men from various American horror comic covers with what appears to have been a *locandina* for a gothic Italo *giallo*. However, more outrageously deceptive by far was Video Laser/ Gourmet Video's '80s Uruguayan PAL Beta/VHS version of **VIRGIN**, entitled **EL INFIERNO DE LOS SENTIDOS** (*"Inferno of the Senses"*), which was packaged to resemble an out-and-out fetish-B&D-S/M porno, complete with leather masks and bit-gags on the cover! Copyrighted to Eurociné Video International, **AVATLD** was released in Japan on Beta/VHS by the label Inferno (#INS-101), bearing the same much-used Spataro cover artwork

and English ad-line (see above) seen on many other releases of the film worldwide. At some point, in conjunction with the film's production company Eurociné, France's *Mad Movies* magazine put it out on French DVD under the title **UNE VIERGE CHEZ LES MORTS VIVANTS**. AVATLD was first released on domestic DVD ("Widescreen Director's Cut") by Image Entertainment in 2003 as part of "The Euroshock Collection". The same year's Netherlands DVD release by Dutch FilmWorks (DFW) reportedly contains the film's "uncut and uncensored" edition, but when that term is used in relation to a film with so many different versions/ cuts extant as **AVATLD** has—there are at least *three* "official" ones, according to reports—it doesn't really say much. In his online review (dated August 2013) of the below-mentioned Redemption disc edition, Richard Whittaker of *The Austin Chronicle* called **AVATLD** "one of the most infamously mutilated underground favorites", which was the long-time Holy Grail of JF completists. (Hardcore Francophiles looking for the most complete "legit" version need to consult Thrower's & Grainger's seemingly definitive book *Murderous Passions – The Delirious Cinema of Jesús Franco, Volume 1: 1959-1974* [London: Strange Attractor Press, 2015], which is currently available on Amazon and elsewhere.) Having previously (2002) released it in the same disc format (in French, with English subtitles), Arrow Films of the UK later reissued the film on PAL Region 2 DVD in 2011, with German dialogue (?) and English subtitles. The disc versions to beat currently seem to be either Kino Lorber's 2013 Blu-ray edition of the film or Redemption's Blu/DVD, latter of which comes complete with the even more "sexed-up" alternate cut of the film known as **CHRISTINA, PRINCESS OF EROTICISM** ("Franco's Director's Cut"), which features the— *ahem*—"big black dildo" scene depicted on page 65. For the same Redemption release, in the featurette entitled "Mysterious Dreams", Jess Franco himself gives one of his final interviews prior to his death, and there are a number other special features besides. As part of their retro Wizard Video reprint line (visit *www.wizardvideocollection.com*), in addition to flogging signed reproductions of said vid label's iconic 'Eighties "big boxes" (for "only" about $50 a pop!), Full Moon Features is currently offering frameable 11" x 17" prints of Spataro's original poster artwork—though curiously, the repro's artwork is copyrighted in the fine print to one Stephen Romano, who presumably only did the new design/layout work for it (?)—complete with revamped title logo/fonts/credits and with an all-new off-color tagline (*"She's Going Down"*). It sells for about ten bucks (+ $5 S&H) on Amazon. Okay, we are outta here. See you next month!

Splintered Visions: Lucio Fulci and His Films

Written by Troy Howarth,
with special collaboration from Mike Baronas
Midnight Marquee Press (*www.midmar.com*), 2015

Any typical monster movie fan nowadays can rattle off two-dozen-or-more zombie films without skipping a beat. For me, that is a tougher job, because I have had no particular love of that particular way-overkilled subcategory of horror film since around the mid-1990s. For me, Romero's flicks aside, undead flesh-eaters carry no especial interest, unless there is some sort of supernatural element involved in their genesis, which makes things more interesting, in my opinion. I'd had my fill of frantic, fast-moving zombies after Danny Boyle's **28 DAYS LATER** (2002, UK) pretty much ripped-off its "gimmick" from Umberto Lenzi's **NIGHTMARE CITY** (*Incubo sulla città contaminata*, 1980, Italy/Mexico/Spain), and nobody even noticed. My kind of zombie films are those which sprang from the macabre imagination of splatter maestro Lucio Fulci. Granted, he didn't actually make as many as a lot of fans might like to think he did, but the ones he did make are mostly tops in my book. And since this is a book review, I must say that, clocking-in at over 350 pages, Troy Howarth's tome on the work of the Italian director is impressive indeed, and it fits right into this ish, considering it's our "Quasi-Zombie" number and all (as if Jolyon Yates' hideously beautiful cover art—whose inspiration source, needless to say, was the most famous specimen of the titular monsters from Fulci's own **ZOMBIE** [*Zombi 2*, 1979])—didn't already alert you to this fact).

Now, Fulci didn't make a whole *lot* of zombie films, if you take into account his long career in the Italian film industry. He got his start back in the early '50s with films like the Classical era costume spectacle **THE SINS OF POMPEII** (*Gli ultimi giorni di Pompei*, 1950), whereon he was not involved in directing the film as much as he was the assistant to the second unit director. Before Fulci became "The Godfather of Gore" to throngs of gorehounds (believe me, I dated such a girl back in the '80s, and when we went to the drive-in, she was sure to check the ads in the local papers to see if any of "*that* Italian's films" were playing) he was responsible for numerous comedies, musicals, westerns (and some darn good ones,

Dr. Freudstein (Giovanni de Nava) in the process of "checking-in" his newest set of body parts (Paolo Malco); from **THE HOUSE BY THE CEMETERY**, Fulci's near-brilliant—and unwittingly (?) Lovecraftian—horror opus

Janet Agren literally loses her mind in **CITY OF THE LIVING DEAD**

to boot!), mysteries, and police dramas. He struck gold of course, with **ZOMBIE** in 1979, and as the director is quoted in *Splintered Visions* as saying, "The zombies in my movies derive from Jacques Tourneur's **I WALKED WITH A ZOMBIE** *[1943, USA]*, they are born of pure fantasy and horror traditions..." In that respect, his variation on the undead is my personal favorite. He would later expand his field slightly with the Lovecraftian horrors of **CITY OF THE LIVING DEAD** (*Paura nella città dei morti viventi*, 1980), **THE BEYOND** (*...E tu vivrai nel terrore! L'aldilà*, 1981) and **THE HOUSE BY THE CEMETERY** (*Quella villa accanto al cimitero*, both 1981). Some weirdo zombies even popped up fleetingly in my third-favorite Fulci horror film, **CONQUEST** (1983), which also happened to be his one-and-only stab at the S&S ("sword and sorcery") fantasy genre, too.

Mr. Howarth really knows his material, and his book, which is loaded with intimate details and anecdotes about its subject, makes for a fascinating read. I especially enjoyed the interviews, along with some of the more insightful technical material which he and his collaborator Mike Baronas have unearthed. *SV* is lavishly illustrated (in full-color) with rare posters—including scads of Italian *locandina*s—as well as lobby cards, production and publicity stills,

Nun possession turns gloopy in **DEMONIA**

and some very welcome "private" snapshots of the director and his cast, crew and family. It goes without saying that if you enjoy Fulci's work as much as I have done and still do, from his weird comedies like the sci-fi spoof **002 OPERAZIONE LUNA** (1965, with Franco & Ciccio), his sadistic western **MASSACRE TIME** (*Le colt cantarono la morte e fu... tempo di massacre*, 1966, with Franco Nero), his classic *giallo* thrillers **ONE ON TOP OF ANOTHER** (*Una sull'altra*, 1969), **A LIZARD IN A WOMAN'S SKIN** (*Una lucertola con la pelle di donna*, 1971) and **DON'T TORTURE A DUCKLING** (*Non si sevizia un paperino*, 1972), to his later work within the supernatural horror genre, such as **DEMONIA** and **CAT IN THE BRAIN** (*Un gatto nel cervello*, both 1990) and **VOICES FROM BEYOND** (*Voci dal profondo*, 1991), then this book is for you. And while you're at it, why not grab copies of Volume 1 (covering the years 1963-1973) of the author/MidMar's in-depth overview of the Italo psycho-thriller genre, *So Deadly, So Perverse: 50 Years of Italian Giallo Films*, which was also published earlier this year. Likewise from 2015—Troy's been a busy boy indeed lately!—is *Tome of Terror: Horror Films of the 1930s*, which he co-wrote with the knowledgeable Christopher Workman. Midnight Marquee intends to publish separate volumes in the *ToT* series covering (decade-by-decade) every horror film ever made in the whole wide world since the beginning of cinema. Quite the ambitious undertaking, you might think…possibly even a next-to-*im*possible one. Yet if anyone would be game to give it a go, it's the prolific and seemingly tireless Troy Howarth!

Even if you are not a huge fan of Italian cinema, reading about Fulci's weird and winding trip through his career in *Splintered Visions* will give you some of idea of just what it was like trying to get films made back when—well—Italian filmmakers were actually still producing exploitation movies by the droves which could stand proudly shoulder-to-shoulder alongside the best that the world had to offer, rather than the slow trickle of "meaningful" Italocentric social dramas and/or Art Films which seem to be all its domestic movie industry produces these days. Sure, that kind of more "highbrow" material definitely does have its place, but give me the heydays of the Roman commercial cinema from *circa* 1960 to 1985, any day.

Splintered Visions: Lucio Fulci and His Films does a most creditable job of recapturing that era, and the author's love and enthusiasm for the material—even at such times as a particular film under discussion is far from one of his favorites, or might even be one of his *least* favorites—really radiates from his prose. ~ **Tim Paxton**

A Monster is Loose!–in Tokyo is currently out of print from Charles E. Tuttle Books, although there is talk of a reprint in the near future. Meanwhile, Betsy Grant has published two volumes of her late husband's work that are available either from *amazon.com* or directly from her website:

http://bvgrantstudio.com

In 1969, Vernon Grant drew upon his ten years of Army life to create 64 cartoons for his book, *Stand-By One!* The topics range from preparing for battle to sexual themes to references to the Viet-Cong and the weather. *Stand-By One!* is available at *http://www.amazon.com/Stand-By-One-Betsy-Grant/dp/194258606X*

Adventures of Point-Man Palmer in Vietnam is Vernon Grant's story about U.S. Army life in the 1960s as told through his cartoons with his unique sense of humor. Grant's biography opens the book. Illustrations include cartoons drawn for the *Pacific Stars and Stripes*, as well as a previously unpublished cartoon story about the need for radios for the foot soldier. *Point-Man Palmer* is also available at *http://www.amazon.com/Adventures-Point-Man-Palmer-Vietnam-Betsy/dp/098997846X*